PRAISE FOR

THE AMARE WAVE

"Dare to think differently, open your heart, and be your best—this epic book will show you the way in business. Read it now."
—MARSHALL GOLDSMITH, only two-time *Thinkers 50*
#1 Leadership Thinker in the world

"With brilliance and rigor, this book shows you how to prosper differently by making love—not war—the new way of business."
—CHIP CONLEY, hospitality entrepreneur and
New York Times bestselling author

"*The Amare Wave* is all about my favorite topic: love in leadership. I love it when Moshe Engelberg writes 'Imagine business is personal. Business leaders love themselves, their people, and their customers, and customers feel genuinely valued.' What a lovely concept! For more about why love is so important in business— and how you and your organization can be part of the wave—read this book. You'll love it!"
—KEN BLANCHARD, coauthor of *The New One Minute Manager*®
and *Leading at a Higher Level*

"*The Amare Wave* sounds an inspiring wake-up call to business leaders everywhere: love works. Dr. Moshe Engelberg makes a clear case that you don't have to sacrifice profits to make the world better. This book will show you why love belongs at the foundation of your enterprise, and how to make that happen. If you are jaded or frustrated with how businesses operate, read this now. It will uplift you and change your thinking forever.'"
—STEVE FARBER, CEO, The Extreme Leadership Institute;
author of *Love Is Just Damn Good Business* and *The Radical Leap*

"I have never read any book that reaches the boundaries of thinking about business as love. *The Amare Wave* is an innovative next-generation idea that will not only help businesses foster a loving philosophy, it will help our new generations rethink business in an entirely different way. Dr. Moshe Engelberg has started a movement to think about business as love and for business leaders to ask themselves two questions: Do we love our customers? and Do our customers love us? He is changing the business-as-war framework to business-as-love transformation! After teaching in a school of business for almost twenty-five years, I am making this book required reading for all my business students!"

—ROBIN MCCOY, PHD,
School of Business, University of San Diego

"Twenty-first-century workers (human beings) are naturally repelled by nineteenth-century leadership practices that inherently oppress, deplete, and undermine human well-being—and they're demanding a new wave of heart-driven thinking. *The Amare Wave* arrives just in time."

—MARK C. CROWLEY, author of *Lead from the Heart:
Transformational Leadership for the 21st Century*

"Finally! *The Amare Wave* answers the question: "Why do we feel great after doing business with . . .?" The amazing interactions we enjoy with these companies is the result of them loving their customers. Moshe Engelberg has delivered insights into how to transform your company to do just that. By exploring yourself through Mirrors, observing others through Windows, and committing by walking through Doors, this book challenges forward-thinking leaders to take the next step. Ride the Amare Wave!"

—JIM TENUTO, strategist, A Squared;
CEO, Renaissance Executive Forums

THE
AMARE
WAVE

Big Amare !

— Moshe

THE AMARE WAVE

Uplifting
Business
by
Putting
Love to Work

BOOK ONE OF THE AMARE WAY® SERIES

MOSHE ENGELBERG, PhD

with STACEY AARONSON

ANGEL
MOUNTAIN
PRESS

Angel Mountain Press
info@angelmountainpress.com

ISBN: 978-1-7332847-0-7 hc
ISBN: 978-1-7332847-1-4 pbk
ISBN: 978-1-7332847-2-1 ebk

Library of Congress Control Number: 2019913758

Editing and book design by Stacey Aaronson

Printed in the United States of America

SOMETIMES IN THE WAVES OF CHANGE,
WE FIND OUR TRUE DIRECTION.

This book is dedicated to my mother,
for her deep and abiding family love and her unwavering
support of whatever it was that I was doing.
May her spirit soar in the most celestial heights.

AUTHOR'S NOTE

The Universe, My First Customer

Walking with my cousin Ginger on the beach at La Jolla Shores—a stretch I've walked on hundreds of times over the years, maybe thousands—I was updating her on a book I was writing on love in business.

"That sounds great!" she said.

Shifting to the topic of inspiration, I shared that when someone tells me they're writing a book, or making an album, or creating something, I immediately and happily give them a twenty-dollar bill and tell them they just sold their first one. "Every time," I told her, "the person is stunned and says something like, 'You're actually buying one?! Wow!' and something shifts with the new validation that their creation is worthy."

As I'm telling Ginger how much I enjoy doing this, and how I find it to be an inexpensive and powerful way to lend support, about twenty yards ahead I spot what looks like money. I instantly think three things: 1) Is that a bill there? In all the times I've walked here, I've never seen money at the water's edge like that. 2) If it is, it's probably a dollar bill. Someone must have dropped it. 3) The next wave will probably take it. If not, the people walking in front of us will likely pick it up.

In the moment, I did not connect the sighting to the story I was literally still telling Ginger as we continued walking, but that was about to change. The people in front of us passed right by the bill, not even looking down. When we reached it, lying in the ebbing tide was . . . a twenty-dollar bill. Utterly astounded and immensely grateful, I picked it up. I had just "sold" my first book—to the universe, my first customer.

Since then, I carry around that twenty-dollar bill as a reminder that this book is meant to be.

WAIT! DON'T SKIP THIS PAGE!

"I like this book," you might be saying, "but it's longer than most. What's up with that?"

Hey, we get it. We know you're busy and want to get to the point. We could have written a book half this length—and we almost did—but here's why we didn't:

We've read a lot of business books that powerfully inspire us but don't always help us understand the "why" behind the problems and solutions, or encourage us to look deep into ouselves, or aid us in knowing precisely how to take effective action. We wanted *The Amare Wave* to be different.

So when you reach the "end" of the main content on page 237, you don't have to sift back through the book to decide what you want to implement. Why? Because what follows is a ready-made roadmap for you:

- A recap of all the reflective activities
- Key Takeaways from each chapter
- Dozens of Getting Started Action Steps

We hope you'll agree it was worth the extra pages. ☺

CONTENTS

————

PART TWO
PITTING US AGAINST THEM:
BUSINESS THE WARLIKE WAY

PART THREE
JOINING US WITH THEM:
BUSINESS THE AMARE WAY

PART FOUR
SETTING YOURSELF UP FOR SUCCESS

IMAGINE

Imagine a business world where love is the driving force. Business as war is in the distant past; all the fighting, violence, greed, and suffering it entailed is a collective memory that serves to remind us of what we have willingly abandoned. Business as love feels good and nourishes humanity.

Imagine that businesses know they exist to provide value to society. Business as love is highly profitable without being heartless and mean; profit at any cost represents the old ways. Maximizing shareholder return is an important byproduct, not the main goal. Competition is respected for challenging us to be increasingly better at what we do.

Imagine that businesses are purpose-driven and committed to lasting relationships with their many stakeholders. Companies are in it for the long term, and they manage people and resources accordingly. Managers and sales reps are not pressured to sacrifice everything to hit their monthly numbers. Shareholders and investors take the long view too.

Imagine that the "Golden Rule" is cherished and honored, and that it is the backbone of business culture. Company success is measured by how well people are treated and how well its higher purpose is fulfilled. Profits are important in their proper role as an enabler of increasing value to society.

Imagine business is personal. Business leaders love themselves, their people, and their customers, and customers feel genuinely valued. What is good for business is good for people and society; therefore, politicians who are "good for business" are good for society. Business is a unifying influence, not a divisive one.

magine business leaders are tuned in to the company's higher purpose as well as their own. There is no business persona that allows leaders to be less than their genuine selves at work. They know themselves, show up authentically and unafraid, and lead with personal values intact.

magine that companies put their people first and treat them well. Employees love their work, feel uplifted, and in turn are uplifting. Customers are valued and made to feel special every day, and they don't worry about being ripped off. Customers give their business to companies that make business love.

magine love as the new necessity in business. It's the leading edge, pushed forward by leaders who know their truth and are committed to do what is best for the highest good. Success, then, breeds success. As others adopt it and it becomes widely understood and valued, the wave of love-centered companies grows in size and power. It becomes the norm, the default expectation.

magine love is not only the new necessity in business, it is simply how business is done in the twenty-first century and beyond. Love in business unifies us, lets us prosper without suffering, and makes our world a better place.

Think this is impossible?

Read on.

I
WROTE
THIS BOOK
TO
ALLEVIATE
SUFFERING
IN
BUSINESS.

INTRODUCTION

I t was 1992. I was close to completing my dissertation and finishing grad school—an intense research-based PhD program in Communication at Stanford. At thirty-three years old, I was married with three young children, and we were decidedly picky about where we wanted to raise our family. I had considered a career in academia, but after completing and enjoying a couple of small consulting projects while in grad school, I was leaning toward full-time consulting.

As I investigated opportunities, I discovered rather quickly that within the big firms at the time, there was an accepted—and to me, disturbing—language. Management consultants were classified into one of two groups. Those who brought in business were called hunters; those who did the work were called skinners. These labels kept echoing in my mind. *Hunters and skinners.* The language sounded brutal and heartless. *What does that make customers?* I wondered. I wanted to make money and do good work, but I didn't want to hunt or skin. Why would I think in terms of killing my clients?

So I started my own firm and vowed to be different.

Then, I forgot.

For the next two decades, I worked mainly with government agencies and large and small nonprofits—and time and again, I observed the same fundamental problems: good organizations that were underknown and undervalued, products and services that weren't selling, marketing campaigns that were misguided, talented people who were frustrated and burnt out, and customers who were feeling ignored and disconnected. During those years, the underlying problem was almost always the same: the organizations were focused more on themselves than on those they were here to serve. In short, they were product-centric, not customer-centric—so that's what I focused on rectifying.

After about fifteen years into my career as a consultant, I had the opportunity to expand into working in the private sector with global medical technology companies, healthcare systems, and startups. Here, too, people and organizations were frequently stuck in a paradigm that did not enable them to be their best or do their best, and that frustration resulted in diminished business performance and customers consistently being deprived of value. Only in the private sector, it got worse. Whereas the nonprofits and government agencies were mostly aligned with the communities they were striving to serve, several of these private sector companies were antagonistic toward their customers. When one client confided that his company actually hated their customers, a light bulb went off in my mind. How could anyone be in a business where they hated the very people they were there to serve, the people who provided their income? This was Disconnect #1.

There had to be an effective solution, I thought. At the same time, the words my colleagues and clients used suddenly felt harsh in a way I hadn't absorbed before: *capture* customers, *crush* the competition, *conquer* the market. I had slipped into using that same language over the years as well, but I hadn't paid much attention to it. It was simply the common vernacular. This pervasive violent language in business was Disconnect #2.

On top of all that, as my spiritual practice was deepening and integrating notions of unity and oneness, I was witnessing how the fighting energy of business led to separateness, greed, and suffering. Disconnect #3.

I began to analyze these three interrelated disconnects, striving to uncover the root cause of all the unhappiness and suffering I was seeing in business. After pondering it for quite a while, it finally came to me. Inherent in most of the problems I'd encountered in all my years of consulting was one foundational element that had gradually become watered down and was now consistently missing—one that took me a while to hone in on but that finally clicked:

Business was missing love.

When this realization sank in, it became clear that what I had been witnessing over the years was that business "success" was about dominating, controlling, and subduing, much like the savage language of those management consulting firms I encountered at the beginning of my career. Companies were predators, customers were prey; competitors were meant to be crushed. This all-consuming focus on being first to market, on beating the competition, on capturing market share, on hitting quarterly numbers—at any cost—was all extremely warlike.

When I unveiled this dynamic, I found it very disturbing and immediately felt compelled to find a way to invite and inspire good organizations to move away from being warlike in business, and instead embrace being love-like. Sounds like an easy enough transition, right? After all, we're hardwired for love. But being love-like in business isn't the paradigm we've been taught, and most of us haven't had business mentors who have modeled this kind of foundation or interplay. Yet I was beginning to see a shift occurring in a small and growing number of large and small businesses alike—a subsiding wave of this warlike model being replaced by a new, emerging one anchored in love. Using the Latin word *amare* for love, I call it the Amare Wave.

This book is your personal invitation to join it.

WHO IS THIS BOOK FOR?

When I first started thinking about expanding this love-based framework into a book, I naively thought it would be for anyone in business, regardless of their role, their experience, their values, or their goals. After all, in today's world, who couldn't use the message that business is not war and that putting love at the heart of business is a much better way to go? As a marketing strategist for almost three decades, I should have known better. No product or service is for everyone.

As time went on and this book came into shape, I thought more about roles in business. I realized that the ideas I present here are most applicable to current and aspiring business leaders who need to set vision, establish culture, and inspire their people. However, some parts of the book are also useful to company VPs and directors responsible for shaping business strategy, making mission-critical decisions, and building significant relationships, where they can pass business love down to managers as strategic and tactical direction. Other parts may be helpful to managers who need to tailor strategy to their projects and execute on tactics—passing business love *up* the ladder as the approach they want to take in satisfying company/upper management goals. Ideally, the book will help all three groups remain in alignment with a company's guiding vision and business strategy that is built on love. (Though I mostly use the word "company" in the book, the content applies to any type of organization that could benefit from the uplifting effect of putting love to work, including nonprofits,

NGOs, and government agencies.) On a deeper level, I believe that where you are in your mind and heart is a better way to consider who this book is for, and if you feel it is for you. Based on my research and understanding, I have identified three main profiles of people this book will serve.

1. YOU'RE ON THE PATH

This book is for you if you are already on the path of love in business. You know this approach is for you. You're living it and have already chosen to be a force for good. You may read this book because you want to feel uplifted and connected on your path, or you may want reinforcement and support. You would like to have more ideas and tools, along with the momentum to grow and expand within your organization—and, more broadly, in the business world. Maybe you are a change-maker or a way-shower, and therefore have a desire to encourage and inspire others to join in. You get it and you are committed.

2. YOU FEEL SOMETHING IS OFF

This book is for you if you feel something is missing in business, even if you don't know what it is. That "something" that feels off might be inside you, or inside your organization. Either way, you know the problem is systemic. You are perhaps frustrated and disillusioned, but deep inside you still hold hope. The idea that business is not war resonates with you; you have felt the pain and experienced the suffering that model requires, and you have seen the consequences and costs. The idea of love in business may appeal to you, or it might be a little off-putting. Maybe you're drawn to it but aren't convinced it will work in the hard-hearted world of business. Bottom line, you're interested in reading this book not because you are certain it is for you, but because you are interested and open to hearing more—and because you *want* this way to work. On a personal level, you know you can be happier and more fulfilled. On a business level, you know your company can *be* and *do* better. On a macro level, you know business needs to shift. You know the world desperately needs healing, and the time is now to become part of it.

3. YOU LOVE TO LEARN

This book is for you if you are a new student or perennial seeker. As a new student, you want a solid foundation and you want it to include ideas like love in business—before you become jaded or are told it can't be done. As a seeker, you like to learn about new approaches and different ideas in business and in life, and this growing movement appeals to you. You will take what you learn here and test it against other ideas; you will experiment and learn more as you apply a few of the principles, tweak others, and reframe or combine some. Hopefully, you'll share what you learn and contribute to our collective knowledge and practice, feeling exhilarated by riding this new wave.

No matter which of these profiles applies to you—and you may fit into more than one—one message is universal: The energy of most business today is fighting, not loving. Business is missing the uplifting energy of love, and this leads to suffering.

When we see clearly how catching the Amare Wave has the power to alleviate suffering, real change for the better can occur. The result is a more harmonious, more grounded, more collectively cooperative model of business that has the goal of benefiting not only shareholders and those at the top, but every person the business serves, those inside the company who make that service happen, and indeed the collective consciousness of humanity.

HOW THIS BOOK IS ORGANIZED

The Amare Wave is presented in four parts.

PART ONE, THE WAVE IS HERE! poses the question: Why Love? Why Now? and explores the positive role of money in doing business the Amare Way, along with the transformative role and evolving consciousness of business in society.

PART TWO, PITTING US AGAINST THEM: BUSINESS THE WAR-LIKE WAY, explores the long-established business as war paradigm, how it became pervasive, and how we are growing tired of seeing stories of evil in business make headlines. It also uncovers the detrimental characteristics, actions, and effects bred within a "business is war" mentality, awakening awareness of what has often gone unnoticed or unspoken in the business environment, inspiring a spark for change.

PART THREE, JOINING US WITH THEM: BUSINESS THE AMARE WAY, explores the importance of alignment, the seven principles of the Amare Way Philosophy, the ABCs—Authenticity, Belonging, and Collaboration—that constitute the Amare Way Practice, and ends with The Amare Way Manifesto.

PART FOUR, SETTING YOURSELF UP FOR SUCCESS, helps you turn five common traps into stepping stones, gathers all the reflective activities and assessments throughout the book into one place, and gives you Key Takeaways and Getting Started Action Steps for becoming a cultivator of love and catching the Amare Wave.

HOW TO USE THIS BOOK

Throughout *The Amare Wave*, I provide ample opportunities for reflection, perspective, and planning. Through the following three portals, you are invited to make the topic of putting love to work highly relevant, both to you personally and to your company.

MIRROR: I invite you to see yourself and your organization in the ideas presented throughout this book, whether it looks pretty or not. These exercises are not meant to be merely a superficial reflection, but a deeper awareness of your experiences, thoughts, and feelings. Within these revealing activities, I encourage you to find yourself and discover your place in catching the Amare Wave. This is where open minds and hearts are important, along with a willingness to be vulnerable and a desire to be authentic.

WINDOW: I invite you to see into the varied experiences of diverse individuals and businesses. Here you will learn what qualities they embrace, what actions they take, and what results they get. This is where you get to peek into both misguided perspectives and their consequences, as well as into how loving organizations thrive!

DOOR: I invite you to step over the threshold from ideas into action to be more love-like in business and doing things the Amare Way. You will find ways to take small or big steps—whichever best suits you—to change yourself and your company for the good.

Opening people's minds to a love-centered view of business, inspiring societal change to support business as a social and economic enterprise that fosters love, and providing concrete ways for people to join the movement of putting love at the core of their business is what this book aims to do.

To be relevant and meaningful on multiple levels, I converged and drew deeply from many sources: my nearly thirty years as founder and head of a boutique research-based consulting firm; conversations with a wide range of kind and smart people; my own decades-long personal spiritual journey, dozens of influential books (see Recommended Reading); and the wisdom of both ancient and modern-day thinkers, authors, poets, business leaders, consultants, researchers, and practitioners whose work illuminates our evolution to a higher level of consciousness. My hope is that this book will help further crystalize the emerging love-based paradigm for organizations of all kinds, as well as advance its successful implementation.

As this shift occurs, the results will not simply render greater business success and prosperity for its practitioners. We will also experience more happiness and fulfillment as a society, and less suffering across the board.

Finally, I propose that experiencing more love in our lives will support the viability of the human race on earth and grow our collective consciousness in a positive way, enabling a more loving, authentic, inclusive, and collaborative way of being and doing, in business and in life.

Onward and upward! Let's do this.

PART ONE

THE WAVE IS HERE!

Get ready to be strong, be great, be amazing.
—UNKNOWN

CATCH
A
wave
AND
YOU'LL BE
SITTIN'
ON TOP OF
THE WORLD.

—THE BEACH BOYS

CHAPTER ONE

CATCHING THE AMARE WAVE:
WHY LOVE? WHY NOW?

A mighty wave, growing in momentum and force every day, is propelling good organizations away from the fear-based "business as war" fighting paradigm, and toward a fresh, love-centered approach that uplifts society and increases prosperity. A healthy number of companies are riding this wave and profiting greatly. In fact, I bet you can name five off the top of your head right now, simply based on your own experience as a customer. Think about it: which organizations uplift you a little bit whenever you do business with them? Which companies do you feel a connection with and want to grow bigger and better? These are the businesses that likely operate with *amare*.

So, what exactly is *amare*?

In its most basic translation, from both Latin and Italian, *amare* means love. In a deeper sense, *amare* also carries layered and more profound meanings, qualities that resonate with the growing movement of this wave: maintaining cohesiveness between people, breaking through walls of separation, focusing on aspects that unite us, recognizing the humanity in each other, rejecting indifference, honoring the other, reciprocating respect, renouncing cruelty and degradation, and being grounded in a desire to better each other's well-being. In sum, *amare* operates to preserve the integrity of humanity and to reduce suffering.

When I use the word *amare* throughout this book and within this growing movement, I want to be clear that it encompasses not only love, but every one of these indispensable qualities. And for you language aficionados, you may find it interesting that *amore* is the noun form of love in Italian, and *mare* is the word for sea. When you marry the two, you also get Amare—combining loving respect for all humanity with the movement of the sea. All of this beautiful etymology lends to the expanding shift toward the "business as love" paradigm I call the Amare Way. You can think of this paradigm as your "ticket" that grants you access to the "ride" we call the Amare Wave.

Whether you realize it or not, this is an incredible time to be in business. We have an amazing opportunity before us: by embracing the fortifying and honoring aspects of *amare* I just described, we become better equipped to let go of the pervasive warlike approach to business—one that is rooted in fear and sustained with an energy of fighting—and instead choose to do business within a paradigm that thrives on the uplifting and unifying energy of love. Think of it as an operating system that elevates business to its rightful place, where it not only improves well-being for others— which is the fundamental reason why business, any business, exists—but it also functions and generates prosperity within a model that no longer perpetuates suffering.

From a big-picture perspective, it is still early days in terms of transforming twenty-first-century business into a love-centered paradigm. This presents tremendous growth potential for business leaders and companies alike. The Amare Wave gathering momentum right now is propelled by a multitude of successful companies and those telling their stories, continuously growing and reaching toward countless more companies across the globe by resonating with their known truths and deepest yearnings.

As a result, love-centered companies that do well by doing good are receiving more and more attention. The wave cannot be ignored because the positive results are too consistent and compelling to write off as an aberration or as unachievable. In fact, researchers have taken notice of these pioneering organizations and have begun to document and share the process and outcomes, which has lent credibility and emboldened confidence. For example, the research-based book *Firms of Endearment* lists a diverse mix of over seventy public and private organizations from the US and other countries that ascribe to a love-centered philosophy—and with great financial results—which is motivating others to adopt recommended practices.

Other books, such as *Reinventing Organizations, Saving Capitalism, Peak,* and *Principles,* similarly spread the word about successful values-based approaches to business. There is also a spate of business books that are explicitly about love: *Lovability, Love Is the Killer App, Love Is Just Damn Good Business, Lead with Luv, Customer Love,* and *LoveMarks,* to name a few. Founders and CEOs of a wide range of companies—Chobani, TOMS, Geisinger Healthcare, KIND, Airbnb, and more—are telling their stories through TED talks, books, conferences, and podcasts about successfully putting love to work. We even see huge companies like Costco consistently resisting the pressures of Wall Street and choosing to do things in their own principled and generous way with great success.

Throughout this book, we will look at various love-centered companies, and I believe you'll be heartened and energized to see the paths they have forged—and the success they have achieved. I'm likewise hopeful you'll feel excited and confident about catching their momentum and surfing the Amare Wave—what I consider to be what oceanographers call a "deep water wave," in that it draws its power and momentum from many contributors. By integrating diverse and complementary principles, practices, and proof points from other areas of life—ancient wisdom traditions, behavioral science, and popular entertainment to name a few—the appeal and relevance of love-centered business reaches deeper and wider, hence strengthening the wave even more.

What's exciting, too, is that disciplines like positive psychology and servant leadership are taking hold in all kinds of businesses, as are a plethora of other ideas and practices that support the energy of love in business. A few examples of these are emotional intelligence, mindfulness, and meditation; co-creation, collaboration, and transparency in teamwork; and being purpose-driven, compassionate, and happy at work. The blending of Eastern and Western traditions is also adding energy to the wave, as we see advice within companies from contemporary spiritual leaders like the Dalai Lama, Thich Nhat Hanh, Deepak Chopra, and Eckhart Tolle, along with ancient wisdom from works like the *Bhagavad Gita* and *Tao Te Ching*.

Plato famously said in *Republic*, "What is honored in a country is cultivated there. Borrowing from that maxim, we assert that:

What is honored in a *company* is cultivated there.

In short, you no longer need to do business within a paradigm that perpetuates suffering.

If you've ever felt dissatisfied, misaligned, or even disheartened by how you and your company act in business, and by how those actions affect people's lives and society at large, you understand what I mean when I use the word "suffering." While some of us experience this infrequently, others experience it on a regular basis.

For example, do you sometimes dread the day to day? Resent your customers? Desire anything but having to interact with your employees or colleagues? Cringe at how ethics are conveniently "bent"—or worse, nonexistent? Are you ever exhausted from the constant fighting to win, the cutthroat battles with competitors, or the pressure to hit your numbers at any cost? Perhaps you suffer from the choices you make, and even more so when you realize your choices make other people suffer. You may even feel that you're not the person you want to be at work, and with that comes a pervasive sense of unhappiness that spills over into the rest of your life.

But what I want you to grasp as you read this book is that when love is at the core of business, it's easier for love to be at the core of life too. You're not in conflict with yourself, acting one way at work, and another way outside of it. The joy you derive from doing work you love, leading others with love, serving people with love, providing products and services rooted in love, elevates your quality of life to a much higher level. This is because the essence of being love-like in business is connection, deep and enlivening connection. It's about understanding what people need on a profound level, allowing them to be truly heard in expressing those needs, and bringing honesty and integrity to meeting those needs. When you cultivate and operate with this positive energy, you are much more likely to be fully aligned with your vision, value proposition, financial goals, higher purpose—and, of course, with yourself. In short, you get to be *you*.

This is cause alone for catching the growing momentum of the Amare Wave. But there's another huge benefit too, one founded in a truth that many of us have missed in prior decades:

**Business is a social enterprise that exists
to provide value to society.**

In other words, business makes life better for people by meeting important needs. Meeting important needs is a loving act. Hence, *business makes love.*

Think about it: most businesses, products, and services were created out of a desire to improve something for others. Because improving things for others is a loving desire—which is rooted in our layered meaning of *amare*—most businesses were conceived out of love.

Now, in exchange for that love-based product or service, businesses receive something in return, typically money. But let's be clear: **no company exists expressly to make money.** Money is an *outcome* of being in business, not the *reason* for being in business. This is why being grounded in *amare* creates such a powerful shift. Instead of being solely focused on dollars, businesses can focus on contributing to the well-being of others, fostering positive brand recognition, and cultivating loyal and lasting relationships. In other words, the "give and get" between parties is the fundamental value exchange that creates commerce and sustains society. And bonus: being love-like is a powerful source of favorable differentiation and distinction in business. The win-win? Companies that effectively "make business love" also make more money.

When we consider these reasons that *business as a social enterprise* exists and how it provides value to society, we are then able to evaluate why *our own* business exists and how *we* provide value.

Consider this illustration:

Imagine "business" as an enormous building—one the size of a large city with multiple floors and an intricate labyrinth of companies, each occupying a certain amount of space on each of the floors. As a social enterprise aimed at making lives better for people, and prospering by doing so, this massive building—or rather, this representation of "business" as a whole—serves society in the most favorable ways possible. Each company within must agree to operate ethically, contribute positively, and embrace bettering some aspect of life for its customers while appreciating the prosperity that brings. Now imagine that any company who either overtly or covertly eschews these values drains life from the building. If there are enough of these draining companies, the capacity of "business" as an entity is diminished. The whole building weakens, and society suffers as a result. But the more people who see the value in running a conscious, *amare*-based company and commit to doing so, the more the enterprise of business thrives. In turn, the companies comprising that entity and those they serve grow and thrive. Bottom line, when the overriding goal is to use business as a means to truly make life better for people, and when individual organizations sincerely embrace this mentality, business as an enterprise can be the greatest agent for awakening us to the power of love, which our world is so desperately in need of now.

**When we use the word "love,"
we define it as energy that uplifts and connects.**

I want you to now imagine placing your own business into the illustration. Can you see how your business—no matter how big or small, prosperous or fledgling—is integral to keeping the harmony within the "building" alive? And, how crucial you are in helping the social enterprise of business function at its optimum? When you do, you will see how *your* individual business plays a significant role in strengthening the Amare Wave and radiating the love-centered paradigm outward.

When millions of people are giving and receiving this love-centered vibration through business, it affects not only us as individuals, but it raises our collective consciousness as well—that is, the set of shared beliefs, ideas, and moral attitudes that operate as a unifying force within society. As a result, business as a social enterprise not only has the power to serve humanity with love, it has the power to move us from unconscious to conscious—or rather, from moving mechanically through our careers to living and working in full awareness and conscious choice—and in the most promising of ways.

If you can imagine yourself—and your company or organization—on the peak of this wave with a magnificent view of what business as love looks like, you can begin to feel the optimism of what this movement on a grand scale could hold. While we can't know how long this wave will last, we can be motivated by the fact that the life of this movement is in our hands as business leaders, investors, workers, and even customers. We have the power to make it last, and there is no reason why we can't make a conscious choice to grow the wave through the twenty-first century and well beyond.

WHY NOW?

One of the guidelines for finding one's purpose, or dharma, is paying attention to the times, what is happening around us, and what is needed in our world right now.

At this moment in history, the ingredients of fighting energy—resistance, fear, hate, greed, violence, and intolerance—are permitted, legitimized, and even perpetuated at the highest levels of business and government. Meanness and lying are pervasive and often without obvious consequence. We see this in many parts of the world. The result is a non-virtuous cycle because the response to fighting energy is typically more fighting energy, and all of it causes a great deal of suffering. While these warlike ways are not new, they are more emboldened, widespread, and visible, which makes them less deniable. In other words, we cannot bury our heads in the sand and pretend this is not currently happening. What we *can* do is transmute the negative energy to motivate positive change.

In part, this pattern reflects the harsh reality that war has been and still is, unfortunately, a huge part of our collective culture. I recently read a striking statistic that there hasn't been a single day without war somewhere in the world for thousands of years. In America alone, we have been at war on some level for

226 of our 243 years, which means that as a country, we've spent over 90 percent of our existence fighting.

Across political parties, religions, and ideologies, many find this way of operating reprehensible and not at all representative of what they believe in, what they value, and what they hold dear. Many people are "done" with the status quo and are actively working to improve society and reduce suffering. You may indeed be one of them. This trend is showing up directly in business with movements like Conscious Capitalism, structures like Benefit Corporations, metrics like TSI (Total Societal Impact), and models like the sharing economy. And we have powerful and high-profile social movements like #MeToo and Time's Up that are making harassment, sexual violence, and incivility punishable and no longer acceptable, especially in work settings. "Business as usual" is riding a wave of change.

Demographically, we also have a generation of elders—that is, my cohort of baby boomers—with myriad lessons to share about challenging the dominant culture and remaking society, in part with the power of love. Gen Xers (born 1965–1980), who are now holding powerful leadership positions in business, have the opportunity to learn from boomers and the traditionalist generation that preceded them, and to apply those lessons today.[1] Perhaps even more aligned in terms of values are Generation Y/Millennials (born 1981–1996), who are widely demanding a balance in life, with passion and energy to take on the challenges of normalizing the Amare Wave as the way of modern business. This is what Generation Z (born 1997–2015) can grow into and further strengthen.

Yes, though it may sound cliché, there is reason for hope, optimism, and a brighter future. And part of this positivity comes from the answer to a critical business question: Will this heart-centered, soulful approach be profitable?

A BUSINESS
ABSOLUTELY
DEVOTED TO
SERVICE
WILL HAVE
ONLY ONE
WORRY ABOUT
PROFITS.
THEY WILL BE
EMBARRASSINGLY
LARGE.

–HENRY FORD

CHAPTER TWO

THE POSITIVE ROLE OF MONEY
WITHIN THE MOVEMENT

In a recent conversation with an exec from one of the world's biggest tech companies about the idea of putting love at the center of business, I received this initial reaction: "Sure, sounds nice. But unless it increases our profitability, I don't care."

Maybe that's your mindset too, as it is for many leaders. I get it. Money matters, and it matters a lot. The good news is that financial gain is an integral part of being an Amare Way company, hence **the short answer to the profitability question is YES, putting love at the center of business *is* profitable.**

Companies that are love-centered—and have all the business essentials in place—do very well financially. But even if it intuitively makes sense to us that being more love-centered would be profitable, sometimes we need to see hard evidence before we can consider making what may be a significant change. So if you're thinking, "Show me the money!", you got it.

Let's take a look at the numbers of six large US-based companies that have been paragons of the "business as love" paradigm, even if they don't expressly use the word *love* to describe it.

TRADER JOE'S, the midsize grocery store chain, with its raving fans (including *moi!*) and unique business model, consistently outperforms its competition, selling nearly twice per square foot of Whole Foods.[2] A recent report estimated that Trader Joe's generated approximately $13.3B in nationwide sales in 2017[3] and is expected to generate $9.67B by 2021[4] – all without any paid advertising. Since its founding in 1967, its focus has been bringing affordable, healthy food to the masses—80 percent of which is from their own private label – while making every interaction genuine and aimed to benefit the customer.[5]

USAA, a financial services company frequently recognized for their exemplary customer relationships and the loyalty that results, has earned a higher return on equity for thirty-four consecutive quarters, compared to other large banks.[6] As of 2017, they were serving over 12 million members[7], generating $2.4B in profit with $155B in total assets.[8] Founded in 1922 to provide auto insurance to Army officers, USAA still focuses its mission primarily on serving members of the US military and their immediate families.

SOUTHWEST AIRLINES has been at the customer love business (LUV is actually their ticker symbol!) since their inception in 1967. Their tremendous success is the stuff of legend.[9] Their annual revenues more than doubled in the last ten years, from $10.35B in 2009 to $21.96B in 2018.[10] They now carry more domestic passengers than any other US airline. Notable in 2018[11] were achieving their forty-sixth consecutive year of profitability with a net income of $2.5B, employees earning $544MM in profit sharing, and returning approximately $2.3B to share-holders.[12]

REI, the consumer cooperative that sells top-notch outdoor gear, has shown consistent year-over-year revenue growth since 2003 and is now 18 million members strong. In 2018, eighty-one years after its founding, REI reported a record $2.78B in sales, while adding one million new members.[13] Over 70 percent of its profits went right back to the outdoor community, supporting employee retirement, helping fund trail work, returning dividends to its members, and supporting nonprofits that get people outdoors.[14] Since its inception, REI has worked to awaken a lifelong love for the outdoors for everyone, through sustainable growth and reinvestment into the communities it serves—all inspired by the company's unchanging belief that "a life outdoors is a life well lived."[15]

COSTCO, the retail warehousing giant – known for inspiring loyalty among employees and customers, and focusing on value while resisting pressures from Wall Street to put money first – had a total sales increase of 9.7 percent to $138.4B for the 2018 fiscal year.[16] According to Motley Fool, as of November 2018, Costco's stock was up 91 percent over the past five years vs. the S&P 500's 56 percent gain, and with the 30 percent increase that key rivals Walmart and Target achieved.[17] Costco scored top marks for online shopper customer satisfaction, putting Amazon in second place after holding the top spot since 2010.[18] The score validates Costco's customer-first culture and proves once again that customers love to shop at Costco.

TOMS has made hundreds of millions of dollars by giving shoes away. Through its ubiquitous "one for one" campaign, TOMS donates a pair of shoes for every pair purchased – more than 86 million pairs of shoes since 2006[19] – with annual revenues approaching $400MM. In 2014, when the company was eight years old, 50 percent of the company was acquired by Bain Capital at a $625MM valuation.[20] Their trademarked one-for-one business model has been adopted by dozens of other successful companies, with products ranging from eyeglasses (Warby Parker) to medical scrubs (Figs). Their numbers demonstrate that it's possible to achieve tremendous financial success with a business model that is, as author Dan Pink puts it, "expressly built for purpose maximization."

As you can see, some of the biggest names in business today are not only intensely customer-focused, but they are making a significant difference in the world and reaping remarkable profits doing so. With their transparency, admirable ethics, and love-centered missions, these companies are showing the world what it means to engage in socially responsible business models that are sincerely focused on making life better for people—and yes, that make a lot of money in the process. I view these highly profitable and long-time industry leaders at the forefront of the Amare Wave —and they are not alone.

A steady stream of research shows that people prefer products and services that are good for them and good for society. For example, a 2015 Neilsen study on sustainability found that 66 percent of global consumers say they would pay more for brands that are good for the planet. Customers want their purchasing decisions to be aligned with their values, and those values include doing good for the community and the world.[21] The idea of aligning profits with purpose to help business make a positive impact on the world is a key aspect of "conscious capitalism," a discipline growing in popularity.[22]

There is also rigorous and compelling evidence of the financial success of love-centered companies in the book *Firms of Endearment* that I referred to earlier by Raj Sisodia, David Wolfe, and Jag Sheth. Their research compares the return to investors delivered by publicly traded companies they classified as firms of endearment (FoEs)[23] to the return to investors delivered by the S&P 500 companies overall. You'll be heartened to know that the FoE companies outperformed the S&P 500 **by more than 8 to 1 over a ten-year period**. In percentages, they returned 1,026 percent to investors over a decade compared to a return of 122 percent for the S&P 500 companies—a huge difference.[24] And I suspect that the differential would be even greater if they had compared FoEs with companies that are deeply entrenched in the business as war paradigm.

These results were a great surprise to the researchers. Sure, they expected and predicted correctly that FoEs would be widely loved by their customers, employees, and other stakeholders. But they did not expect better financial performance. If anything, they anticipated lower profitability: "After all, they (FoEs) pay their employees exceptionally well, do not squeeze their suppliers, deliver great products and experiences at fair prices to customers, are conscious of their environmental impact, and spend significant resources in the community—surely, all this should lead to a reduction in profits and thus the stock price."

But that wasn't what they found at all.

Chief among the behaviors of the cited companies is that they emphasize humanity and espouse being more authentic, heart-centered, and soulful in business. These highly effective companies have adopted proven leadership and organizational management principles and practices that are consistent with a "business as love" paradigm—and the ideas and their applications have been shown to enable companies to fulfill their higher purpose; consistently deliver on their value proposition; earn the enduring trust of employees, customers, and other stakeholders; outperform competition; *and* show healthy profits.

The reality is that companies committed to *amare*-like principles—using frameworks like conscious capitalism, servant leadership, Teal organizations,[25] or similarly spirited models—are by far in the minority as of now. But the number of companies adopting these approaches and catching the Amare Wave is increasing, supported in part by compelling evidence of superior financial performance.

PUTTING PROFIT INTO PERSPECTIVE

Now that we've made the case that a) profitability is essential for love-centered companies to be successful, and b) love-centered companies are generally (and sometimes exceedingly!) more profitable than competitors, let's quickly put financial performance into proper context within the business as love paradigm.

First, let's be perfectly clear: profitability is but one indicator of success, and not the most important one. In a business as war paradigm, profitability is the dominant measure of success. But in a love-centered model, increasing profitability is not the leading driver of business decisions, nor is it the overriding indicator of business success.

This brings us to two important points:

1. The measure needs to fit the paradigm.

If we allow profitability to become the exclusive governor of whether to adopt a love-centered paradigm, there will be misalignment. It's like requiring proof that the new paradigm is better, but with the proof based in the thinking and values of the old paradigm. Einstein famously said that "we cannot solve our problems with the same thinking we used when we created them." By design or not, this dynamic tethers us to the "business is war" model.

2. Insufficient profit is not the problem.

The problem we're solving with a shift to a love-based paradigm is not how to increase profitability. Many companies are very good at maximizing profits already. The problem we're solving is how to make business be both good for people *and* for profits—and to reduce suffering.

Remember: Just because increasing profitability is not the problem being solved does not mean that the solution—a love-based paradigm—will not increase profitability. In fact, it can and it does.

MEANINGFUL VALUE AND HEALTHY RETURN

In business, we all want to make money. To convince stakeholders that our company, product, or service under consideration is a worthy investment, we create a business case that shows it provides *meaningful value* and will generate a *healthy return*.

But what do these two terms mean?

A traditional market-driven view of **meaningful value** is that it exists when you offer something people want and will buy. A **healthy return** means that sales will generate a good profit. The markers of a strong business case, then, are projected demand and profit.

In the business as love paradigm, however, the definitions are different.

Meaningful value, rather than being merely about market demand, goes beyond any particular product or service to your higher purpose of providing value to society. Why?

Because providing value to society is why your company exists.

How does this redefine healthy return?

Healthy return becomes measured not solely by the profits on your goods and services, but also by the advancement of your higher purpose. Profitability, then, becomes a necessary but not sufficient part of the business case.

If this is still a difficult concept to grasp in terms of running a financially profitable company, let's return for a moment to TOMS.

In theory, it may seem monetarily counterproductive to give away a pair of shoes for every pair you sell. But founder Blake Mycoskie wasn't thinking in those terms. For him, providing shoes to those in need was the primary goal, and he found a way to accomplish that through selling shoes with his "one for one" promise. Because people feel good about giving, and they are able to do so by simply enjoying a pair of shoes for themselves with no additional contribution, people flock to TOMS. Of course, style, quality, and sustainable materials matter too, and TOMS has that covered as well. But what's important here is to understand that this company, valued at $625 million only seven years after its founding, began with, and has always maintained, a core mission to provide shoes for people in developing countries. It's never been about money, yet TOMS continually enjoys and sustains solid profits.

Yes, we are still in a relatively early stage of the "business as love" paradigm, and yes, the statistics thus far are undeniably energizing. As such, I hope you feel confident that catching the Amare Wave can make your company a lot of money, while having conscious capitalism at your company's core and keeping profitability in its proper perspective.

In the next chapter, we'll briefly explore business and the evolution of consciousness, which shows just how capable we are of making positive change—and how the timing couldn't be more perfect.

HUMAN
SELF-UNDERSTANDING
CHANGES
WITH
TIME,
AND SO ALSO
HUMAN
CONSCIOUSNESS
DEEPENS.

–POPE FRANCIS

CHAPTER THREE

BUSINESS AND THE EVOLUTION OF CONSCIOUSNESS

Although the big picture appears rather bleak at times, there is great reason for optimism.

Yes, it may be true that corruption in many businesses is over the top, that violence is permeating every nook and cranny of society, that our climate is in deep crisis, and that decency seems to be a thing of the past. It's not hard to feel justified in concluding that things are hopeless, that our world is simply falling apart.

Yet, there is another perspective, an empowering and pragmatically optimistic one—one in which we can see the good.

In Ralph Alan Dale's masterful introduction to the English translation of the *Tao Te Ching*, the central text of Taoism, he points out that what is upon us now is the birth of the next evolutionary phase of consciousness, known as *synthesis*. To put this into context, the first phase of human consciousness was highly cooperative and went on for millennia. It was called the Yin phase because it was grounded in the more peaceful and receptive yin energy—and thereby named *thesis*, i.e., the main premise by which society ran. Then came its negation in the much more combative Yang phase, called *antithesis,* which has defined the past 10,000 years or so. The next and impending phase, *synthesis,* will reconcile and unify the best of the thesis and antithesis phases, and eventually, over time, will become the prevailing thesis.[26]

Presently, we are in the latter days of the *antithesis,* where—ironically—the very advancements developed in this phase pose dire threats. As Dale explains:

> Life today is an expression of the decline and fall of this second great phase, which accounts for the enormous social and individual trauma of our time. Although societies have come and gone in the past, there is a new ultimate danger which the present disintegration of civilization presents: the intolerable juxtaposition of social pathology and high technology, a volatile mixture which can lead not only to the end of civilization, but also to the possibility of our very species' extinction.

Frightening, I know. If unchecked, the consequences would, in fact, be devastating. I believe we know deep inside that this existential threat is true because we can *feel* that times are different, that there is an urgency to alter course. However, what's empowering is the knowledge that we have the potential to transform our social pathology.

One of the changes that can make the biggest difference is being more loving in business. This evolutionary shift is similar in spirit to what big-picture business thinkers envision: what Daniel Pink calls the Conceptual Age, what Raj Sisodia and colleagues call the Age of Transcendence, and what Frederic Laloux calls the time of Teal Organizations.

Because we can actively choose how we operate in business, we have the power to help usher in the synthesis phase *through* business.

What does this mean? That the imminent prospect of a transformation into a much healthier and sustainable next phase of business is upon us!

As Dale explains, the *Tao* describes this third evolutionary epoch of consciousness as the Great Integrity, characterized by engagement with life and transcendence of our inhumanity, and envisioned as a quiet revolution that a) confronts and purges our pathologies caused by the overabundance of yang, b) embraces the yin energy of our total humanity, and c) liberates us to function with the full potential of our species, a potential that has taken millions of years to ripen to readiness. In the process, we will overcome the pervasive lack of engagement and tame our ability to dehumanize that helps drive the business as war paradigm (explored in depth in Part II), which is a direct outgrowth of the combative Yang phase.

In short, *synthesis* entails ditching warlike actions for love-like behaviors, and being elevated to embrace the spirit of *amare* in its varied forms, all of which are grounded in a desire to better our own and each other's well-being and improve society.

As a reminder, amare encompasses all of the following:

- maintaining cohesiveness between humans
- breaking through walls of separation
- focusing on aspects that unite us
- recognizing the humanity in one another
- rejecting indifference
- honoring the other
- reciprocating respect
- renouncing cruelty and degradation

In *The Soul of America: The Battle for Our Better Angels*, Pulitzer Prize–winning author John Meacham makes a historical case for these levels of positivity:

> To know what has come before is to be armed against despair. If the men and women of the past, with all their flaws and limitations and ambitions and appetites, could press on through ignorance and superstition, racism and sexism, selfishness and greed, to create a freer, stronger nation, then perhaps we, too, can right wrongs and take another step toward that most enchanting elusive of destinations: a more perfect Union.

What enables us to get through such immense challenges as the Civil War, abolishing slavery, the women's suffrage movement, the resurgence of hate groups, and isolationism? To Meacham, it is the triumph of hope (what I call love) over fear, sanctioned by strong and committed leaders, enabling us to endure times of madness, overcome injustice, and grow together—or, as President Lincoln said, let our "better angels" prevail.

I firmly believe that this same love and leadership *can* and *will* carry us through—albeit painfully at times—today's extreme challenges in business and life.

Circling back to Dale, he concludes his Introduction to the ancient *Tao Te Ching* by stating:

> How unbelievably privileged we are to be the generations assigned the ultimate task: to be the midwives of our own rebirthing!

In this spirit, I believe the growing momentum toward a more evolved and holistic model of business is an integral component of a successful transition to this next level of consciousness.

Yet the vast majority of companies still operate with a warlike mentality, enabled and rewarded by Wall Street investors, government regulations, media coverage, and other powerful forces. To recognize what sustains that, and to better equip us to consciously move business in the direction of love, let's take a clear-eyed look at the current, widely accepted warlike paradigm of business—the Us Against Them model—so that we can better understand why we've become so immersed in a pattern that instead of uplifting society, fundamentally causes a great deal of suffering.

PART TWO

PITTING US AGAINST THEM: BUSINESS THE WARLIKE WAY

Business is war. I go out there, I want to kill the competitors. I want to make their lives miserable. I want to steal their market share. I want them to fear me and I want everyone on my team thinking we're going to win.
—KEVIN O'LEARY,
INVESTOR ON THE TV SHOW *SHARK TANK*

WE
FORGET
THAT OTHERS
ARE
HUMAN
BEINGS
LIKE US,
STRIVING
FOR THE
SAME
GOALS.

CHAPTER FOUR

A SHORT IN THE HARDWIRING: HOW WE'VE ADOPTED A BUSINESS AS WAR MENTALITY

To make sense of the momentous shift toward a "business as love" paradigm and put the Amare Wave into context, it's vital to first understand where business has largely been anchored for centuries—with its corresponding attitudes and practices—and why.

The truth is, we often don't even recognize we're steeped in a mentality that treats business as war. It may start with common and seemingly innocuous language, such as talking in terms of battle plans and capturing market share. In the daily grind, you may compromise your own ethics to look better to your investors, or lose sight of the real reason your business exists, allowing key decisions to become misaligned. You may likewise put out some slightly misleading marketing messages to increase sales and hit your monthly numbers. All of this can devolve into dehumanizing people—treating employees as commodities, customers as prey, and competitors as enemies. Some businesses take their warlike mentality a step further: Do whatever it takes to maximize short-term profits without regard to how others are affected, even delighting in watching the competition go down.

These attitudes, language, and behaviors of the "business as war" paradigm have become so ingrained in our culture, they are not only tolerated or accepted, but to a large degree are expected, admired, and rewarded.

How did this come to be?

I'm not a historian and don't pretend to be, hence this book does not endeavor to present a comprehensive history of business trends, or even address the growth of capitalism and free markets, per se. Instead, I believe it's more useful to put the "business as love" and "business as war" paradigms into the context of our broader human journey by stepping way back in time.

As I briefly touched on in Chapter Three, ancient Chinese philosophy partitions human evolution into two main phases, the first being the Yin epoch and the second the Yang epoch. The Yin epoch lasted millions of years and was characterized by mostly communal living and a predominance of intuitive right-brain functioning. There was a sense of harmony and integration with nature and the greater whole; we cared for each other because it helped us survive. For the same reason, our social structure was egalitarian and cooperative.

In contrast, the Yang epoch of approximately the past ten millennia has been represented by coercive civilizations, the predominance of left-brain analytical thinking, and a corresponding alienated consciousness dominated by the ego. This phase emerged as agriculture created the capacity for the many to create a surplus that enriched the few, who then controlled society. Some historians refer to the transition from traditional hunting and gathering to farming in permanent settlements—which marked the advent of the Yang epoch—as the First Agricultural Revolution, or Neolithic Revolution. The fact that food could now be farmed to meet demand fueled global population growth and seeded a dynamic of always "needing" more, which could come from one of two perspectives.

ARE YOU HERE FOR THE WORLD, OR IS THE WORLD HERE FOR YOU?

A compelling and related way to think about the evolution of humanity and these two ways of living are compellingly presented in Daniel Quinn's controversial novel *Ishmael*. In it, he characterizes people as either Takers or Leavers.

Leavers correspond to the dominant culture in the Yin epoch, or those who generally belong to traditional tribal cultures that live simply and in harmony with the rest of life. They subscribe to the same ecological rules that govern other species, with a harmonious premise: "We are here for the world."

Takers (aka our civilization and the dominant culture in the current Yang epoch), in contrast, see it as their birthright to rule the world through conquest, domination, and unchecked growth. For Takers, the premise is aggressively Yang: "The world is here for *us*." This lets them (us) justify doing whatever they want to the world and without any concern for others. While Takers think they have used technology to outwit nature, in reality they are depleting the planet of natural resources and will eventually plummet into extinction (which we are, frighteningly, witnessing in our time).

It is during this Yang phase of existence that instead of needing to care for each other to survive, it has become advantageous to the few to dominate and subdue the many. In short, we exchanged our natural harmony with the universe in the Yin epoch for gratification of our egos in the Yang epoch. In agriculture as well as in other business sectors, this process catalyzed—then normalized—a warlike approach in which greed for self eclipsed service to others. As a result, success metrics apart from money, power, and prestige largely became devalued.

Fast forward to the mid-nineteenth century for a more modern evolutionary perspective and observe the teachings of Darwin. As you know, his theory of evolution powerfully shaped the thinking of science and society. From a business perspective, his theory was taken—or rather mis-taken, in my opinion—as an admonition for dominating markets, crushing competition, and doing whatever it takes to come out ahead. It is probably no surprise, then, that the Darwinian notions of survival of the fittest and natural selection became quite warlike in their application.

A hundred years or so later, this mentality manifested in numerous corporations becoming hyper-focused on maximizing shareholder return as their main objective. The idea, widely attributed to economist Milton Friedman in the 1960s, during a period when when economists were newly wielding major influence in politics and business,[27] was that by narrowly focusing on the singular goal of maximizing profitability for shareholder return—and rejecting the notion of businesses having "social responsibility" to the public or society—corporations would optimally increase productivity and improve economic growth and well-being. This, like Darwin's theory, was used to put money front and center in business and justify a "whatever it takes" attitude, which perpetrated correspondingly rancorous behaviors.

In brief summation:

1. We have the backdrop of the last 10,000 years of our human journey in which business came to be fueled by an alienated and greed-driven social consciousness, through which the few subordinated the many.

2. We have the dominant theory of evolution being interpreted to condone bellicose behaviors in business as natural and necessary to not only survive as the fittest, but to eliminate competition, both at any cost.

3. We have the legacy of a highly influential economist whose advice led to prioritizing shareholder return above all else, which in turn was used to focus on short-term profitability and rationalize all kinds of warlike actions to achieve it.

These forces, coupled with many others, righteously enabled—even "ennobled"—the business as war paradigm as *the way* to do business.

THE BUSINESS AS WAR PARADIGM

According to *Warfighting*, the US Marine Corps' basic manual:

> War is a state of hostilities that exists between or among nations, characterized by the use of military force. The essence of war is a violent clash between two hostile, independent, and irreconcilable wills, each trying to impose itself on the other. Thus, the object of war is to impose our will on our enemy. The means to that end is the organized application or threat of violence by military force.

Now let's apply the same description to competition in business and add customers into the mix, changing a few words as needed.

> **Business** is a state of hostilities that exists between or among **companies**, characterized by the use of **corporate manipulation**. The essence of **business** is a violent clash between hostile, independent, and irreconcilable **competitors**, each trying to **eliminate** the other. Thus, the object of **business** is to **crush our competitor enemies in order to dominate markets and impose our will on customers**. The means to that end is the organized application or threat of **annihilation by corporate manipulation**.

What is your first reaction to this warlike description of business? How does it square with your beliefs? We often act and talk like business is war and think that's okay. But when we look at how war is actually defined, do we really have a sound analogy? Do you want to go into work every day and tell your people to treat competitors as the enemy to be annihilated? Do you want to impose your will on customers with predatory intent, hostility, and violence?

Like in battle, business as war requires a degree of detachment in order to make choices and carry out acts that would otherwise be unconscionable.

Blatantly cheating customers, lying to shareholders, stealing from the company, raping the environment—the list is, sadly, a long one. Sun Tzu, author of *The Art of War*—which many business leaders esteem as their bible for strategy—says, "All warfare is based on deception." If business is war, that means we must depend on deception to win in business too.

What enables us to do these things in business—lie, steal, deceive, and more—when, for most of us, these behaviors are in direct opposition to our stated values?

One answer is **moral disengagement**.

Social psychology recognizes many forms of moral disengagement, all of which lead us to act as though accepted ethical standards don't apply to us in certain situations, often perpetuating horrific acts and great harm. The documentary *The Sultan and the Saint* posits that moral disengagement through dehumanization is what prompts one group of people to harm another group of people. After all, if "they" are not human like us, the logic goes, then the rules for how to treat humans who are like us don't apply.

Take the Three-Fifths Clause of the United States Constitution of 1787, for example, wherein slaves were measured as three-fifths of a person to determine the number of congressmen each state would send to the House of Representatives. This "less than human" assessment sustained—among other deplorable actions, such as treating African Americans as chattel to be bought and sold—the dehumanization and debasement of all members of the black community. The same was true in the Holocaust, in which non-

Aryans were considered subhuman and were forced to live in unforgivable conditions, endure unimaginable suffering, and perish in concentration camps. There are, unfortunately, numerous other examples of tremendous harm inflicted on specific cultures, tribes, and peoples that has been fueled by moral disengagement through dehumanization during the Yang epoch of human history.

In business, moral disengagement through dehumanization occurs when we reduce customers to a data point or market share, employees to assets to be deployed, and competitors to faceless enemies to be destroyed. We forget or ignore that "they," like us, are all human beings with multiple commonalities, which makes it much easier to engage in and rationalize all kinds of otherwise unacceptable behaviors.

But what drives us to disengage?

At the core, its fear—fear of losing, fear of difference, fear of embarrassment, fear of failure—fears that are typically unfounded and irrational but have been perpetuated by a multitude of influential forces—political, social, economic, and more. Throughout history, we have seen that fear is a powerful energy that can propel us to do crazy things, often with an irrational yet comforting sense of justification that resists any challenge and questioning.

If you've ever thought of your competition as a mere entity to be conquered, or customers simply as market share to be captured—and if you've perhaps forgotten along the way that your competitors are, like you, a team of human beings striving for the same goals you are; and that customers are, like you, individuals looking to business to meet their needs and thereby make their lives a little better—then you have likely participated in the disengagement I'm speaking of. Most of us have.

There's a related psychological quirk at play here, all too common to us humans. Research in psychology demonstrates that as human beings, we are highly capable of tolerating and living with **inconsistency**. For example, many of us believe we should eat nutritiously or exercise regularly, but we don't do it. The reality is that our beliefs about health and our actions don't always align, yet we somehow manage to tolerate those inconsistencies and stay on the same unhealthy path.

Same with attitudes and behaviors at work. Consider how often we as individuals say one thing and do something different. We believe we should stop texting at work and focus on business, but don't do it. We believe we should treat our customers well, but don't do it. We believe we should only invest in companies that are aligned with our moral values, but don't do it. Misalignment is a fitting word for these choices.

This is a dynamic that is not only evident at an individual level, but at an organizational level as well. Think, for example, of companies that proudly declare their guiding values: honesty, innovation, teamwork, and so on. You see the words on gilded signage in the boardroom, on posters in meeting rooms, on screensavers, on annual reports. These stated "values" show up everywhere—except, in practice. And that's the rub.

If you ever took an introductory psychology class, you may remember learning about "cognitive dissonance theory." Popularized in the late 1950s and '60s, this and similar theories posited that we have a strong inner drive for our attitudes and behaviors to be in harmony, and that when we have inconsistencies—or dissonance—between attitudes or behaviors, we will make changes to eliminate the dissonance and restore consistency. While that drive for consistency may be strong, so is our ability to live with inconsistency. Turns out we draw on all kinds of mental tricks to enable us to be inconsistent, such as being unaware of the dissonance, denying it, suppressing it, rationalizing it, etc. It is our capacity for inconsistency that allows moral disengagement in its many forms to take hold. It is also this capacity that lets us live out of alignment with ourselves, be inauthentic, and participate in the paradigm of "business as war," even when we disagree with it.

MIRROR
Measuring Your
"Business as War" Beliefs

The wording of the questions in this mirror exercise is one-sided by design to help you expose your beliefs to yourself. Be honest, even if you don't like what comes out. Respond to each on a 1 to 5 scale, with 1 being Strongly Disagree and 5 being Strongly Agree.

- Business is war.
- We need to fight to win in business.
- The world is here for us.
- Greed is good in business.
- Making money trumps everything.
- Competitors are enemies to be destroyed.
- Customers are prey to be captured.
- Employees are commodities.
- Business is "us" vs. "them."

Based on your answers to these questions, place yourself on the scale below with regard to how you view business as war—with 1 seeing business completely as war, and 10 not seeing business as war at all.

BUSINESS AS A REFLECTION OF GOOD AND EVIL

Another factor that influences "good" people to engage in less than admirable behavior is our daily exposure to both contemporary and age-old tales of good vs. evil. While these stories can't be blamed for our behaviors and are not inherently bad in and of themselves, they do serve to perpetuate the business as war paradigm and an "us vs. them" mindset in some surprising ways.

Take the ancient biblical story of the Garden of Eden and parallel tales of the painful birth of humanity, stories that go back several thousand years. Literary classics like *Macbeth, Beowulf, Crime and Punishment, The Hobbit, The Wizard of Oz, Lord of the Flies, East of Eden,* and *Star Wars* squarely pit good against evil; more recently, the *Harry Potter* series and *Game of Thrones* do the same. While these are but a handful of examples, this contrast shows up everywhere and every day: in the news, in sports, in entertainment, in war, in religion, in politics, in healthcare—and certainly in business. One reason that it's so ubiquitous in our culture is that these stories of good and evil engage our brains at a powerful and primitive level as we relate them to our very survival. Conflict and its resolution is a centerpiece of effective storytelling and sense-making.

Why is it useful to think about good and evil in relation to business? Because we are highly driven to find meaning in our lives, and the contrast between good and evil helps many of us to do that.

But if the common motif is that good always triumphs over evil, why would anyone in business choose to take the so-called evil route? Aren't we more inclined to want to be the good guy? The one who is celebrated and admired?

Yes, most of us want to be on the side of good when it really matters; however, there are several compelling explanations—all rooted in the idiosyncrasies of human psychology—for how our penchant to side with good over evil gets transmuted, or turned on its head.

First, as a society, we tend to romanticize war. And it makes sense. War requires valor and courage. War protects our interests against defeat and keeps us safe from harm. War also has heroes and villains, which seems to create a clear case of "us vs. them" and "good shall triumph over evil." In war, therefore, we must be on the side of good ("us"), which puts our enemies ("them") on the side of evil.

Now, when we apply the metaphor of war to business, we similarly romanticize warlike notions. It may sound like this:

> Our business leaders require valor and courage to do whatever it takes for us to win. Our company is protecting shareholder interests against defeat, providing security for our employees, and eviscerating our competitors. It's "us" vs. "them." This means our company ("us") must be on the side of good, which puts opposing forces ("them") of all types (competitive, regulatory, etc.) on the side of evil. Therefore, we are triumphing over evil. We are part of something righteous and important, and shall be victorious!

How bizarrely noble these notions can sound, even if they're far removed from the brutal realities of waging war. With this subtly distorted mentality, we allow ourselves to admire and condone warlike behavior in business. Further, our capacity to tolerate inconsistencies in our beliefs lets us compartmentalize the suffering that warlike behavior in business causes, and ignore the bad behaviors entailed so that these realities do not consciously interfere with our romantic notions about waging war in business—or enjoying the spoils that come with winning.

This mindset is also fed by our deep desire to belong to something meaningful, something bigger than ourselves. Think about it: war provides a focal point and rallying cry around which people come together. For those in favor of the cause the war presumes to further, there is a necessary sense of righteousness and urgency, whether real or manufactured, that adds import to the sense of belonging.

Natural disasters and serious health problems can elicit a similar sense of belonging. For example, when communities are dealing with dramatic and unexpected catastrophes like hurricanes, tsunamis, earthquakes, or wildfires, everyone tends to engage with one another and is committed to the greater good.[28] Families likewise unite around dire health situations, like when someone is diagnosed with a deadly disease, or tragically killed in a car accident.

But when business leaders call on "war" as their frame of reference, it "rallies the troops" around a "crisis"—like the enemy (aka competitors) stealing market share. In the process, people almost always lose themselves and their personal values. Everyone in the company then belongs to the holy war of crushing and eradicating those who threaten their dominance—which in turn justifies exerting whatever violence is necessary to achieve it, no matter how distasteful, immoral, or harmful. This brings us back to the issue of partaking in moral disengagement.

From an *amare* perspective, the real lesson here is how important belonging is to all of us, and how powerful an enabler of all kinds of behavior it is—including behavior that falls more on the "evil" side than the "good" side. And to be clear, it's not merely belonging—it's belonging to something we perceive as noble and bigger than ourselves, which meets a fundamental human need—to be assured that who we are and what we are doing matters.

And that's not all. (We sure are complicated creatures!)

On top of the many ways we distort reality and tolerate misalignment in ourselves and our companies, as well as latch on to unhealthy opportunities for belonging, we also frequently grapple with what is called the skewed power of relativity.

How Bad Is Bad?

As human beings, most of us find it easier to navigate our lives with absolutes of what constitutes good and evil, right and wrong, rather than an ever-changing set of rules. But in reality, our boundaries frequently shift for what is good and right, and what is evil and wrong, based on the particular circumstance.

For example, is it bad to place ads that intentionally mislead customers to increase sales? Of course it is. But is it as bad as selling customer data without permission, or stealing directly from customers, or embezzling millions from your company?

You might say, "These are all deplorable." But if you compared them, would you consider certain ones worse than others? I ask this because although yes, even if all of them are wrong, how bad we consider something usually changes as our anchors or reference points change.

What does that mean?

The field of behavioral economics, pioneered by Israeli psychologists Amos Tversky and Danny Kahneman, demonstrates how reference points generate cognitive biases that can powerfully and easily cause our judgments to shift and affect the decisions we make. For example, when a small business owner is fined $10,000 for unethical business practices, that seems bad because it's compared to a reference point of zero dollars, or no fine. But when the messaging shifts the reference point to a maximum $100,000 fine, $10,000 seems not so bad after all—and that can correspondingly make the unethical business practices seem not so bad. In other words, this shift in reference points ultimately compromises the deterrent effect of the fine on the business owner's future behaviors: i.e., why not do it if it makes money and the negative consequences aren't so bad?

Changing reference points can make it easy to rationalize our actions and ratchet down our judgments of how "bad" something really is. This is the skewed power of relativity at work.

We have numerous mental tricks for rationalizing our bad behaviors and seemingly putting ourselves on the side of good with "us against them" stories. For example, many people who cheat on their taxes, drive well over the speed limit, or lie about their kid's age to get cheaper theater tickets would easily judge these common and widely practiced infractions as "not so bad." How? By believing that the government has "more than enough money and doesn't need more of mine," or "everyone's driving this fast so it's not that dangerous," or "movie tickets are overpriced anyway . . . they can afford to lose a few bucks on a child's ticket." Essentially, we criticize the system, comfort ourselves that what we're doing is normal and common, and convince ourselves we're simply getting even. Us vs. them. Good over evil.

For some people, all of these justifications seem perfectly rational. No one's getting hurt, right? But is that really true? Are we making these decisions because we believe no one will ever know, and therefore we won't have to be accountable? Or if we did get caught, the consequences wouldn't be life shattering?

Maybe.

Does that make it right? No.

Do we feel conflicted every time we do it? Depending on the person and the situation, that could be a resounding *yes*, a detached *no*, or an *absolutely not* imbued with righteous indignation. Or if the person doesn't even notice anything wrong, then the answer is a confused, *conflicted about what?*

These same kinds of rationalizations frequently make their way into everyday business practices and onto the sliding and malleable scale of what is and is not acceptable. As a result, when we operate in this fashion and "get away with it," it opens the door to potentially get away with more.

It is this same psychology that Malcolm Gladwell cogently explains in *The Tipping Point*: Little things set the stage for big things to happen. Once we justify and normalize one seemingly minor misdeed—say, cheating on the corporate tax return—the momentum may be hard to stop. If tax cheating isn't so bad, how bad can it be to mislead investors by altering pro forma financial statements a little bit? To manipulate annual reports to shareholders? To engage in deceptive marketing practices to lure customers into paying for services they can't afford or don't need? And so on.

This is partly what I mean when I say there's a short in the hardwiring of many businesses today. When these types of practices become commonplace, other companies, seeing no major negative consequences, follow suit and maybe even set industry standards. The practices become so deeply entrenched that they become "business as usual," which also makes them practically invisible. While this pattern doesn't always happen, it sometimes becomes an epidemic with grave consequences, like the subprime mortgage crisis and major recession of the late 2000s.

The bottom line is, when organizations embrace a warlike mentality, and the goal is to trample the competition through deception (remember the quote I gave earlier from *The Art of War*), then the "absolutes" of right and wrong, ethical and unethical, good and evil become skewed in favor of "winning" at all costs. **The more this occurs, the more the lines are blurred, and as long as businesses "get away with it," the more this way of operating is normalized.**

But who controls these situations in which "sliding ethical scale" decisions are made? In her book *Mindfulness*, Harvard professor Ellen Langer states:

> Social psychologists argue that who we are at any one time depends mostly on the context in which we find ourselves. But who creates the context? The more mindful we are, the more we can create the contexts we are in. When we create the context, we are more likely to be authentic.

This is fine when we're mindful and choose to run an equally mindful business. Then our values, decisions, and actions are more likely to be aligned and authentic to who we are. But what if we're not so mindful? Or what about when we work in a business environment that encourages deception, or even relies on it? We have a few options: we can try to change things; we can seek out another job or industry more aligned with our values; we can cave to the expectations with some or a lot of inner conflict; we can believe in the justification for the actions (remember, that's how we win in war!) and adopt the common behavior of everyone around us in our company or organization; or we can ignore it all and be complicit in doing business as war.

For most of us the majority of the time, the context exerts a powerful influence on our behaviors. Interestingly, what influences our decisions—to be ethical or not, warlike or not, or loving and compassionate or not—is *not* merely shaped by our personality and disposition as is widely believed. Rather, as research in social psychology has shown, it is powerfully shaped by the *context* or *situation* we're in. In fact, we frequently over-attribute others' behavior to their personality, disposition, or character, instead of to the demands of a particular situation. It happens so often that psychologists have a name for it: fundamental attribution error.[29]

Being Good, Doing Good (Sometimes)

Fundamental attribution error (or FAE) is another example of how we as human beings are subject to being illogical, irrational, or just plain wrong in our thinking—and not be aware of it in the moment. A classic example is the priest rushing in the rain to give a sermon on compassion and not stopping to give a homeless man a dollar, though in less stressful situations, he absolutely would. Or the harried employee coming in late to a meeting; you may malign his or her character, but if you're the one who is late, you come up with all kinds of situational explanations.

Ethical questions get raised every day in business for both big and small issues: Should we inflate our numbers to get a better bond rating? Should we steal top people from our competitors by revealing made-up dirt about their company? Should we sell customers products at full price knowing the products will be obsolete next month? Should we fudge our hours to get more vacation time? Should we take some stickies from the supply room since we just ran out at home?

Once again, I'm not implying that decisions made to intentionally deceive customers, harm the competition, or pilfer from your company's bottom line are excusable. What I'm aiming for is creating awareness for how these "circumstantially acceptable" business practices come about under the powerful influence of the context or situation, and how they can so easily get way out of hand.

For example, while I was doing research for this book, within a one month period—in April 2018—there were three major corporate scandals dominating the news:

- CAMBRIDGE ANALYTICA AND FACEBOOK: For collecting personal information of 87 million users without permission and using it to influence voter opinion

- THERANOS: For being charged with massive fraud by the SEC, after raising over $700 million based on false claims of having developed revolutionary technology for blood tests

- WELLS FARGO (again!): This time being fined $1 billion by two federal agencies for a) charging customers with car loans for insurance without telling them, even if they were already insured; and b) charging customers for extending mortgage-rate locks, even if the delay was the bank's fault

All three examples are illustrative of business gone bad, propelled by a desire for fortune, fame, or both. To put it simply, these companies blatantly engaged in lying and stealing. Greed was the catalyst, with deception and fraud as the mechanisms. Such is the nature of business as war.

Exactly one year later, in April 2019, all three were back in the news: Facebook for trying to influence how many billions would be an effective fine for the Cambridge Analytica scandal; Wells Fargo for the abrupt "retirement" of its new-ish CEO (three years) in the wake of accusations that their culture and behaviors had not yet improved sufficiently; and Elizabeth Holmes, the disgraced CEO of Theranos, said to be seeking investors in Silicon Valley to start a new company—this while awaiting trial for criminal fraud and likely years in jail.

To further show the prevalence of this pattern of behavior grounded in the fear, greed, hostility, and deception of the business as war paradigm, we could look to the drama of the international "trade wars"—and to two other companies making front page headlines:

- Boeing, one of the world's largest airplane manufacturers, for hiding from their customers automation software problems that led to deadly and preventable crashes of two of their 737 MAX planes, killing 346 people.[30]

- Purdue Pharma and the Sackler family that controls it, facing a burst of high-profile litigation for their extensive role in knowingly and deceptively creating the national epidemic of opioid addiction, misrepresenting OxyContin's addictive qualities and potential for abuse, manipulating physicians and blaming patients, and more recently for further worsening the opioid crisis in part to make more money selling treatments for the addiction problem their company helped create.[31]

Clearly, these are all examples of business out of balance—out of touch with its purpose, out of alignment with its customers, and certainly not operating from love. This is precisely what business as war looks like, where winning—i.e., money, fame, and power—

crush other considerations and vindicate any behavior, no matter how much pain and suffering it causes.

Because headlines of fraud have become so commonplace, when we see these stories, we may simply roll our eyes over "another one." Or we may become incensed and if it's appropriate, refuse to do business with a particular company. Either way, I believe we've become sick and tired of seeing companies commit these deceptive acts, which is but one reason why the climate is ripe for change.

I do wish to note here that I am not equating being warlike with being evil. Companies that go evil are typically warlike in their thinking and actions; however, companies can be warlike and *not* evil. In fact, some warlike companies can be good, upright, and ethical in many respects. But be aware that it's far more difficult to uphold these values, because the warlike mindset of "winning at all costs" is such a convenient and alluring way to justify bad behavior and override impulses for good.

MIRROR
Measuring "Good" in Business

1. Is your company ethically good?
   Under what conditions?

2. Does your company compromise its values?
   Under what conditions?

3. Is your company generally warlike?

Based on your answers to these questions, place your company on the scale below with regard to how "good" it is in business—with 1 ranking low, and 10 ranking best.

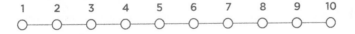

PROMOTING OPPOSITION THROUGH PREDATORY LANGUAGE

As I shared in the Introduction, one of the most striking impressions I had of some large management consulting companies early in my career was the way that those who brought in business were called hunters, and those who did the work were called skinners. In our business culture, it is certainly easy to get caught up in this kind of violence-laden and predatory language. I've caught myself using phrases like "capture market share" and "fighting competitors," and in strategy sessions with clients on business development, new product innovation, or positioning and branding, I've often heard things like:

> *How do we hunt down our target customers?*
>
> *What market segments can we exploit with our solutions?*
>
> *How can we steal customers from our competitors?*
>
> *What's our plan of attack for capturing more of our customers' wallet?*

Over time, I became increasingly disturbed at the predatory nature of these metaphors, especially in relation to customers, i.e., those we serve who give us money. *Exploiting* customers. *Capturing* customers. *Stealing* customers. *Hunting down* customers. Really? We think and talk about customers in terms of violence, and that violence is what we aim to *do* to them?

Maybe I felt this more strongly because several of the clients posing these questions were in the humanitarian business of health and well-being. But for any company, this kind of predatory language promotes an adversarial relationship dynamic in which the business aims to overpower, dominate, and subdue its customers. In short, the business only "wins" when the customer is beaten.

We all know that language is immensely powerful and that it has lasting impact. This recognition led Marshall Rosenberg in the 1960s to create the Nonviolent Communication (NVC) process— also referred to as Compassionate Communication because the core premise is about understanding, valuing, and meeting people's basic human needs by replacing any kind of violence in language with responsible and compassionate words.

Think back to your early years: If perhaps a teacher—even once—said something hurtful to you, such as "You're just not smart in math," or a parent said, "Why can't you be more like your brother?" you know that those words can be internalized and negatively affect you for years. The same holds true for the *positive* words that get through and stick. The words people say shape us continuously throughout our lives. In business, you have no doubt experienced this, either as the one speaking or the one receiving the message. Words can edify, encourage, embolden, enlighten. They can also denigrate, dishearten, disrupt, and destroy.

Violence-laden language always hurts business, rather than helps it.

Even if all a business cares about is making money, treating customers as prey is not the optimal path to success. Why? Because the relentless stream of predatory thinking and corresponding language in business causes suffering. It promotes an attitude of fear, self-protection, and unkindness that serves no one. It also breeds contempt, while diminishing respect and gratitude. And worst of all, little by little, it hardens people's hearts. The *amare* alternative is thoughtful choosing and using of words that convey compassion and caring rather than violence and predatory intent.

WINDOW

A Shift in Language Promotes a Shift in Perspective

Sister Mary Jean Ryan recognized the power of language and long ago institutionalized a non-violence language policy at SSM Health, the nonprofit Catholic healthcare system she led as CEO for many years.[32] In an open letter to employees, physicians, and board members, here's how Sr. Ryan set the tone:

> "We know all too well that violence exists in our nation and the world. Every day, those of us in healthcare tend to the victims of violence in our hospitals and emergency rooms. Most certainly the violence will not end until we each take responsibility for promoting non-violence in our personal lives and in our communities."

She went on to say that people at SSM can make a difference in reducing violence and promoting safety, in part, with their choice of words.

> "One way is to be aware of our own language and the language spoken in our homes and offices. You may be asking, 'How can that make a difference?' Don't underestimate the power of language. We each can choose to speak to those close to us or to strangers in ways that create happiness and inspire, as opposed to language that demeans people or creates unhappiness."

Her conclusion connected simple changes in language to their purpose as a healthcare system:

"Our overall goal with language is to help create healing environments for patients, their loved ones, and for
ourselves. At first glance, it may seem like a small thing,
but it is something every one of us can do to make a
difference and to make the world a kinder place."

Sr. Mary banned the use of language in SSM Health that
gratuitously indicated violence, in everything from business
strategy to community presentations. For example, instead of
capturing markets, SSM *secures* markets. *Target* audiences become *intended* audiences. *Take a stab at it* gets replaced with
give it a try. SSM Powerpoints don't use *bullet* points, they have
information points. She wanted her employees to recognize that
their words had power and should be used to strengthen their
culture of healing body and spirit.[33] [italics added]
Indeed, our words reflect our thoughts and shape our actions—and they have significant consequences on those around us.

I recognize that within the culture and times in which we live,
predatory language is deeply entrenched in our daily lives. It's
pervasive in popular entertainment, advertising, competitive
sports—and need I even mention politics! But the fact that warlike
language is ubiquitous in our culture and common in business does
not make it right, necessary, or acceptable.

A story on PRI's *The World* called "How Gun Culture Permeates Our Everyday Language" opens with some relevant questions:[34]
Have you ever found yourself "sweating bullets" because you were
"under the gun" at work? Ever hatched a "bulletproof" plan? Or
taken a "shot in the dark?" Told a joke that totally "misfired?" Ever
had an idea that was "shot down" right on the spot? If you have,
did you "stick to your guns?"

In the story, Bob Myers, a cultural anthropologist who studies
language, violence, and culture, points out that this pervasive "gun

speak" has so permeated all levels of American culture, we often don't even notice we're using those kinds of expressions. The article raises the question: If the expressions are so common that they are stripped of violent intent, does it matter that we use them so casually? Myers responds that though he scientifically sees a strong association, he does not see the evidence to claim direct causality, i.e., that using violent language is why we as a nation have so many killings. But it is clearly a contributing factor, as he suggests when he raises the provocative question that if instead of "gun speak" we routinely used all kinds of racist words and expressions without thinking about it, would we be more racist or accepting of racism? My guess is yes. And by extension, if compassionate language was the order of the day, would we not be far more love-centered in our world?

In the same way that I took part without initially being aware of it, most of us use some predatory language in everyday conversation and don't even notice it as such. But that's no longer an excuse. It's time for us to both *notice* and *choose* our language consciously. We have reached a time when there is no longer space for a violence-based paradigm that uses predatory language in relating to customers or competitors. Being rooted in fear, this language is not only self-defeating, but it perpetuates a negative mindset and wears people down. In addition, it does not genuinely serve employees, meet customer needs, or sustain healthy relationships. And, through the insidious and sometimes invisible damage predatory language causes, it can greatly reduce profitability over the long haul. As the main conveyance of our thoughts and beliefs, language truly matters.

If you want to change the world, change the metaphor.

—JOSEPH CAMPBELL

MIRROR
How Predatory Is Your Language?

1. Have you noticed the violence in the language of business?

2. When you think about how pervasive this language is in business, does it bother you?

3. Is violent or predatory language commonly used in your company?

4. Do you tend to use warlike euphemisms in your work?

5. Do you believe business needs this kind of language in order to motivate people?

6. Do the words you use in business match your values and beliefs?

7. Can you imagine eliminating violence-laden language in your company?

8. Do you believe business can be highly profitable without resorting to warlike language?

9. Will you commit to replacing predatory words with more compassionate language?

Based on your answers to these questions, place yourself on the scale below with regard to how prevalent predatory language is in your work world—with 1 being highly prevalent and 10 being nonexistent.

DOOR

Here are a few ways to reverse predatory language and begin promoting compassion and inclusiveness.

- Start becoming aware of the words you use, with whom, and under what conditions. Pay attention to how you react when you use or hear others use violent and predatory language at work.

- Set an expectation that when anyone notices this kind of language, they can safely and without judgment make note of it. Notice and praise when it happens.

- Challenge your team to identify predatory words in your vernacular and replace them with more love-based and still impactful words, similar to the example of SSM Health. Make a chart to show the "old" and "new" language.

- Set formal communication policies that ban language that connotes violence and provide replacement words. Make clear the connection between these policies and your company culture, values, and purpose.

As evidenced from this chapter, there are several reasons we've fallen into the trap of a business as war mentality, often without our knowledge. But unfortunately, these alone don't paint the full picture. While I certainly don't want to place too much energy on the negative, in order for us to break away from warlike habits, we must recognize that there's more at play.

In the rest of Part II, we'll explore how other demeaning personal qualities, ingrained beliefs, and being ruled by fear energy play a significant role as well—and how seeing and understanding these dynamics is a first step toward making conscious choices.

THE MORE
HONEST
YOU CAN BE
WITH
YOURSELF,
THE MORE
OPEN
YOU CAN BE
TO MAKING
POSITIVE
CHANGE.

CHAPTER FIVE

IF YOUR BUSINESS IS MISSING LOVE, ARE **YOU** MISSING LOVE?

Fear of vulnerability. Incivility. Arrogance.

Our environment and the context we're in have promulgated—unwittingly or not—a business as war paradigm, supported by some powerful mental acrobatics and psychological quirks common to us humans. And if these three common and insidious elements in our personal attitudes and behaviors, in particular, feel unsettlingly close to home, it's because they're indeed a few of the strongest contributors.

This chapter title asks if you are missing love, but this is not about psychoanalyzing how much love you've received from your family, or how your upbringing has influenced your business habits—there are plenty of resources that endeavor to help people get to the root of those things. This is instead about looking at who you are now, in terms of love and business, and the three topics mentioned above.

A lack of love, particularly love for self, often informs the characteristics we absorb and project to others. For this reason, I invite you to reflect on whether any or all of the three beliefs and habits we'll explore in this chapter lend to how you operate in the world and in business.

You may find that some of these habits are so deeply rooted that you don't even realize on an intellectual level how embedded they are in the fabric of your being. This is not a criticism; it is simply a call to look closely at yourself for a better—and even possibly more compassionate—understanding. And with that, the possibility for change in the most positive of ways for yourself, your company, and those you work with and serve in business.

FEAR OF VULNERABILITY

Research professor Brené Brown's profound work on vulnerability in the last decade has brought this previously taboo topic more to the surface than ever before. Even if you haven't read any of her work or seen her speak about the subject in her viral Ted Talk entitled The Power of Vulnerability, you know that being vulnerable involves exposing ourselves to others in a way that may feel uncomfortable—and that exposure may cause us to feel things we don't like, open the door to pain and criticism, or lead us to see parts of ourselves we're not proud of.

One of the culprits is our ego-driven primitive brains that rule in situations where they don't belong. Said another way, we allow the fears, fueled by the drive of our egos, to supersede our willingness to be vulnerable, often without our even knowing it. For example, instead of sharing real emotion with your team over a deflating quarterly report, you show a tough front and drill them for mistakes that have been made. Or perhaps you have to speak to an employee about a habit that's annoying others—a habit you yourself had to conquer—but refuse to admit you've encountered the same challenge during your talk with him.

Dr. Brown points out that these fears of revealing certain parts of who we are may carry an unwelcome byproduct: shame.

So to protect ourselves and avoid what can sometimes be a crippling feeling of shame, people numb their vulnerability. In business, this is more the norm than the exception because of how protective we tend to be of our role, status, and reputation.

In addition to numbing, we also frequently:

- intellectualize our feelings away
- seek more and more control rather than surrendering
- busy ourselves so there is no space for tuning in
- hide behind perfectionism

Unfortunately, we are quite talented at donning armor against our own uncomfortable feelings. When we do, we choose comfort over courage.

There are two problems with this pattern.

First, as business leaders, we lose out on the myriad benefits of showing vulnerability at work, which allows us to fully be ourselves. As a result, we don't receive the trust that being transparent and authentic generates, or the deeper connections that come from exposing our flaws. Further, we don't generate the best solutions—those that develop when we own our mistakes and admit we don't know it all. When we model behavior and create a culture that tells our people, "Don't show your vulnerabilities here. Weaknesses and mistakes are forbidden," we don't get the quality from ourselves or our team that comes about when people feel safe to be themselves.[35] Bottom line: fear of vulnerability shrivels up people's willingness to be honest, to take risks, and to be whole, which is diminishing to everyone and everything in business.

Second, numbing vulnerability numbs *all* of our feelings, because, as Brown explains, we're not capable of selectively numbing one single emotion. In other words, as we numb what may feel like shame, we also numb compassion, joy, gratitude, happiness, and of course, love. In so doing, we create a dangerous cycle of misery and suffering for ourselves, and we project that suffering onto others. What's more, as numbness makes it increasingly difficult to find and feel purpose and meaning in our work and in our lives, we turn to other mechanisms to cope. It makes sense, then, that Brown says we are the most obese, addicted, and medicated cohort in human history.

Let's take a look in the mirror here to gauge how you feel about vulnerability. Remember to be honest—the more honest you can be with yourself, the more open you can be to making positive change.

MIRROR
How Vulnerable Are You at Work?

---

1. Do you believe vulnerability is good for business?

2. Do you believe vulnerability is more a sign of weakness or strength?

3. Do you know how to be vulnerable at work?

4. Under what conditions do you show vulnerability at work?

5. Do you hide things about yourself or your actions for fear of criticism or rejection?

6. Do you sometimes feel fearful or insecure in business and are afraid to show it?

7. Do you know what it feels like to be vulnerable and accepted at work?

8. Do you trust others at work enough to show your vulnerabilities?

9. Do others at work trust you enough to show you their vulnerabilities?

10. Do you demonstrate to others that it is okay to be vulnerable at work?

Based on your answers to these questions, place yourself on the scale below with regard to how willing you are to be vulnerable at work—with 1 being not at all willing, and 10 being fully willing.

1   2   3   4   5   6   7   8   9   10

I realize these can be tough questions to answer. In merely thinking about them, you may feel unsettled inside. But I have good news: **you can embrace vulnerability and make it work to your advantage in ways you may have never imagined.**

Brown calls people who embrace vulnerability *wholehearted*. They feel worthy of love, belonging, and connection, and they believe what makes them vulnerable makes them beautiful and special. Wholehearted people view vulnerability not as uncomfortable or excruciating, but simply as necessary. Being vulnerable does not mean you are weak or submissive; rather, it means you have the courage to be yourself and the willingness to deeply connect with others, even when it's difficult.

For my writing partner, Stacey, this quality didn't surface until she was able to make a profound admission.

WINDOW
The Cloak of Perfectionism

For whatever reason, from the time I was a toddler, I was a staunch perfectionist. My family never imposed it on me; in fact, they often begged me to let up on myself – but to no avail. I was blessed with a natural affinity for reading, math, and language and took great pride in doing well in school . . . but with that came a fear of making mistakes, which I interpreted as looking stupid. Because of this, I would go to great lengths to prove I wasn't wrong – even when I was – all to try to uphold my reputation of being smart. I wasn't an arrogant kid, but this fear of vulnerability could cripple me, even sometimes to the point of avoiding certain decisions so I wouldn't make the "wrong" one.

Early in my management career, I encountered a person who could never be wrong about anything – and it drove me absolutely crazy. It wasn't until I saw myself in her that I realized I could be equally annoying at times, giving me a major wakeup call. Startled into awareness, I vowed to not only own being wrong from then on, but to do a complete 180° flip and be gracious about it. At first, it was tough. What would people think of me? I'd hidden under my cloak of perfectionism for so long that I felt incredibly exposed.

But, as soon as I began this gracious – and even sometimes laugh-at-myself – approach to making a mistake, or not having the answer, or making a poor choice, I was amazed at how much better I actually felt! By not making people uncomfortable in my defensiveness, they related to me better, and I relished letting go of my previous necessity to be "right" most of the time. The result? It was one of the biggest win-win shifts I've ever made – and both my life and my business have benefitted tremendously.

Imagine a business culture that embraces vulnerability. Not only can you can show up as *you*, but customers feel seen and valued as they are too. In a recent issue of *Entrepreneur* magazine[36], consultant Angela Kambouris made the case that being vulnerable is the boldest thing a business leader can do. As examples, she cites Sheryl Sandburg sharing leadership lessons in resiliency and coping after her husband's sudden death, and Howard Schultz being highly emotional and transparent about the need for serious change if Starbucks was going to survive when it had fallen to the lowest point in its history.

Vulnerability is the key to business,
opening yourself up and showing people who you are.

—MARCUS LEMONIS, STAR OF CNBC'S HIT BUSINESS SHOW,
THE PROPHET

DOOR

To begin getting in touch with your vulnerability:

- Humbly own and admit your mistakes—out loud. You may be surprised just how much respect people will have for you when you do this.

- Reject being a know-it-all. No one likes being around a person who thinks they're smarter than everyone else.

- Embrace that everyone has feelings of vulnerability on some level, whether they're hiding them or not. Be unafraid of showing yours so that others feel comfortable showing theirs.

Hopefully, you can see the value of vulnerability at work and its connection with making business love. And, conversely, you can imagine what kinds of behaviors show up instead when fear of vulnerability is the norm . . . which leads us to the second detrimental behavior I address in this chapter: incivility.

INCIVILITY

Rude actions. Dismissive comments. Hostile behavior. Leaving messes for others to clean up. Not responding kindly to greetings. Being ungrateful for favors. These are just a few examples of how incivility shows up in life—and in business.

Christine Porath, Georgetown University professor and author of *Mastering Civility: A Manifesto for the Workplace,* has shown that once people are treated rudely, they are three times less likely to help others. In other words, the bad feelings spread. And once people are infected, so to speak, it's hard to bounce back. The negativity can last for a single day or for much longer periods, depending on the prevalence of incivility in the environment. Once this atmosphere of detachment and rudeness is established, it requires repeated efforts to win back trust and re-energize relationships.

When work relationships are destructive and de-energizing, Porath says, performance suffers.[37] Her research shows that among workers treated with incivility:

- 78 percent said that their commitment to their company declined.

- 66 percent said that their performance declined.

- 25 percent admitted to taking their frustration out on customers.

- 12 percent said that they left their job because of the uncivil treatment.

To add to this, the organizational training company, ELI, points out that well before companies get in trouble for illegal incivil behaviors like harassment and discrimination that generate multimillion-dollar lawsuits and grab national headlines, they have established a culture of *legal* bad behaviors such as rudeness and bullying.[38] Enabled by leaders "looking the other way," incivility continues to accelerate, which saps morale, distracts employees, and cuts into productivity. While these outcomes aren't typically the outward goal of those acting with incivility, they nonetheless occur to the company's detriment.

How would you honestly answer the questions in the following Mirror activity?

MIRROR
How Incivil Are You at Work?

1. Do you act rudely to your coworkers?

2. Do you make hostile or condescending comments?

3. Do you ignore or exclude people in your workplace?

4. Do you make jokes at other people's expense?

5. Do you ever resort to bullying and meanness in your interactions?

6. Do your words or actions make others uncomfortable?

7. Do you smile or say hello to coworkers?

8. Do you acknowledge coworkers when you walk by each other?

9. Do you say thank you when someone does something kind for you?

10. Do you put your phone away during meetings?

11. Do you speak up when you witness incivility?

Based on your answers to these questions, place yourself on the scale below with regard to how incivil you tend to be toward others—with 1 being all the time, and 10 being never.

Again, it can be difficult to hold this mirror up to yourself. But if you realized in this exercise that you indeed practice some acts of incivility, you have an opportunity to think about the deeper reasons why—and then focus on how you can flip them to more loving behaviors that will endear, rather than repel, you to others in the workplace and beyond.

Besides civility being a good practice for its own sake, it has a heavy influence on how your team interacts with your customers, suppliers, and others important in the running of your business. When your staff is constantly bombarded with incivility, it carries over to customer interactions—whether in person, or by phone or email—and can negatively affect the entire customer experience. It comes across not only through *what* employees say and do, but also *how* they say what they say and do what they do. Customers typically sense incivility immediately and when they do, most will take their patronage elsewhere if they have a choice. Nobody wants to be treated rudely, let alone when they are choosing to give you their business. And while your employees may not possess the disposition for rudeness as individuals, remember that our choices to behave in a certain way are often influenced by particular situations. If your team is treated with disregard, they may very well internalize this standard, believing that treating customers poorly is likewise acceptable for them, because it is to you.

But when a company operates with kindness, and civility is the standard among the leaders and staff, it is much more common for all team members to extend courtesy to the people you serve—and for those people to forge stronger loyalty to your products or services.

DOOR

To begin overturning incivility in the workplace:

- Model civility yourself.
- Employ Sam Walton's "ten-foot rule" — smile and make eye contact when you are within ten feet of a coworker or customer and say hello.
- Establish specific expectations, providing appropriate rewards/consequences for both civil and uncivil behaviors.

- Offer enlivened training for how to treat employees, suppliers, and customers as a key step to improving civility in your workplace.
- Set an uplifting tone the company embraces as a whole.

ARROGANCE

By my count, more business leaders have failed and derailed because of arrogance than any other character flaw.

−HARVEY MACKAY, BESTSELLING BUSINESS AUTHOR

Often spurred by fear of vulnerability, our third adverse behavior is defined as an attitude of superiority that comes from an inflated sense of self-importance and underlying sense of inferiority. If you ever find yourself being overbearing and contemptuous of others, being bullying and mean, or being unwilling to consider other perspectives and unable to take criticism to heart, this section will be particularly important.

Arrogance can be learned through observing others in business, through cultural conditioning, and through consequences of personal experience. But it can—ironically—also manifest as an unintended consequence of efforts to build self-esteem. It can further emerge when egos override emotional intelligence, or when a person is fearful or insecure and doesn't want to show it, like in the classic bully syndrome.

Arrogance often develops as companies become successful and slip into thinking the business exists simply to better the business.

Sadly, arrogance has often been lauded as a positive leadership trait in corporate America, quite visibly in Silicon Valley in recent years, with notorious stories of ruthlessness and greed. It is not uncommon to witness arrogance misconstrued as confidence or strength of character, and thereby celebrated as a good thing. But don't be fooled: arrogance may be associated with single-mindedness—which can reap certain benefits with the right focus—but it in no way demonstrates strength of character. Yes, some arrogant leaders have created highly successful companies, but arrogance is clearly not a necessary or even desirable ingredient for success. In other words, arrogance and confidence should not be considered some kind of package deal in garnering respect.

What typifies the most successful business leaders, and arguably our greatest world leaders too, is *humility*. A defining trait of what Jim Collins dubbed Level 5 leaders—those able to take a company from good to great—humility is the antithesis of arrogance. In fact, research shows that companies with humble CEOs not only have **reduced turnover** but **increased employee engagement**.[39]

Think about it: wouldn't you rather work for someone who is approachable and kind than someone people would rather avoid?

Paul Graham, CEO of the startup accelerator Y Combinator, turns arrogance on its head in the *Business Insider* article, "Why 'Arrogant Jerks' Become Rich and Successful in Silicon Valley":

> It's certainly possible to build a multi-billion dollar startup without being a jerk. We've funded several, and the founders are all good people. In fact, based on what I've seen so far, the good people have the advantage over the jerks. Probably because to get really big, a company has to have a sense of mission, and the good people are more likely to have an authentic one, rather than just being motivated by money or power.[40]

We can conclude two things here:

1. Arrogance is not confidence, and is not necessary for business success; in fact, it hurts productivity in many ways.

2. Having an authentic sense of mission, and aligning with a higher purpose beyond financial profit, helps temper arrogance, and is part of what I hope *The Amare Wave* inspires in you.

Let's do another Mirror activity to see if arrogance may be a factor for you.[41]

MIRROR
How Arrogant Are You at Work?

---

1. Do you generally believe you know better than everyone else?
2. Do you ever become overbearing or threatening in your dealings with others?
3. Do you find yourself contemptuous of others?
4. Do you criticize others in a threatening or hostile way?
5. Do you find it difficult or even unbearable to honestly consider others' perspectives?
6. Do you find it a waste of time to explain your decisions to others?
7. Do you get defensive when your opinions are challenged?
8. Do you equate arrogance with confidence or strength of character?
9. Do you use arrogance to try to bolster your self-esteem?

Based on your answers to these questions, place yourself on the scale below with regard to how arrogant you tend to be toward others—with 1 being all the time, and 10 being never.

I realize this is a particularly tough set of questions for most business leaders because of what they expose, and I applaud you for your honesty (and vulnerability!) in answering them. If you've been entrenched in this way of thinking or being for a long time, you have taken an important first step—but you know it takes more than admission to turn yourself around.

So, what to do?

Avoiding—or countering—arrogance requires among other things, balance. The great sage and Talmudic scholar Rabbi Hillel who lived about two thousand years ago, likely overlapping with Jesus, is famously quoted as saying, "If I am not for myself, who will be for me? But if I am only for myself, who am I?"[42]

In that vein, companies that wish to eschew arrogance and build a safe workplace culture can adopt the following healthy practices. We all know of people and companies who embrace these qualities, and we prefer to do business with them. You can be one too.

DOOR

To begin overturning arrogance in the workplace:

- Recognize the need to take care of yourself, along with your culture, your people, your customers, and your balance sheet.

- Project that you are not only for yourself but that you are part of a much larger ecosystem.

- Remember why you exist—to carry out your higher purpose, not solely to make money.

- Adopt the "No Asshole Rule" coined by Stanford professor and author Bob Sutton in his book of the same name, which sets a clear standard for what is and is not tolerated.

- Catch yourself when you notice you're disregarding others' opinions as if they don't have merit and asserting your own instead, and then stop and apologize for interrupting. Then, listen without the belief that your idea/solution is inevitably better.

- Humbly view your purpose as sacred and your employees and customers as worthy of love, which is what leads team members, investors, partners, and customers to support the company too.

In summary, if your business is missing love, it's likely that some degree of love is indeed missing within—whether that manifests as an inability to be vulnerable, a disregard for others, or an inflated ego. And if you're honest with yourself, you know instinctively that no one likes being around people who put up a tough front, are rude or indifferent, or project an inflated sense of self-importance. Not only do these behaviors make it difficult to be authentic and trusting, but also to meaningfully connect. All of these ways of being deplete energy and can diminish our—and others'—self-worth if we allow it.

The good news is that even when these qualities are ingrained, they're not insurmountable; all of them can be turned around.

In Chapter Twelve, I will provide you with additional ways to make vulnerability an asset, usher in civility with kindness, and replace arrogance with humility. But for now the succinct takeaway is this: When companies enable their people to be "real" at all levels within an organization, customers trust them more and want to engage with them, which is precisely what catching the Amare Wave is all about.

Once we can achieve that, we are much better prepared to recognize—and to not fall prey to—the influence of another factor that permeates the business world: that of fear energy.

THERE
ARE
TWO BASIC
MOTIVATING
FORCES:
FEAR
AND
LOVE.
–JOHN LENNON

CHAPTER SIX

IS FEAR ENERGY RULING YOUR BUSINESS?

I f you've been in the work world for a while, you're almost certain to have experienced the "business is war" mentality, simply because, as we've already discussed, it's a paradigm we've been immersed in for a long, long time in modern society. As a result, you may very well know what it takes to succeed in a "business is war" world. It may have even made you rich.

Yet, despite our successes, many of us are tired of operating in this way. We don't want to do business is war anymore, even if it can make us a lot of money. We've seen how it causes too much suffering, personally and societally, and how it makes us compromise our values and be untrue to ourselves. Perhaps worst of all, it takes away some of our humanity and our connection to the greater whole.

The bottom line? Deep down, we know business can be better, and still be highly profitable. It's the dueling motivations of fear and love that trip us up.

FEAR ENERGY VS. LOVE ENERGY

The best way to think about these two energies is not to go within the mind, as we so often do when striving to understand a concept, but rather within the body. This is because the energy of both fear and love is felt as heightened physiological arousal. With love—whether in personal situations or at work—our bodies actually feel *expanded* when we are filled with this energy, giving us a sense of alignment with our true selves. Fear—whether from real danger or the anticipation of bad things happening—also directly affects the body, only in a way that makes us feel *constricted*. This type of energy pulls us out of alignment with our true selves and our higher good, thereby diminishing us.

You can think of the energies of love and fear as differing in terms of their frequency and vibration. While this may sound like "woo woo" language, the idea that everything is energy and expressed in frequency and vibration is actually a central tenet of quantum physics. Engineer and physicist Nikola Tesla famously said:

"If you want to know the secrets of the universe, think in terms of energy, frequency, and vibration."

This is where physics and new-age thinking join hands: love vibrates at a high frequency, and fear vibrates at a low frequency. As human beings, we sense and respond differently to love and fear vibrations, even if we don't know how we do it and science cannot yet fully explain it.

Have you, for example, ever had a sudden and strong reaction that you couldn't logically explain when meeting someone new? That's you tuning into and reacting to that person's energy, or their vibrational frequency.

It's fascinating that from an evolutionary perspective—as our brains have grown and our prefrontal cortex has evolved to give us greater cognitive power and language—our ability to understand

and choose the energy of love has increased. It makes sense that exercising our propensity for love demonstrates our more noble and evolved selves, as well as our natural state of being. But on the flip side of that is fear, which elicits our fight/flight/freeze response, involving our more primitive lower brain stem. It's no surprise that when we exercise this survival mechanism, one rarely needed in the modern world, we show our more primitive selves.

While we all have the unique capacity for both love and fear, consider for a moment what I said about the energy of love being expansive, and the energy of fear being constricting. Now imagine, for example, in what state employees are likely to fully engage, contribute new ideas, and put forward their best work. The answer, I believe, is obvious.

When we are afraid, we pull back from life. When we are in love, we open to all that life has to offer with passion, excitement, and acceptance.

−JOHN LENNON

Now, there are some who say that fear is a useful tool for managing and motivating people in business—and it is true that fear can be effective at driving us to do things in certain circumstances, precisely because fear triggers our primitive brain to respond in unthinking ways (think flight, fight, freeze, or faint). However, as decades of research have demonstrated, using fear as a leadership strategy or management tool comes at a tremendous cost that well overrides whatever short-term gains it may produce, creating a multitude of problems:

- trust is diminished
- people become insecure about their jobs
- any healthy sense of cohesiveness disappears
- self-esteem suffers
- feelings of helplessness, alienation, and sometimes anger take hold

- people feel intimidated and frequently silenced, which counters creativity, open-mindedness, and the willingness to critically challenge each other's ideas—and sometimes even has deadly effects

Malcolm Gladwell, in his investigation of Korean Air's unusually high crash rate in the 1970s and 1980s, showed that fear of speaking up can lead to real tragedy—in this case, when co-pilots wouldn't challenge their captains' decisions, which led to numerous crashes and hundreds of deaths. We see the same dynamic at play every day when employees feel threatened into silence as they watch ego-driven CEOs take their companies into bankruptcy and worse.[43]

The issue is not whether fear can motivate—it can. The real issue is whether you want to live with the energy of fear driving your business, and driving *you*. If you are truly in a dangerous situation where your life is at risk—such as being robbed at gunpoint—then your fear-based instincts activate to protect you. But many of us work in a culture of fear even though there is no life-threatening situation. Think about it: how often is a fear-based work culture upheld through misperceptions, exaggerations, or ruminations that lead us to imagine the worst-case scenario of how our actions will be judged, what people think of us, and what may or may not happen *to* us, or *because* of us? When this occurs, fear-based thoughts like the following emerge and become strong influences:

My company doesn't value me.

The Board will dump me if we don't hit our numbers this quarter.

My people don't respect me and think I'm weak.

My boss probably doesn't think I'm good enough to get promoted.

Our customers probably don't think our products are as good as our competition's.

Since I'm not as creative as [insert name], I probably won't last in this job.

Our competition is going to put us out of business.

I doubt that we can ever penetrate that market.

It's going to be an uphill battle to surpass [X] company's reputation.

Now, these may be legitimate beliefs; various factors could make them true. But what's critical to observe is that there are two ways to approach them: one is fear-based, and one is love-based. Let's take a look at what constricted, fear-based thinking could motivate:

My company doesn't value me, **so I better suck up to them**.

The Board will dump me if we don't hit our numbers this quarter, **so I'll doctor our financials to look better**.

My people don't respect me and think I'm weak, **so I better get mean and show how tough I am**.

My boss probably doesn't think I'm good enough to get promoted, **so I might as well just do the minimum and forget about moving up**.

Our customers probably don't think our products are as good as our competition's, **so we've got to find a way to make their products look less appealing**.

Since I'm not as creative as [insert name], I probably won't last in this job, **so I might as well hang it up now**.

Our competition is going to put us out of business, **so we need to come up with a strong campaign to lure their top people over to us.**

I doubt that we could ever penetrate that market, **but I bet we could if we threw some products together and made them seem a lot more eco-friendly than they actually are.**

It's going to be an uphill battle to surpass [X] company's reputation, **but if we dig up some dirt on them and make it public, we might be able to make some strides.**

Do you see the direction fear moves people toward? Can you feel the constriction as you read these statements? *Giving up. Degrading others. Stealing employees. Using unethical tactics. Igniting ugliness.* It's all terribly diminishing. Yet, over thousands of years, and with a tremendous amount of conditioning, we have allowed fear to be an acceptable and even desirable motivator for achieving business outcomes that have zero to do with our basic survival. This has become part and parcel of warlike business culture, expressed through a skewed perspective of good and evil, the use of predatory language, fear of vulnerability, and projection of incivility and arrogance—in short, behaviors and beliefs that feel good to no one, as we discussed in Chapters Four and Five.

Now let's look at these same dilemmas viewed with love-based energy responses.

My company doesn't value me, **so maybe it's time to realize we're simply not in sync and look for a job where there is alignment and better opportunities.**

The Board will dump me if we don't hit our numbers this quarter, **so I'm going to ask for their input; after all, they might have some great ideas they'll be happy to share.**

My people don't respect me and think I'm weak, **so I need to adopt better ways of coming across and relating to them that are authentic and will put me in a more favorable light.**

My boss probably doesn't think I'm good enough to get promoted, **so I'm going to ask for a meeting with her to see what I can do to make myself more valuable.**

Our customers probably don't think our products are as good as [X] company's, **so it's time to infuse some better qualities into them, such as being more eco-friendly.**

Since I'm not as creative as [insert name], I probably won't last in this job, **but that could change if I focus on combining my analytical talent with her creative talent – we might make a great team.**

If we're not careful, our competition is going to put us out of business, **so we need to ask our customers what they need that we're not providing, then take their input and make some positive changes.**

I doubt that we could ever penetrate that market, **but I bet we could if we created a new product line that has all the integrity of our service offerings.**

It's going to be an uphill battle to surpass [X] company's reputation, **but it would be great to be on par with them – there doesn't need to be a clear number one as long as we both offer distinct value.**

Can you feel the sense of expansion in these statements, particularly in contrast to the fear-based examples that preceded them? Each of these take what could be construed as requiring defeatist or subversive action and instead apply an uplifting action—an action more based in our multilayered definition of *amare*.

In providing these sample scenarios, I want it to be clear to you that outside of the rare life-threatening situation, you always have a conscious choice when you are afraid. You can:

1. Give in to the fear and let it take over your thoughts, words, and actions.

    OR

2. Observe your feeling of fear without judging it, then consciously move yourself out of the constriction of fear energy and toward the expansiveness of love energy.

I'm not saying it's easy, especially after so many generations of conditioning that has us feeding our fears or acting within one of its many disguises. And for men in particular, we need to get over our hang-ups about tuning in to and talking about our emotions. However, there are numerous ways to move from fear to love, some of which follow. I recommend you try different ones to discover what works for you.

DOOR

In the moment of awareness that you are lapsing into fear, one method of shifting states is through interruption:

- take a deep breath
- change your cognition to a better feeling thought
- say to yourself, "Stop!"
- wash your face
- swig some water
- physically move your body
- any other interruption that works for you

Although it's easier to recognize the process of shifting from fear to love in extreme situations, you likely know how good it feels. Consider this example:

> You're walking toward a hotel to give a speech to a large group. You're nervous and sweating, lost in a plethora of self-induced thoughts about how you'll screw up in front of so many people. Suddenly, a car swerves to avoid a bicyclist and almost hits you, screeching to a stop inches from where you're standing. You are stunned for a moment, then quickly recover and with a deep sigh of relief, feel immense gratitude for being alive. You are almost giddy as you look around smiling, noticing how beautiful the trees are, how bright the colors are, the richness of all the sights and sounds surrounding you. The debilitating fear you had moments ago is utterly gone. You feel alive, uplifted, and connected.

The same thing happens in less dramatic situations, simply by providing yourself with an interruption. Choosing the vibration of love doesn't require heart-stopping events like a near car accident to wake up the possibility.

Fear, on the other hand, rarely feels good. Its denigrating and separating nature confines us to a limited realm of possibility. Sure, we're hardwired to remember and respond to fear-based information because eons ago, it helped us stay alive on a daily basis, as in "Lions are on the prowl over there in that savannah—avoid it!" But in business, while there's certainly nothing wrong with feeling fear sometimes—we all do—you may find that it is your guiding force, rather than an occasional visitor.

> *Fear is the cheapest room in the house.*
> *I would like to see you living in better conditions.*
> —HAFIZ, 14TH-CENTURY PERSIAN POET

FDR, in his inaugural presidential address, famously said: "The only thing to fear is fear itself." What he meant by that is when people operate out of fear, it does more harm than good. At the time of his presidency, he was referring to masses of Americans rushing to their banks to withdraw all their money, which served to further damage a fragile economy. Today, we see something similar occur when businesses, believing that operating under fear-based energy is what will help them attain what they consider to be the realm of success, do more harm than good.

What scares you? Is it when you pitch a new idea to investors? When you make a mistake that costs the company a lot of money or some degree of embarrassment? When you need to make major decisions? When you think you are getting laid off or need to lay someone off? When a bully at work flies off the handle? When your company's stock value drops precipitously? When your performance is being evaluated?

All of these situations may be threats to your pride and personality, yes—but not to your life. Yet fear tends to awaken the beast of the ego, which will not only trigger you, but *want* you to immerse yourself into the fear, to make up worst-case "what if . . .?" stories. That is how the ego nourishes and protects itself. Spiritual teacher Eckhart Tolle calls this the "pain body"—a semi-autonomous entity that seeks more suffering to feed and grow itself.44 It is important to notice when this happens so that you can consciously step away from ego-based reactions and decisions. Why step away? Because operating from the ego tends to drive defensive, *constricted* reactions, which often translates into hostile behavior. If you think about your own experiences, you'll realize this is true. Coming from ego may be fine when you truly need to protect yourself from immediate danger, but other than that, it doesn't tend to serve us all that well in the bigger picture.

Let's explore this a bit further by giving your honest answers in the following Mirror activity. Be aware of how your immediate responses *feel*. Are they constrictive or expansive?

MIRROR
Fear/Ego Responses vs. Love/Heart Responses

---

1. You pitch a new idea that isn't well received. Your response is:

2. You make a mistake that costs your company a lot of money or some degree of embarrassment. Your response is:

3. You get laid off during an economic downturn or other restructuring within the company. Your response is:

4. A bully at work flies off the handle at you. Your response is:

5. Your company's stock value drops precipitously. Your response is:

6. Your performance is evaluated and you don't believe it reflects the work you've been putting in. Your response is:

7. A customer says something nasty, but true, about your company. Your response is:

Based on your responses to these questions, place yourself on the scale below with regard to how often you tend to react from fear vs. how often you react from love—with 1 being always from fear, and 10 being always from love.

I want you to really think about your first response to these scenarios. Did you feel defensive, angry, even vengeful? Did you begin imagining the retribution you would mete out, or the lies you might tell to shift blame? If so, you were having an ego response, which is, unfortunately, the norm for many of us. But before you get down on yourself or decide you're a bad person for wanting to tear into someone or react with hostility, remember that in every reaction you have a *choice*.

Between stimulus and response there is space. In that space is our power to choose our response. In our response lies our growth and our freedom.

—VIKTOR FRANKL (PARAPHRASED BY STEPHEN COVEY)[45]

You can carry out the warlike behaviors your ego is erroneously prompting you to perform to defend yourself, or you can re-evaluate your response and bring yourself into a space that more encompasses the spirit of *amare*. If that's feeling a bit foreign to you right now, here's how this might look.

You pitch a new idea that isn't well received.

EGO RESPONSE: Believe your boss/team must be narrow-minded and stupid. Give one or all the cold-shoulder for a while. Have a poor attitude toward future projects.

AMARE RESPONSE: Remain unattached. Ask to speak with your boss/team to respectfully, without hostility, find out exactly why they didn't care for the idea. Is there a way to improve on it? Do you perhaps need to explain it better? Or is it truly not the best idea, and that's okay — you'll learn from it and do better next time.

You make a mistake that costs your company a lot of money or some degree of embarrassment.

EGO RESPONSE: Find a way to shift the blame onto someone or something other than you.

AMARE RESPONSE: Take accountability for the mistake. Sincerely apologize to all affected parties. Ask others for input on how you might have avoided the error. Offer to work on a way to recover money or reinstate good standing.

You get laid off during an economic downturn or other restructuring within the company.

EGO RESPONSE: Tell off your boss. Rant to everyone who will listen about how unfair the decision was. Threaten to make the company look bad for doing this to you.

AMARE RESPONSE: Have a civil conversation about the decision. Ask what it would take for you to be able to stay, and accept the answer. Empathize with the person who may be in a difficult position of letting you go. See if you can calmly negotiate a fair layoff, if possible, with either compensation or time to find another position.

A bully at work flies off the handle at you.

EGO RESPONSE: Fly off the handle in return. Tell others what a jerk he is, retelling the story to anyone within earshot. Scheme to make his life miserable.

AMARE RESPONSE: Diffuse the exchange calmly, not taking it personally. Ask if he's okay. Offer that something must really be bothering him to go off this way on you. Ask if there's anything you can do to help.

Your company's stock value drops precipitously.

EGO RESPONSE: Call yourself a failure. Deflect responsibility from yourself and blame the team. Panic and take on undue stress.

AMARE RESPONSE: Breathe. Accept that the situation may be out of your control. Know that the stock market fluctuates and that your shareholders won't necessarily sell immediately. Ask your team for ideas. If you do have control, see it as a time to get creative and grow.

Your performance is evaluated and you don't believe it reflects the quality of work you've been putting in.

EGO RESPONSE: Become angry and defensive with the reviewer. Assume he's an idiot and doesn't have a clue. Believe he's out to get you.

AMARE RESPONSE: Respectfully ask how your performance was evaluated. Calmly present your side. Ask with genuine interest if there's something you can do to receive a better review next time. Show your gratitude to the reviewer for the guidance you found helpful.

A customer says something nasty, but true, about your company.

EGO RESPONSE: Get snippy with the customer. Defend the comment and say it's not true. Tell the customer, with an attitude, that she can take her business elsewhere.

AMARE RESPONSE: Empathize with how she feels. Make every effort, with kindness, to fix the problem. Assure the customer you will bring her concern to the right person's attention. Be sure you have her information, then follow through on updating her.

As you read these contrasting responses for each scenario, be aware of the feeling you have inside. Which one feels better? Even if the *amare* response is a bit unnatural for you, do you notice how much better it feels not to be primed for war, as in the ego responses? With practice, an *amare* response can actually become your default. And even if it's not, remember you always have the power to take a moment to breathe and adjust your state before responding to any situation. By learning to shift your responses away from the ego and make decisions more from the heart, you also receive the bonus of transmuting fear into an opportunity for growth—making you more conscious of *you*.

The moment we stop running from the demons in our heads, and instead we choose to love them; when saying yes to life, both shadow and light, our suffering is done and we come alive.
—FROM THE SONG "SHEDDING SKINS" BY FIA FORSSTRÖM

One more note:

In honoring and wanting the best for "the other"—your coworkers, customers, and suppliers—you are more likely to be kind, generous, and thoughtful in meeting their needs with integrity. But let me be clear that this does not mean you take abuse and allow someone to beat you down or take advantage of you because you're always striving to be the "nice guy"; that is *not* what I'm saying. It is still always prudent to uphold your values, assert your truth, and stand up for yourself respectfully.

In sum, it's true that we are in control of taming the pervasive fear-based fighting energy within business today and replacing it with uplifting love-based energy that seeks to benefit everyone.

But what if the fighting energy has permeated to a deeper level, where the negativity has become a truly insidious company-wide influence that translates into hate?

CUSTOMER HATRED AS A DEBILITATING FORCE

"We hate our customers," Juan told me rather matter of factly. "Really, we hate them."

To hear someone so bluntly describe his company's relationship with their customers as hate startled me, but I was not surprised. Juan's company was at war with their customers. As a smart and seasoned product manager for a global medical company (we'll call them Ace Medical), he had the insight to see the discord for what it was, and the courage to call it what it was, as harsh as it sounded.

Having consulted with Ace Medical for many years, I understood the dynamic. They did harbor hatred toward their customers. Actually, a more precise descriptor would be contempt. And as a wise old psychiatrist once taught me: Nothing destroys relationships, or is harder to recover from, than contempt.

What happened within this company to spur such loathing?

Ace was a business-to-business (B2B) manufacturing company, and their customers were distributors (aka middlemen) who then sold Ace's equipment to consumers. Simply put, Ace Medical felt trapped in their relationship with their customers. They considered them a necessary evil they wished they could eliminate, like crushing an opposing force in battle. Only in this case, the opposing force also paid the bills.

Why the warlike mentality, you may be wondering? In a nutshell, Ace Medical firmly believed their customers—the distributors—had zero loyalty and took advantage of them. But Ace was afraid to confront them or to change any existing arrangements, fearing these distributors would simply switch to a competitor, which some had in fact threatened to do. In a command-and-control culture, fear of losing customers they disdained was the unspoken dynamic driving the business, perpetuating negative energy that deeply affected employees too. As a result, most employees at Ace Medical did not feel appreciated, valued, or inspired. They certainly did not feel loved by the company, nor did they feel connected with customers.

And what about those customers?

It's no surprise that they, too, sensed the animosity and negative energy. They had choices, but for the most part they opted to stay with Ace Medical because Ace had better equipment and a good brand name. Some stayed because they were afraid to take big risks, as new methods of direct-to-consumer distribution, like Amazon, introduced great uncertainty to business-to-consumer (B2C) distributors. Some simply stayed put until something better (they hoped) came along.

Unfortunately, fear and disdain are contagious within a company. It didn't take long for any new Ace employee to come to the belief that customers were the reason no one liked their job. How could employees possibly feel passionate about their work or deliver their best if they hated the people they were serving?

One product manager actually said, "This would be so much easier if we just didn't have to deal with those damn customers!"

As you might imagine, there was a lot of fighting internally as well as with customers. Putting so much energy into fighting wore people down, and eventually, many good people left. Others resigned themselves to the grind, while a few optimistic change agents tried to enlighten people and change things, but with limited success.

Ace Medical's curse—yes, *curse*—was that they still made money. Being solvent served to reinforce the status quo. It also perpetuated their fear of changing the fundamental way they related to their customers. Yet despite delivering reasonable profits, they were missing big opportunities to innovate and become even more profitable. Instead, they continued fearing and fighting.

Be honest: Does your company hate its customers? Most people in business would quickly say no. I hope for you and your company that the answer really *is* no. But would your customers agree?

When companies love their customers, the customers know it —and the company's staff knows it. But within companies that disdain their customers, it may be less clear. That's because in most companies, antipathy will not be an explicitly stated value, even when it is the *functioning* value. You'll never see "We hate our customers" headlining the annual report or being acknowledged by the leadership team; in fact, they may *say* quite the opposite, championing customer-this and customer-that as corporate rhetoric. This inconsistency between how the company says they are, and how they really are, causes a great deal of confusion internally.

As you can imagine, hating customers is an attitude that becomes reflected in what people think, the actions people take, and the energy behind those thoughts and actions. When companies despise their customers, for example, employees will talk, or at least whisper about it. Some may even deny the negative attitudes, though they are being demonstrated in thoughts, words, and deeds. But the bottom line is: when hate is honored in whatever fashion, more hate will be cultivated.

Why this hostility? Because a) business leaders often simply project what they know, and b) rarely are business leaders criticized for being tough and aggressive (unless they are women, but that's a different story). In fact, business leaders, like politicians, are often lauded and rewarded for talking tough and engaging with others through fear and intimidation. This creates two problems:

1. Tough often morphs into hostility, meanness, and greed— conditions that do not garner the benefits of being love- like and kind to employees, customers, or other stakeholders.

2. The energy of the business-as-war paradigm is fear, which is almost never acknowledged because we pretend being tough means being unafraid. Instead, the fear is used as fuel for fighting—for market share with competitors, for

turf and recognition with other employees and business units, for better deals with investors and partners in the supply chain, and for support against customers who dare to ask for better products, services, and experiences.

As a result, greed and corruption frequently become the dominant ethos and culture of the company. Again, though it's not always evident, this warlike mindset is fueled by fear—fear of losing, fear of failure, fear of being looked down on, the list goes on —with the explicit goal to make as much money as quickly as possible and at any cost. Once again, customers are simply prey to capture, subdue, use, and expend. To be clear, this is not "values be damned"; these *are* the values.

When business leaders become afraid, they often mask it with aggression, which is used to justify and perpetuate warlike thinking and actions. Other times, companies inadvertently drift from their good values and mission into negative practices, and then fall into deeper and deeper holes. In some circumstances, the negativity develops out of desperation, as if it's the customers' fault the business is failing.

MIRROR
Gauging Customer Hatred

---

1. Does your company hate, disdain, or dislike its customers?

   If you answered yes:

2. In what ways is that conveyed to employees?

3. In what ways is that conveyed to customers?

4. Hate is fueled by fear. Does your company operate out of fear?

If you answered yes:

5. How do you see it manifested toward employees?

6. How do you see it manifested toward customers?

Based on your answers to these questions, place yourself on the scale below with regard to how your company feels about its customers—with 1 being hateful toward them all of the time, and 10 being loving toward them all of the time.

Even if you uncovered some hatred going on in your company through the Mirror activity, the good news is that no company *needs* to feel hateful and contemptuous toward their customers—or toward their competitors. There is no requirement for any business to be warlike in thoughts, words, or actions for any reason. Not only does that hatred cause far too much suffering, it is unnecessary. Whatever success showing contempt for customers may generate for some, it comes at too high a price for the people involved, the customers affected, and society at large.

If you believe it's tempting to allow a company's financial goals to justify hating, mistreating, or otherwise taking advantage of their people or their customers, consider the extreme example of the broker depicted in *Wolf of Wall Street*—a man who, along with his firm, unabashedly connived customers out of their life savings to profit themselves. This is "shareholder capitalism"—as some call it—at its worst. Think, too, about the actions of the banks that were "too big to fail" in the major recession of recent years. The question is not so much how they made fortunes through meanness, greed, and corruption. We know it *can* be done. The questions are: 1) What personal price did they pay to make those fortunes? And 2) How much would have they made by treating their customers with *amare*?

WINDOW

A Peek into Extreme Business Greed with Mr. Incredible

There's a great scene in the movie *The Incredibles* that illustrates how managers pressure their people to focus on money and shareholders, even when it cheats or hurts customers. In this scene, our hero, the kind-hearted Bob Parr (Mr. Incredible), is being yelled at by his mean boss Mr. Huph for authorizing payment on a customer's insurance claim.

MR. HUPH: Parr! You authorized payment on the Walker policy?!

BOB: Someone broke into their house, Mr. Huph. Their policy clearly covers–

MR. HUPH: I don't wanna know about their coverage, Bob! Don't tell me about their coverage. Tell me how you're keeping Insuricare in the black. Tell me how that's possible, with you writing checks to every Harry Hardluck and Sally Sobstory that gives you a phone call.

The conversation continues when Huph's secretary calls Bob into Huph's office.

MR. HUPH: Sit down, Bob. [pause] I'm not happy, Bob. Not happy. Ask me why.

BOB: Okay. Why?

MR. HUPH: Why what? Be specific, Bob.

BOB: Why are you unhappy?

MR. HUPH: Your customers make me unhappy.

BOB: What, you've gotten complaints?

MR. HUPH: Complaints I can handle. What I can't handle is your customers' inexplicable knowledge of Insuricare's inner workings! They're experts. Experts, Bob! Exploiting every loophole, dodging every obstacle! They're penetrating the bureaucracy!

BOB: Did I do something illegal?

MR. HUPH: No.

BOB: Are you saying we shouldn't help our customers?

MR. HUPH: The law requires that I answer no.

BOB: We're supposed to help people.

MR. HUPH: We're supposed to help *our* people! Starting with our stockholders, Bob. Who's helping them out, huh?

As you might imagine, this isn't such an extreme example. In fact, precisely this type of exchange between boss and employee leads to another detrimental effect of the business-as-war mindset: the psychological and emotional disengagement of individuals from their company altogether.

FUELING AN ATMOSPHERE OF DISENGAGEMENT

What happens when the leaders of a company operate from a place of fear, embrace fighting energy, and treat business as war? When they lack a higher purpose, become greedy, and lose their way? When they don't foster uplifting experiences or meaningful connection between people?

What happens is *disengagement*. And when that occurs, people just plain stop caring.

If you think about it, it makes perfect sense. Who wants to feel unappreciated, mistreated, and diminished? Naturally, those feelings foster even more negativity in the workplace in the form of poor morale, reduced trust, lost productivity, decreased loyalty, damaged reputation, and a host of other responses that harm people, business, and society. You may not be surprised to learn that disengaged employees cost organizations between $450 and $550 *billion* annually, according to estimates from a study conducted by the Engagement Institute.[46] Clearly, lack of engagement—and even worse, active *dis*engagement—is a serious and pervasive problem.

Jim Clifton, the CEO of Gallup, introduces their 2016 State of the American Workplace report as follows:

> The American workforce has more than 100 million full-time employees. One-third of those employees are what Gallup calls engaged at work. They love their jobs and make their organization and America better every day. At the other end, 16 percent of employees are actively disengaged – they are miserable in the workplace and destroy what the most engaged employees build. The remaining 51 percent of employees are not engaged – they're just there. These figures indicate an American leadership philosophy that simply doesn't work anymore. One also wonders if the country's declining productivity numbers point to a need for major workplace disruption.[47]

I admit, I found these numbers to be staggering. Imagine yourself at a work meeting. Look to your left, then to your right. On average, two of the three of you are not engaged in your work.

From a global perspective, things are even grimmer. An earlier Gallup survey of workplaces in 142 countries found that only 13 percent of employees worldwide—that's 1 out of 8—feel engaged at work.[48]

How does your company measure up on this topic? Notice what factors you consider as you answer the following questions. Pay attention, too, to your emotional responses. If you hold your breath, sigh, wince, or tighten up, think about why that is. Your body won't lie to you.

MIRROR
Where Do You Fall on the Engaged-O-Meter?

Place a checkmark next to all the statements that merit a yes.

- ○ I feel engaged in my work most days.
- ○ I believe in the company mission.
- ○ I feel motivated to do my best.
- ○ I feel seen and heard at work.
- ○ I want to be there.
- ○ I feel valued.
- ○ I believe what I do at work is important.
- ○ I feel connected to the people at my company.
- ○ I feel uplifted by my work.

Based on your responses to these questions, place yourself on the scale below with regard to how engaged you feel at work—with 1 being not engaged at all, and 10 being wholly engaged.

Consider all your answers. If you are highly disengaged, is staying in your job worth it? What would it take to become meaningfully engaged? If your engagement is already high, note what specifically fosters that engagement. How can you deepen your engagement and how much others in your company are engaged?

Customers will never love a company until employees love it first.
—SIMON SINEK, AUTHOR OF START WITH WHY

In summary, both love and fear are highly motivating, but what and how these opposite energies manifest is very different, as we've explored in this chapter.

Overall, the energy of fear is constricting. It tends to shut down our creativity, foster warlike behavior, and inhibit our engagement with our work and company. The dismal engagement numbers I just shared highlight a tremendous need for improvement. Business can't maximize its value and fulfill its societal purpose if its workers aren't engaged.

In contrast, the energy of love is uplifting and connecting, engaging us deeply as human beings and as workers, opening us to opportunity, and leaning into growth and expansion. This is how business as a social and economic enterprise ideally operates—and how business can dare to prosper differently. This is the essence of riding the Amare Wave and what brings us to the heart of this book: how to become a thriving and uplifting Amare Way company.

In Part III, I'll show you precisely how to reach this goal through achieving and maintaining alignment, adopting the Amare Way philosophy, and taking action with the Amare Way practice.

Get ready to be energized!

PART THREE

JOINING US WITH THEM: BUSINESS THE AMARE WAY

*Successful people become great leaders when they
learn to shift the focus from themselves to others.*
—MARSHALL GOLDSMITH,
EXECUTIVE COACH AND AUTHOR

BUILDING
A VISIONARY
COMPANY
REQUIRES
ONE PERCENT
VISION
AND
99 PERCENT
ALIGNMENT.

–JIM COLLINS, BUSINESS AUTHOR

CHAPTER SEVEN

───────────

TO THINE OWN SELF—
AND BUSINESS—BE TRUE:
THE IMPORTANCE OF ALIGNMENT

Jim was a store manager at Einstein's Bagels, a company he describes as not particularly warlike or love-centered, but a decent company somewhere in the middle. They cared about customers and genuinely wanted employees to take good care of them, but unfortunately, money often became more important, and that led some managers to make decisions that compromised doing right by both employees and customers.

Jim, on the other hand, made his employees his top priority as a manager. He wanted them to be happy, to be authentic, to be aligned with the company mission, and to always have what they needed to succeed. The company offered various incentive programs, ran "rah-rah" campaigns to motivate the team, and set clear financial goals for each store and region, with bonuses tied to monthly financial performance. But Jim says that none of that really influenced what he did as a manager, not even the bonuses, because he believed if he took good care of his people, they would do their best to make customers happy, which would then bring in the money. He therefore figured that the money part would work out in the long run—which it did.

Jim's team regarded customers as family—those who came in for coffee and bagels every day were their core family, and those who came in once or twice a week were their extended family. The team loved them all, and the customers knew it. In fact, when Jim was promoted to regional manager, their family of customers surprised him by organizing a going-away party, complete with a big cake and cards signed by all the regulars. Not only was it a beautiful and heartfelt celebration, but it acknowledged for Jim that his customers indeed felt seen and cared for, even loved.

Jim's story is an excellent example of what it means to operate in alignment, and is our segue into the Amare Way framework that is the focus of this part of the book. But before diving into the framework in detail (which I cover in the next two chapters), I lead with this chapter on alignment because it underlies and unifies everything that follows.

In the Amare Way, alignment provides a common ground for connection, commitment, and love between your company, employees, customers, investors, the community, and other stakeholders, based on shared goals and values. Without alignment, you suffer energy drains, confusion, and frustration, which hurt morale, productivity, and performance.

To break it down simply, alignment encompasses the following:

1. Consistency and integrity across:

    - your corporate vision, strategy, and execution
    - your purpose, values, and brand identity
    - your value proposition and the value you deliver

2. What you as a company believe, say, and do all match.

3. How your company behaves behind the scenes, when out front doing business, and in society at large. All the ways you show up are situationally appropriate, in sync, and in line with the promises you make.

There is also an energetic aspect to alignment—the vibration we touched on in Chapter Six. Within the Amare Way framework, the priorities you set, decisions you make, things you say, and actions you take are all attuned to and express the same positive energy and vibrational frequency. What does that look like?

Foundationally, real alignment requires buy-in from people at all levels of the company: the people leading, directing, and managing the organization; those designing, making, and selling your products and services; teams in strategy, research, planning, and marketing; customer service people; and administrative staff and support people. In short, everyone in each role in the company needs to genuinely be on board with and commit to the beliefs, aims, and ways of the company.

For that buy-in and commitment to be fully authentic, there must also be consistency between *personal* goals and values and *corporate* goals and values; otherwise, half-hearted efforts, dissension, and absenteeism run rampant.

The starting point for alignment? **Your higher purpose**. Aligning around a sense of purpose gets us outside our limited selves to help us find meaning and connect with things bigger than ourselves.

Naturally, alignment is much stronger when your purpose is something your stakeholders believe in and care about—that is, a shared purpose with mutual benefit. In the Amare Way framework, you want all your stakeholders to buy into the higher purpose of your company and how you do business. When this kind of multifaceted and multi-stakeholder alignment is in place, the uplifting and connecting energy of love can take hold because everyone shows up authentically, feels like they belong and want to belong, acts in line with their intention and words, desires to collaborate and work toward shared aims, and puts forward their best. In Chapters Eight and Nine, you will see how deeply alignment integrates with the Amare Way philosophy, as well as with its pillars of practice: Authenticity, Belonging, and Collaboration.

MIRROR
Is Your Company in Alignment?

Consider how aligned your company is—or isn't—by noting your level of agreement with the following statements on a scale of 1 to 5, with 1 being not aligned, and 5 being completely aligned.

____ There is consistency and integrity across your corporate vision, strategy, and execution.

____ There is consistency and integrity across your purpose, values, and brand identity.

____ There is consistency and integrity across your value proposition and the value you deliver.

____ What you as a company believe, say, and do all match.

____ There is consistency and integrity in how your company behaves behind the scenes, when doing business, and in society at large.

____ All the ways you show up are situationally appropriate and in sync.

Based on your ratings to these questions, place your company on the scale below with regard to how in alignment it is overall—with 1 being completely out of alignment, and 10 being completely in alignment.

What level of company alignment is reflected in your answers? Where are you most aligned? Which, if any, are the areas where you need to focus on becoming more aligned?

On multiple levels, alignment is critical to successfully being love-centered in business and in prospering. And it all starts with you being aligned with, well, *you*.

DOST THOU KNOWEST THYSELF?

"Know thyself." We've all heard dozens of times this adage that dates back to ancient Greece, Egypt, and India. Shakespeare, too, had his take: "Of all knowledge, the wise and good seek most to know themselves." Author Asaf Braverman expounds:

> This two-word imperative traveled from antiquity and throughout history to the present day. Like a golden thread in a multicolored fabric, Know Thyself wove its course through races and cultures, through religious and secular traditions, spanning spiritual and scientific teachings and appearing in art and literature. Indeed, the ancient adage was declared in almost every medium on every continent and in every era.[49]

Yes, being in true alignment means knowing ourselves well. But it's not always apparent to us precisely who we are. Benjamin Franklin concurred: "There are three things extremely hard—steel, a diamond, and to know one's self."

Some people have been living out of alignment and out of touch with themselves for so long they're not even aware of it—and they're not sure what being in alignment feels like. The good news is that for most of us, it's not that difficult to start to recognize, as long as we're willing to be a little vulnerable. That's because if you've been operating out of alignment—either at work, in life, or both—and haven't been cognitively aware of it, I can guarantee you've still *felt* it on some level. It could be there has been inconsistency between what you do and your core values and beliefs. You may have felt like a fraud or a fake, sending mixed messages and generating confusion among your people because they witness you say or do one thing, yet embody the energy of the opposite. You may have also felt lost, or like you don't know who you are anymore. Or you may have simply felt "off." If any of these are true for you, you've definitely been out of sync with yourself.

It's no surprise, then, that when you are *in* alignment, the opposite is true. Your sense of yourself and your role in your business are consistent and healthy, in line with your core values and beliefs. There is less ego and angst, as well as less uncertainty. You have more flow and ease in your life, and you feel more internal guidance. It is as though you are operating from a higher place, in sync with a larger whole. Because your aligned state of being feels connected and uplifted, you feel you are in a state of what some call "unity." I call that state *love*. When you love yourself and how you present yourself to the world, it feels good to be you. Being in alignment with and loving yourself go hand in hand, and you are a more effective leader when you love yourself in a healthy way.

> *Find out who you are and be that person.*
> *Find that truth, live that truth, and everything else will come.*
> —ELLEN DEGENERES

When I was first developing value-based consulting proposals instead of the hourly-based proposals that are much more common in the industry, I remember initially feeling afraid that a prospective client would say, "Are you crazy? Who are you to charge as much as the big firms with thousands of people? No one will pay you that!" It never happened, but it took awhile for me to let that fear go.

Essentially, I needed to discern if I was acting from—you guessed it—fear or love. For example, fear might say, "I think the value is worth $85,000, but can I really ask for that much?" Sometimes I didn't and lowered the fee, all the while feeling "off" inside because I wasn't trusting myself. Or greed (built on fear) might sneak in and ask, "How much can we get away with charging for this scope of work?" Whenever I rationalized the greedy fee as okay and asked for more than I believed the engagement was worth, I felt terrible and became defensive, even shutting down. A better way to handle it would have been to let those questions go and shift to: "What can we do to best serve this client given their current condition?" and "What are the intended results worth to the client?" Once I answered those questions honestly, I could then properly present the clients with the appropriate fee for the value provided.

All these years later, I still occasionally have twinges of those old fears when developing and presenting proposals. But I have learned—through experience and my daily meditation practice—to trust my "makes sense" and "feels right" reactions. In this context, these reactions tell me that my actions are aligned with what will best serve clients, and that my fees are aligned with the value I'm providing.

Unfortunately, in the West, we've traditionally not been taught to value or even think about alignment with self; however, that's changing as practices like meditation and mindfulness continue to proliferate. Still, simply being aware of whether you're in alignment with yourself or not is a huge step. If you lead in business with that awareness, you are on the Amare path.

In many wisdom traditions, you may know that living in alignment with your sacred purpose is a consistent theme. It is a main message in the ancient scripture, the *Bhagavad Gita*, which teaches that when you are in alignment with your dharma—or purpose—you are in the right role and doing the right thing with your life, at least for the time. Stephen Cope, in his exposition of the Gita entitled *The Great Work of Your Life*, expresses this beautifully as:

The unification of thoughts, words, and actions in alignment with our soul's highest calling.

Now, this may all sound great, but if you haven't yet found your soul's highest calling, how do you get yourself into alignment? And even if you're fulfilling what you believe is your soul's highest calling on some level, how do you know you're in proper alignment with yourself?

The following Mirror exercise is designed to reveal both how well you know yourself and how you can get to know yourself better. Through answering these questions, you can learn to achieve greater alignment by pinpointing what you care about, who you are truly meant to be, and what you are meant to do in business and in life. Note that in this particular exercise, it's important to answer the questions without much thinking or analysis, allowing your first instinct to guide you. I would also encourage you to notice when you feel constricted inside vs. expanded, as it is a good guideline for where you are currently aligned (expanded) or not (constricted).

MIRROR
Being in Alignment;
Staying in Alignment

Consider how aligned you are—or aren't—by noting your level of agreement with the following statements on a scale of 1 to 5, with 1 being not at all aligned, and 5 being completely aligned.

Being in Alignment

____ I generally feel in alignment with myself in business.

____ I stay true to my core values and beliefs at work.

____ I feel genuine and authentic as a business leader.

____ I feel connected with something bigger than myself.

____ I feel uplifted—and uplifting—in my leadership role.

____ I feel I am on my right path for now.

____ I know how it feels in my body when I'm true to myself.

____ I know how it feels in my body when I'm not true to myself.

Based on your answers to these questions, place yourself on the scale below with regard to how in alignment you are with yourself —with 1 being completely out of alignment, and 10 being completely in alignment.

1   2   3   4   5   6   7   8   9   10

Staying in Alignment with Yourself

1. What business situations or people tend to strengthen your alignment?

2. What business situations or people tend to pull you out of alignment?

3. What do you do in the moment when you feel yourself being pulled out of alignment?

4. What do you do in the moment when you notice you are not aligned with yourself?

5. How do you enable yourself to stay out of alignment with yourself?

6. What do you do to prevent being pulled out of alignment with yourself?

7. What do you do to get yourself back into alignment with yourself?

8. What do you do to overcome your own resistance to getting yourself back into alignment?

9. What do you do when you notice you are back into alignment?

Based on your answers to these questions, place yourself on the scale below with regard to how you keep yourself in alignment—

with 1 being not so good at staying in alignment, and 10 being excellent at staying in alignment.

As you assess yourself and become more and more grounded in who you truly are—keeping in mind that alignment always feels uplifting, never demeaning to yourself or anyone else—you may or may not like everything about how you are or how things affect you. That's completely normal. Many of us are strangers to our own selves, and holding up a mirror honestly can be jolting. But remember that you always have the option to consciously stay one way or to change. In time, knowing yourself makes it a lot easier to *be* yourself on a regular basis, which is of course the essence of being *aligned* with yourself.

Sure, how you show up in the numerous circumstances of business and life will be different at times. Your role may change from CEO to investor to board member to colleague to friend—sometimes all in one day. You may do most of the talking, then most of the listening. You may take command at times, and then at other times allow and enable others to lead. You may feel confident, nervous, happy, or sad—all of which can be situationally appropriate and in alignment with who you are.

What doesn't change when you are in alignment with yourself are your guiding values and beliefs, and the accordance of your energy, words, and actions. In other words, though you may appear and act differently based on circumstances and roles, you can always remain true to yourself.

WINDOW

A Painful Lesson in Client Alignment

Stacey recounts how, early in her career as a book production professional, she entered a partnership where she allowed herself to be pulled way out of alignment.

"I had decided from the inception of my company that I would never work on a book that wasn't aligned with my values, and I've always held true to that. But in this particular case, it wasn't the book; it was the author. From our first email, I felt a sense of being out of alignment with him: I put forth how I worked; he countered it. I outlined how much I valued trust in each other and the ethics I embraced; he demonstrated unease from being taken advantage of in the past. But because I completely believed in the message of the book – and, erroneously, in my ability to assuage his fears – I overlooked those red flags. What resulted was a constant push-and-pull partnership that gave me an enormous amount of stress for months – and I'm certain he wasn't content on his side either. No matter how much I tried to be positive in our relationship, something would get triggered for him, and vice versa. Had we both simply admitted that we weren't a good match for each other (and I take full accountability for my end of that), I could have shifted my attention to working with another client who *was* a good match, and he could have sought out a provider he more resonated with. Truthfully, I considered leaving the partnership midstream for my own sanity and well-being, but I felt ethically challenged in leaving a client hanging with a half-finished book. So, we both remained focused on producing the best possible book, but getting there was the most misaligned path I've ever experienced in my work in this field.

After the book was finally launched and we parted ways, I vowed that I would never compromise my values like that again, not for any book – even one I sincerely believed in – or for any amount of money. I love what I do and I love the clients I choose to work with – and who choose to work with me – and we both deserve to feel aligned with each other for such a long-term and sometimes fairly intimate commitment. That decision has served me well for years, and it's certainly one I will always hold fast to. Being out of alignment with a client was one of the most disruptive periods of my career, negatively affecting every aspect of my life. I'm glad it happened so that I could learn that valuable lesson, but it's one I certainly plan to never repeat!"

Have you had a similar experience in your work? Have you compromised your values for money or prestige? Or even for the noble aspiration of lending your skills to a project you believed had merit, but caused you to feel like you lost five years of your life? Or to compensate yourself, charged a PITA (Pain in the Ass) tax to extremely difficult customers you only worked with because you felt you "should"?

I would venture that most of us have. In a way, that's a good thing, because, as in Stacey's case, you learn how to never let it happen again. This can be incredibly empowering because no one wants to loathe their work, and knowing how to avoid that feeling of being out of alignment can keep you from going down that road.

It all comes back to a topic we've discussed at length: having shared goals and values. For business love to happen, there must be alignment in what your company wants and cares about, what employees want and care about, and what customers want and care about. Ideally all stakeholders, and every player, in the value chain—from design and manufacturing to sales and distribution—will be aligned with meeting customer needs in ways that are uplifting. Even in a small or one-person company, this is an integral part of building a complete culture of business love. This is why, even if you *desire* to be an Amare Way company, but part of your value chain is fear-based and warlike in its business approach, it will have a detrimental effect. Can it be mitigated? To some degree, yes. It will cost you, though—and not only in time and money. The conflicting energy caused by a mismatch in goals and values can take a great deal to overcome. Furthermore, because that energy is not aligned with your company and culture, it may also call your authenticity into question, which then threatens people's ability to trust you.

Truly knowing yourself, as a precursor to alignment, means you are honest about who and what you are, what you value, what uplifts you, and what de-energizes you. Returning to Jim at the beginning of the chapter, we saw how he was aligned with taking excellent care of his team, who then took excellent care of their customers, and not so aligned with prioritizing hitting certain numbers. In his case, the former led to the latter organically, and he experienced favorable results on all fronts. Had he taken the course of other managers he knew, he would have been way out of alignment with himself.

I believe we have an inner guidance system that wants harmony in all aspects of our experience, which is why being out of alignment doesn't feel very good. We have all experienced pressures to conform in business and in life, sometimes to things we don't believe in or even abhor. Being love-centered in business can be an antidote to misalignment because it creates space to be *in* alignment on a regular basis. In other words, being committed to *amare* in all its forms can give you the courage to *not* conform when it would be inconsistent with your core being. Once you are living within the uplifting and connecting energy of business love, you will be empowered to show up fully aligned—inside and out—in all aspects of your life. You go beyond *knowing* who you are to *being* who you are, which is where the real action happens.

"Know Thyself" was written over the portal of the antique world.
Over the portal of the new world, "Be Thyself" shall be written.

—OSCAR WILDE

One note of caution: Once you've stepped over the threshold between unawareness and awareness of your own alignment, you can't go back. Ever. The threshold will have disappeared. So what does that have to do with being in alignment with yourself? Simply this: To allow a lack of alignment to continue once you are aware of it, you must ignore, deny, or rationalize how you are behaving. By extension, ignoring or denying your lack of alignment causes you to shut down part of yourself. It also requires you to pretend things are not what they are, which of course is inauthentic. And rationalizations? They can be endless. You might, for example, convince yourself that sacrificing alignment is worth it because of the money you'll make, or the prestige it will garner you, or the satisfaction you'll get from aggressively showing your power. More perversely, you may rationalize that you don't deserve alignment, perhaps because of a legacy of past deeds enabled by misalignment, and thereby continue to live out of sync with yourself.

This is why it's crucial to understand that if you regularly tune out your inner signals, you likely will not be aware when you are out of alignment with yourself—at least until something so big happens, it will be undeniable even to you. This is usually a crisis that portends a major shift in energy, which none of us desires to be our wakeup call.

In the best case, people who know you well will recognize if you are regularly out of alignment with yourself, and they will have the courage and compassion to tell you. If you are a leader in this situation, be sure your leadership style does not preclude others from respectfully giving you that kind of feedback. And be sure you have not created a culture where being out of alignment with yourself is the norm and even rewarded. The more you are in tune with your values and staying in line with them, the more you will find yourself living your true purpose and inspiring others to do the same. And—bonus!—the more you will prosper.

WINDOW
Finding Alignment with Brain-Gasms

Ryan was a high-ranking mergers and acquisitions (M&A) executive with a global financial firm, leading the integration of companies they acquired. Despite his professional success, he felt something was off. Ryan was in a daily manic cycle of intense outward work, then escaping inwardly when he came home. He knew this would eventually result in big regrets with his family, but he felt extremely grateful for his success and financial abundance. He also had deep attachments to being a strong financial provider for his family above all else, and it was like jumping off a cliff to think about changing what he was doing.

While the work satiated many ego needs, the way Ryan was approaching it was getting in the way of meaningful connections with his family and community, and he recognized that this work was no longer aligned with his purpose. Though Ryan wasn't yet sure what his purpose was, he knew M&A in financial services was not it. Driven to search for a more satisfying path, he bought a large yoga studio that was about to shut down.

Soon after, while participating in an intensive professional development program, Ryan had an experience of profound clarity and total bliss, a state Eastern wisdom traditions call *samadhi*—and what he called a "brain-gasm." It lasted intensely for a couple of hours, then lingered more softly for a couple days.

He believed a brain-gasm like that could only mean he was definitely on the right path; he then grew to recognize and trust more subtle forms of guidance as he made business decisions. At the same time, Ryan's decision criteria for how to sustain and grow the business shifted. "Will this make money?" was not his first question. Rather, it was "Will this be fun and meaningful for our members?" If the answer to that first question was yes, then he turned to, "How can we do it in a way that makes a reasonable profit?" He asked the questions in this order because the core of his calling was to help people improve their lives and have more fun; making money was a byproduct. His brain-gasms gave him the certitude that it all was authentic, uplifting, and aligned.

And it's working from a money perspective too. When Ryan took over the yoga studio as an owner, it had a strong foundation but was in significant financial distress. Though he says the future is still uncertain for his venture, Ryan was able to immediately triage losses of approximately $40K monthly, and in the two years since, he has helped grow sales revenue from $1MM to over $2MM annually.

In the remaining chapters of Part III, where we will bring to life the philosophy and practice of the Amare Way framework, you will quickly notice that alignment regularly shows up. This is why we began with this topic—because alignment is the integral force that underlies and unifies what it is to ride the wave of being love-centered, and of prospering, in business.

I
STRONGLY
BELIEVE
THE
BUSINESS
OF A BUSINESS
IS TO
IMPROVE
THE
WORLD.

—MARK BENIOFF,
COFOUNDER AND CEO OF SALESFORCE

CHAPTER EIGHT

THE AMARE WAY PHILOSOPHY: GROUNDING YOUR BUSINESS IN SEVEN FOUNDATIONAL PRINCIPLES

The idea of love in business is, thankfully, not exclusive, secret, or new. What *is* new and different is how the Amare Way framework unifies diverse ideas and connects familiar dots in a way that I hope makes the concepts and practices easy for you to understand, relate to, and implement. After all, the notion of moving from being warlike to love-like may resonate with you, but without tangible guideposts on which to ground your efforts, running a love-centered business may sound like a lot of fluff that is ambiguous at best. I also realize that for some companies, adopting the Amare Way may feel particularly challenging—because of deeply embedded habits that require what may seem like "too much work" to break. However, I firmly believe any company can adopt the Amare Way and be highly successful, given the right mindset, heart set, and skill set, along with the right opportunity. The Amare Way framework aims to give you precisely the foundational tools you need to do that, while feeling energized and confident about the transition and believing wholeheartedly in the value of *amare* as you move forward.

The Amare Way framework for business success consists of two primary components:

1. a business **philosophy** comprised of seven simple and timeless principles

2. a business **practice** comprised of three ABC pillars rooted in the uplifting and unifying energy of love

Functionally, this framework is an ecosystem, in that all stakeholders—owners, employees, investors, suppliers, partners, customers, and the community at large—affect and are affected by all of the others. This means there are interdependencies and relationships that are constantly evolving and changing to assure alignment and to balance the needs of everyone involved. Like in a healthy biological ecosystem, flexibility, adaptation, and consideration of others is therefore required in order to survive and thrive.

In this chapter, I will outline the first component, the Amare Way philosophy, which will lay the foundation for creating your Amare Way company. Once you are familiar with these principles, I will introduce you in the next chapter to the second component, the ABC practice, which builds on our seven principles.

THE AMARE WAY PHILOSOPHY

The seven essential principles of the Amare Way philosophy are grounded both in the wisdom of the ages and what are proving to be contemporary best practices. They are:

1. Treat one another well.

2. Inspire connection.

3. Get on purpose.

4. Respect money.

5. Choose love over fear.

6. Take the long view.

7. Prioritize relationships.

1. Treat one another well.

In business as in life, we are all human beings. And regardless of title, station in life, culture, ethnicity, or age, we all desire love and kindness, respect and understanding. This is the essence of the Golden Rule, that in various forms is a centerpiece of many diverse religions and wisdom traditions: Do unto others as you want done unto you. In business, this applies not only to your employees and customers, but to suppliers and competitors too. And if "do unto others" feels untenable in any way, you may find value in the flip side of the maxim.

Two Sides of the Golden Rule

In reality, some companies will not be ready for a Golden Rule that affirmatively states how to be. Instead, they may need to start with how *not* to be. According to legend, this is the hidden message of the sage Rabbi Hillel's "on one foot" teaching, a story that goes like this.

A man asked Rabbi Hillel to teach him the entire Torah – the five books of Moses – while standing on one foot. Hillel, in wanting to impart the very essence of the Torah said, "What is hateful to you, do not do to your neighbor. That's the whole Torah. All the rest is commentary. Now go and study."

For businesses embarking on the Amare Way, we might put Hillel's teaching this way: "Don't do to customers what you wouldn't want done to you as a customer."

The lesson is that companies need to start where they are currently and not aim too high too soon. As Rabbi Joseph

Telushkin explains,[50] Hillel did not say to love your neighbor as yourself. That would have been too hard for this new student to accomplish off the bat. In the same vein, if you treat customers poorly, first stop that negative practice; don't expect your company or people to do a sudden 180. It would likely fail or result in inauthentic and forced behaviors that are not uplifting for anyone. Instead, make the transition step by step.

To cite a contemporary example, when Google began, its code of conduct included "Don't be evil." In 2016, when Google formed Alphabet as a parent company, it replaced that motto with "do the right thing." Shifting from a proscription (what *not to do*) to a prescription (what *to do*) is telling and promising, as long as "doing the right thing" is rightly understood by Googlers and justly rewarded by the culture.

While one of the keys to fostering an Amare Way business hinges on the age-old Golden Rule, it must expand beyond that. We do this by offering two things: empathy and compassion.

Empathy allows us to "get" the other's perspective, on both a thinking and feeling level. Unlike sympathy, which is more about rationally understanding the other's situation, empathy is about being in a person's shoes and feeling something of what they feel.

Research from the Center for Creative Leadership found that within a company, "managers who show more empathy toward direct reports are viewed as better performers in their jobs by their bosses." There is also evidence that when customers are empathic toward employees—most likely a reciprocal reaction to when they feel employees empathize with them—they will be more forgiving of dissatisfying experiences and less likely to turn away from the company.[51]

Compassion is the understanding, connection, and feeling of caring we have for the suffering of others. It has also been defined as "holding space for anything, without judgment." Compassion creates happiness too. As the Dalai Lama said: "If you want others to be happy, practice compassion. If you want to be happy, practice compassion."

Psychologist Jonathan Haidt has shown that in the workplace, feeling uplifted through compassionate acts—a state of being he calls elevation—leads to greater loyalty. When leaders were compassionate, their employees were uplifted, which in turn led employees to feel greater loyalty toward the compassionate leader, and to act more compassionately to other employees, as well as to customers.

In business settings, there is a long history of characterizing "soft skills" like empathy and compassion as signs of weakness, of being feminine, or of not being tough. In short, for many years, the prevailing ethos was that these practices don't belong in business and that they hurt profitability. Yet nothing could be further from the truth.

Based on the law of reciprocity and the science of human behavior (or the notion of karma, if you prefer), you will reap benefits from treating others well—because when you are good to others, they are more likely to be good to you. It's not only human nature, but it's a survival instinct in our highly social, interdependent world.

Here is what **treating one another well** looks like in relation to business:

- **Put yourself in others' shoes:** Ask yourself how you would react if what you did or said to a colleague or customer was being done or said to you—*if* you were in their position. This is empathy at work.

- **Filter your words:** Before you speak, submit your words to what some call the three gates of speech. Is it true? Is it kind? Is it necessary?

- **Slow down:** In tough situations, take a breath—actually stop long enough to breathe in and breathe out—before you react. This helps you ground yourself and find compassion.

- **Tune in:** If you sense misalignment, harshness, incivility, or lack of respect for others, acknowledge it, apologize if appropriate, and reframe things to better honor the other person's humanity.

- **Offer compassion:** If a colleague or customer is going through a rough time, rather than merely seeing their problem as a disruptor to business, show them you care by asking what's going on, expressing kind words, or offering some one-on-one time.

- **Remember** *amare*: Keep top of mind the meaning of *amare* that is "being grounded in a desire to better each other's well-being." This sets the stage for treating others well in business and life.

As you can imagine, adopting this one simple idea of the Amare Way philosophy, and sincerely putting it to work, can dramatically change your business.

2. Inspire connection.

We are all interconnected, for connection is the nature of our being and is fundamental to operating effectively as a society. Recognizing this enables us to see and appreciate each other and our shared goals and values. Lucky for us, business provides numerous opportunities for connection: every point of contact, every inter-action, is a chance to inspire meaningful connection—and it works so well because it appeals to us on a deeply personal level.

Now, some say love doesn't belong in business; in fact, there's a famous line in the movie *The Godfather* that says: "It's not per-sonal, Sonny. It's strictly business." **But make no mistake: Business *is* personal.** How we are wired as human beings does not change when we put on our CEO hat, or physician hat, or product manager hat, or employee hat. The same is true when we are a customer, client, patient, or guest. We are people who want to be seen, cared for, respected, and appreciated. As such, we don't shut down our "person-ness" or leave our humanity behind when we go to work, or to the doctor, or out to eat, or shopping. We are al-ways human beings, and the Amare Way nurtures and values our humanity by encouraging authentic connection within the space of business.

Our Biological Aptitude for Connectivity

Barbara Fredrickson, psychology professor and author of *Love 2.0: How Our Supreme Emotion Affects Everything We Feel, Think, Do, and Become*, depicts love as micro-moments of connection – a smile from a co-worker, a happy customer, an inspired idea, shaking hands on a deal – little things that add up in a big way. It is these little bursts of positivity that create instances of connection and uplifting spirals of energy that I call love.

Is there a way to further our ability to connect?

Research in Fredrickson's Positive Emotions and Psychophys-iology Laboratory at the University of North Carolina tells us the answer is YES! She and her team have demonstrated that our "biological aptitude for connectivity" relies on the tone of the vagus nerve, which is measured by tracking your heart rate to-gether with your breathing rate. The vagus nerve helps to orchestrate the *calm and connect* response, which Barbara points out is as ancestral as our primitive *flight or fight* response. She explains it this way: "Your vagus nerve is a biological asset that supports and coordinates your bodily experiences of connection – of love. Outside your conscious awareness, the vagus nerve stimulates tiny facial muscles that better enable you to make eye contact and synchronize your facial expressions with another person. It even adjusts the minuscule muscles of your middle ear so you can better track the other person's voice against any background noise."

Bottom line, the more toned your vagus nerve, the more love you experience in daily life. The good news is that, like muscle tone, vagal tone can actually be strengthened quite easily with practice, by simply doing deep diaphragmatic breathing – with long, slow inhales and exhales through the nose – to stimulate the vagus nerve and slow heart rate and blood pressure, especially in times of performance anxiety. That means we can *biologically* learn to connect better and have more micromoments at work of feeling uplifted, with more positivity and love that generates an upward spiral in our lives.

While the Amare Way is not a religious belief, a type of dogma, or tied to any particular tradition, the notion of us all being somehow connected as part of a greater whole is common to many wisdom traditions and spiritual practices, and is what I believe to be a fundamental truth and central to the Amare Way philosophy. From a quantum physics perspective, we recognize that what connects us beyond our shared goals and values, our desire to be treated well, and to love and be loved is a unifying and uplifting energy that is neither static nor fixed, but rather an ecosystem of universal energy that we affect, are affected by, and exchange with one another through our intentions, interactions, and experiences. Whether called God, Spirit, the Force, Higher Consciousness, Nature, Source, or simply "energy," the Amare Way helps generate, focus, and amplify that energy of love to create meaningful connection within the context of business and commerce.

Here is what **inspiring connection** looks like in relation to business:

- **Smile genuinely when you meet someone's eye** — A sincere smile acknowledges the other person's presence and sparks a feeling of connection on a soul level, whether you know each other well or not.

- **Pay attention to how people respond** — When you ask a customer or coworker how they are, regardless of their status, really listen with your mind and heart. (FYI, the Hebrew words for "pay attention" translate into the imperative of *placing your heart.*)

- **Suspend judgment** — Challenge yourself to interact with coworkers, customers, and critics without judging them or taking things personally.

- **Be genuinely interested in others** — Don't just act interested, *be* interested. If you don't give a damn, it will be evident and you won't connect.

- **Ask questions that inspire sincere and respectful conversation** — Instead of regularly asserting your opinion as if it's the "right one" or the only one that matters, or dominating the conversation, show that you are sincerely interested in connecting, not merely sharing your side of things, particularly when you may have opposing opinions.

- **Actively look for aspects that unite** — Make it a point of relating to coworkers, customers, and other contributors within your business on an interest, background, life situation, event, talent, or goal you share.

- **Recognize the humanity in each other** — Listen attentively with eye contact when others speak, seek to see things from others' points of view, and respect that every human being is here for a reason at this time in history to contribute something of value.

Author Brené Brown has stated that the ability to feel connected is why we are here, that it is what gives purpose and meaning to our lives. This deep-seated human need is beautifully encapsulated by developmental psychologist Erik Erikson:

"Life doesn't make any sense without interdependence. We need each other, and the sooner we learn that, the better for us all."

3. Get on purpose.

As we touched on in Chapter Two, research reported in *Firms of Endearment* and elsewhere shows that companies with a higher purpose do better financially than those without one. Hence, acting "on purpose" is foundational to making business love. It not only adds meaning and motivation to your business, but it keeps leaders on focus, employees staying on task during hard times, and customers coming back.

Finding a meaningful and inspiring higher purpose that goes beyond your products and services, and committing to it for the long haul, is one of the most energizing parts of transitioning into an Amare Way company. If you haven't already grounded your business in such a way, and it feels overwhelming or you're unsure how to choose, the good news is that there are numerous books and experts to help you understand, set, and act on purpose. I find the description of purpose by public health professor Vic Strecher very insightful:[52]

"[Purpose is] a self-transcending goal that you deeply value . . . it focuses the mind and removes extraneous clutter. That it comes from one's core values makes it non-negotiable and authentic."

Strecher also quotes Studs Terkel, author of *Working*, who beautifully balances idealism and pragmatism by saying:

"Work is about the search, too, for daily meaning as well as daily bread, for recognition as well as for cash, for astonishment rather than torpor; in short, for a sort of life rather than a Monday through Friday sort of dying."

Having a higher purpose is like having an inner compass; chosen well, it will be your guiding light in business. But a few words of caution: don't get caught in the trap of coming up with nice-sounding, ubiquitous words that you call your higher purpose and then ignore them; don't misuse your higher purpose to justify unhealthy actions when it is really a grab for money or power; and don't misconstrue "maximizing shareholder value" as a higher purpose. It is an important goal, yes, but it is not a higher purpose. Look instead to one that resonates with your people and your customers—one that is shared, explicit, and aligned with decisions and actions.

A Look at Shared Purpose

Futurist Mark Bonchek, in the *HBR* article, "Purpose Is Good, Shared Purpose Is Better," contrasts companies that express a shared purpose with direct competitors that don't.[53] None of the statements are bad, mind you; they simply differ in the extent to which they are about the company and what they do, versus being about the company's "why" and conveying a sense of belonging together, of unity. Here are two distinct examples that show the difference.

Dunkin Donuts is here to "make and serve the freshest, most delicious coffee and donuts quickly and courteously in modern, well-merchandised stores."

Starbucks exists "to inspire and nurture the human spirit – one person, one cup, and one neighborhood at a time."

* * *

Adidas aims "to be the global leader in the sporting goods industry with brands built on a passion for sports and a sporting lifestyle."

Nike seeks to "bring inspiration and innovation to every athlete in the world." (In the spirit of inclusiveness, Nike adds, "If you have a body, you are an athlete.")

Do you see the inherent difference in the "why" in each pair of companies?

Why does your company exist? Does it have a shared purpose? Who benefits, and in what ways? How might you recast your purpose to be a higher and shared purpose?

To **get on purpose** in your business, consider the following:

- Ask your people what your company's higher purpose is. Then ask them if they believe in it.
- Talk to your customers. Find out if they share your higher purpose and if it inspires them.
- Bring your higher purpose into decision-making. Assess how well your decisions align with your higher and shared purpose.
- Communicate your higher purpose explicitly and in meaningful ways. This can create accountability.

- Live your higher purpose—through your goals, priorities, actions, and through what you say yes and no to.

Bottom line, people naturally align with purpose. Not only are employees more attracted and devoted to companies when they believe in the company's higher purpose, so, too, are customers and investors.

4. Respect money.

As I said in Chapter Two, making money is certainly a core aspect of being an Amare Way company. However, it's crucial that you not view the amassing of money as if it is the *only* thing that matters. So, what does a healthy approach to making money look like for an Amare Way company?

First, it's important to make clear that the *desire* for money is perfectly healthy. The more you have, the more good you can do in the world, and the more you're able to create a comfortable life for you and your loved ones. Once again, **financial abundance is fully aligned with catching the Amare Wave and in running an Amare Way business**. In fact, succeeding financially is—and should be—a must for a new love-based paradigm in business to take hold.

Where we sometimes get caught up is when we let that desire for money override our other values, or cloud our perceptions and priorities. In other words, money isn't inherently bad; it's the behaviors we often justify in *pursuit* of money that can give it the bad rap. Hence, what people who run Amare Way companies do is to indeed pursue financial abundance and the reward of profits, but they do it with their customers' and employees' best interests at heart.

To **respect money** in your business, consider adopting the following guidelines:

- If the action to make money deceives anyone, we don't pursue it.

- If the action to make money harms anyone, we don't pursue it.

- If the action to make money manipulates anyone, we don't pursue it.

- If the action to make money is not aligned with our core values, we don't pursue it.

- If the action to make money unsettles anyone on the decision-making team, we listen and are open to re-evaluation.

- If the action to make money would damage or destroy our reputation should it become public or its motives were revealed, we don't pursue it.

- If the action to make money violates our ethics, we don't pursue it.

If you're truly honest when considering these guidelines, can you see how there is no gray area to sway you in an unhealthy direction when you make decisions around money? A yes to any of them means you don't pursue that action, period. With these as your compass, it's practically impossible to allow yourself to go off track in the pursuit of financial gain. It's truly as simple as that.

While these specific Amare Way questions are not what all love-centered businesses use to make decisions, putting each of these statements into question form (such as, "Does this ad campaign deceive anyone?") allows you to easily make Amare Way–aligned decisions when it comes to the pursuit of financial gain—which, let's face it, is a significant consideration in most decisions.

Remember, business exists to make life better for people. When care and thought—and love—is at the heart of delivering on that goal, money, on some level, typically comes. In fact, the more we treat money as a byproduct of a higher purpose instead of focusing on it as the purpose itself, the more money we are likely to make. No, love alone doesn't achieve profits, but it *is* the guiding force that aligns and energizes all decisions that influence the company's success—and having a healthy respect for money is a vital piece of that alignment.

5. Choose love over fear.

We talked at length about love and fear in Chapter Six, so this is not a new concept. We all know from experience what it is to choose love and what it is to choose fear. As social animals, we thrive when we have love in our lives, and we wither when we don't. I have no doubt that on both personal and professional levels, most of us have at times used fear—or its frequent and more aggressive counterpart, anger—to get what we want from others. We have also likely succumbed to others out of fear, even doing things we knew were wrong.

But making love the heart of the operating system of business requires us as business professionals to not let fear drive us. In other words, we can choose to function out of fear and greed with our more primitive brain, a capacity designed for dangerous and threatening situations; or we can operate out of love and compassion with our higher more evolved brain, our natural and aligned state. We are presented with the opportunity to make the choice every day, every moment. Talk about empowerment!

Our Deepest Fear

Sometimes what we fear the most is something we wouldn't expect: our own success. Marianne Williamson, author, spiritual activist, and 2020 US presidential candidate, has potently said:

Our deepest fear is not that we are inadequate. Our deepest fear is that we are powerful beyond measure. It is our light, not our darkness that most frightens us. We ask ourselves, Who am I to be brilliant, gorgeous, talented, and fabulous? Actually, who are you not to be? You are a child of God. Your playing small does not serve the world. There is nothing enlightened about shrinking so that other people will not feel insecure around you. We are all meant to shine, as children do. We were born to make manifest the glory of God that is within us. It is not just in some of us; it is in everyone and as we let our own light shine, we unconsciously give others permission to do the same. As we are liberated from our own fear, our presence automatically liberates others.

Here's what **choosing love over fear** looks like in relation to business:

- **You aim to uplift, not to intimidate.** You know how to win in business with the intention of elevating yourself and others without fighting with or diminishing others.

- **You make it a point to use love-like language** to inspire your people, and you avoid amping up your team with warlike fighting language to squeeze suppliers, crush competitors, and control customers.

- **You know there is enough to go around and have faith that life conspires to support us all**, hence you realize greed and arrogance have no place in your business or life.

- **You show up whole—without fear of vulnerability—and** not in any way diminishing or hiding from your own power. You are not afraid to shine, or to allow others to shine, because you know everyone deserves to realize and contribute their gifts toward the greater good of the company.

- **You sincerely want similar companies—who are also love-centered and ethical—to succeed**, recognizing that when we all serve our common audience well, everybody wins.

Both love and fear can be linked to productivity gains in business under certain conditions, but Amare Way companies recognize that gains motivated by fear are short term and come at a significant cost. Over time, fear diminishes performance, as it erodes trust and physiologically wears people down. On the flip side, in the long term, love *works* better. And at the end of the day, love *feels* better than fear. Being love-centered is *how* you treat each other well, *how* you generate interconnection, and *how* you stay attuned to the company's higher purpose.

6. Take the long view.

A commitment to *amare* means thinking, planning, and making decisions with the long term in mind. We all intuitively know a long-term perspective makes sense for any serious business, yet it often gets short shrift, especially in a society like ours that is obsessed with immediate gratification, and a business world incessantly pressured for performance today by an impatient Wall Street. Yet, in today's business environment, leaders who embody resilience, perseverance, and vision are those who successfully take the long view, invest in lasting relationships, and gainfully ride the Amare Wave for the duration.

In the last fifty years, many corporations have become hyperfocused on maximizing shareholder return as its main objective. But what does a business culture that makes this its primary focus really accomplish? Sometimes it makes a lot of money for shareholders, sometimes it doesn't. Unfortunately, it leads management to myopically zero in on short-term profits and stock prices, often putting the company's long-term viability at risk. In doing so, leaders tend to think in warlike terms, rationalizing greed and attacking anything that gets in the way of short-term returns. Employee well-being and customer satisfaction, among other things, become yet further casualties of these warlike ways.

"It's All About the Long Term"
Amazon's Commitment

Although Amazon's omnipresence and how the company operates on some levels have become controversial of late, it's worth looking here – in relation to having a long-term view – at the first letter Jeff Bezos wrote to Amazon shareholders back in 1997.[54] In it, he made very clear the company's commitment to the long-term over immediate returns, saying, "We will continue to make investment decisions in light of long-term market leadership considerations rather than short-term profitability considerations or short-term Wall Street reactions." That's a strong and clear statement of intention. Bezos wisely and transparently framed it in terms of alignment, wanting shareholders to be sure that their investment philosophy was consistent with Amazon's commitment to the long term: "Because of our emphasis on the long term, we may make decisions and weigh tradeoffs differently than some companies. Accordingly, we want to share with you our fundamental management and decision-making approach so that you, our shareholders, may confirm that it is consistent with your investment philosophy." He closed with a statement that explicitly recognized that prioritizing long-term results over short-term returns is not for everyone when he asserted: "We aren't so bold as to claim that the above is the 'right' investment philosophy, but it's ours, and we would be remiss if we weren't clear in the approach we have taken and will continue to take."

As Bezos's letter illustrates, creating alignment through shared goals and values, with authenticity and transparency, sets the stage for establishing trust in relationships, and cultivating an enduring sense of belonging and collaboration (which are two of the three Amare Way pillars we will discuss in the next chapter). Notice, too, that he expressed his message with no judgment, just a statement of fact that invited investors to honestly assess the quality of fit—particularly with how Amazon viewed long-term goals.

Here's what **taking the long view** looks like in relation to business:

- You explicitly set and reinforce expectations that your decisions will be based on long-term viability, as in the Amazon letter.

- You let your stakeholders know what it means to them that you are taking a long-term view, e.g., slower and steadier growth for investors, knowing it will not appeal to everyone.

- Your KPIs and internal reward system are aligned with your long-term focus, not merely hitting quarterly numbers.

- You stand up to pressure to conform to Wall Street–like expectations.

- You pay your people well and invest in sustaining healthy relationships with all your stakeholders.

Yes, short-term needs are important and cannot be ignored—bills need to be paid, products need to be delivered, promises need to be fulfilled, and investors need to be happy. At the same time, within the Amare Way, the goal is to not become attached to short-term outcomes (see Chapter Ten for a discussion on this topic), such that you diminish your organization's long-term viability, compromise your guiding values and higher purpose, or shut down your humanity. Instead, taking the long view grounds you with a focus on relationships, leading us into our final principle of the Amare Way philosophy.

7. Prioritize Relationships.

Our last principle, and perhaps the glue that holds the first six together, is recognizing that relationships rule. In fact, the most valuable equity a company has is its relationships—especially those with its employees and customers. As such, the Amare Way culture is all about cultivating and nurturing relationships. How could something about love between two or more parties not be?

Years ago, when my kids were teenagers, I read a great book called *Parent-Teen Breakthrough*. The essential message was that as a parent, I couldn't really make my teenager do much. The breakthrough idea was to focus on the relationship and the associated feelings as what truly mattered, not the homework, friends, driving rules, or bedtime. Those issues, when placed in the context of striving for a good relationship, often became much easier to resolve.

The same is true with customers and other stakeholders. It's not so much about the product quality, the refund, or the wait time. It's about the health of the relationship and the surrounding feelings, which create a context for addressing issues with empathy, compassion, and kindness. As an added bonus, taking this approach is tremendously beneficial for ourselves even as we are in service to others.

When the quality of the relationship is the priority, tendencies you may have to default to arrogance, incivility, or ego become replaced with tendencies toward empathy, compassion, and kindness. Again, these types of responses benefit everyone involved and serve to nurture the relationships that are the backbone of your business.

From Sales First to Relationships First

In the classic film *Miracle on 34th Street*, we see a perfect example of business allowing relationships to become the priority. After years of stiff competition between the two New York City department stores Macy's and Gimbels, Macy's hires a store Santa Claus – the "real" Santa Claus – who begins telling parents (unbeknownst to R.H. Macy and the staff) where they can find their children's wish list of toys if Macy's doesn't carry them or they are too expensive there. Once Macy finds out, he is outraged that their Santa would send customers away – until customer praise starts to flood in. Putting the customer first, particularly during the hectic holiday season, is a surprise and delight to the customers; they can't believe Macy's would be so centered on the needs of its patrons. The praise shifts Mr. Macy's perspective on the value of customer relationships. Taking it even further, he publicly shows solidarity with his rival, Mr. Gimbel, elevating a once competitive relationship to one that is mutually focused on best serving their common customer, no matter which store gets the sale.

This story didn't just make for a great film that over seventy years after its release is still a perennial favorite. It is actually a blueprint for how business *should* be and *can* be here and now, in the twenty-first century and beyond. When valuing and maintaining strong relationships is paramount, all the other pieces fall more easily into place.

Here's what **prioritizing relationships** looks like in relation to business:

- **You think in terms of "we" not just "me."** Literally, you change your thinking by including the word "we" in your thought process—and you mean it.

- **You put people before products and profits**—and you are clear and explicit when and how you do so, which helps others in your company do the same.

- **You regularly ask yourself: How will this decision or this action affect the relationship?** You do this with employees, with customers, with investors, with the community—with all your stakeholders—and you make choices that favor sustaining healthy relationships.

- **When you say or do something hurtful to others at work, you own up to it.** You don't merely apologize, you also make amends and tell them how you will avoid that hurtful behavior in the future.

- **You feature your commitment to relationships in your messaging** to attract employees, and in the customer experience you promise. You deliver day in and day out on putting employees and customers first.

- **You make it easy for customers to be delighted**—through your guarantees, your return policies, your customer service process, your people. Every part of the experience you provide honors the relationship, and you avoid having policies and procedures that are filled with empty words and are disempowering to your people.

As I've highlighted throughout this book, a core tenet of the Amare Way is that the best way to stand out and succeed in a competitive market is through meaningful relationships grounded in love that meet shared goals. When this is your guiding light, the Amare Way will powerfully differentiate your company, and can even become the heart of your culture, brand definition, and value proposition.

If you're like the hundreds of business leaders and managers I've talked to about the components of the Amare Way philosophy, something inside you is likely saying, "Yes, there's something here. I'm tired of the battles. Maybe love *is* the answer; it can only make us better." And while all of these principles are indeed central to creating an Amare Way company, I want to take a moment here to make it abundantly clear that love in business is *not* a panacea.

In a recent conversation with a banker colleague of mine—a thoughtful and fiscally prudent guy whose bank is built on strong relationships—the subject of love as a driver of business came up and resonated with him right away . . . sort of.

"But," he countered, "my bank, even with strong relationships, would be nowhere without good financial products, solid operations, committed people, and effective investment strategies that help our clients grow."

I agree completely. You absolutely need business basics in place, regardless of how love-like or not your company is, which requires:

- offering real value through products or services that solve meaningful problems
- customers who want and buy what you offer
- a sensible business model
- good operations run by good people and sound technology
- sufficient capital

Being love-centered is a vital foundation, no doubt, but it is by no means a *replacement* for all of these business essentials. At the same time, it's important to understand that having love at the core of your business *affects* each of these elements. In other words, adopting the Amare Way framework will influence how you think about value and serving your customers, which in turn deeply impacts your business model and investment priorities. Hence, you will be more guided on the value you offer—and what you make, how you sell, and the multiple ways in which you may prosper.

To help you assess where you stand with respect to the Amare Way philosophy, I've created the following Mirror activity. For each of the seven principles, review the corresponding section in this chapter, answer the questions based on your company's norms, then put all your ratings into the At-A-Glance scorecard. This will provide a holistic view and help you determine where and how to move forward with adopting the Amare Way philosophy: go all in, dip in, or do something in the middle.

MIRROR

The Amare Way Philosophy and Your Company At-A-Glance

For each principle, rate your company on all three criteria. In each box, put a ✓ for YES, a ✓✓ for a strong YES, an X for no, or an XX for a strong NO.

	We believe this	We practice this	We reward this
Treat one another well			
Inspire connection			
Get on purpose			
Respect money			

	We believe this	We practice this	We reward this
Choose love over fear			
Take the long view			
Prioritize relationships			

Now, go down the "We believe this" column and notice which of the principles you do and don't believe and to what extent. Then look across each row to see how aligned and consistent your beliefs and actions are, and how well you reward what you believe in and do. Consider what enables and impedes your Amare Way beliefs, actions, and rewards.

If you're feeling the positive energy (internal feeling of expansion) of adopting the Amare Way philosophy within your company, consider the following options:

- You can go all in with the seven principles and make them your own to fit your culture.

- You can choose with your team a few high-priority principles and integrate those immediately, with an eye toward consistency across beliefs, actions, and rewards. Then you can work toward bringing the others into the fold, integrating additional principles within an appropriate timeframe.

- You can also start slow with investing your energy, particularly if you feel you are light years away from a love-centered philosophy.

  For example, if the "We believe this" is filled with Xs, then it will be a heavy lift to fully adopt the Amare Way philosophy. It can be done, especially if you are doing a corporate reboot of sorts, but it will require incredible fortitude and sufficient resources to keep it going in the face of what may be strong resistance. In this case, consider choosing one principle and invest your efforts there. You'll find that the results will flow over into the other principles, making it easier to incorporate them. Remember, too, that sometimes it's easier to change behaviors than beliefs—as in, "try it, you'll like it."

Now, based on your results in the summary chart, rate your company on the scale below with regard to how aligned you are with the Amare Way philosophy—with 1 being totally unaligned, and 10 being in line with all of the principles.

However you decide to approach it, I recommend that you:

1. Present and discuss these principles and your goals surrounding them in a positively charged team meeting. Doing this ensures that everyone is clear on what each principle encompasses and how it translates into your particular business. **These principles will set the tone of your company culture.**

2. Display the chosen principles (some or all) of the philosophy in a way that is visible to your entire team:

    •   on a large centrally located chart or poster,
    •   on a screensaver or desktop background,
    •   and/or on smaller handouts for each person's office or workspace.

    If you're ready to go full board, include them on your website in your values statement.

Remember: As a leader in an Amare Way company, you establish the tenor of your culture, knowing it's not about *you*, but about something greater than you. *You* bring the Amare Way philosophy to life through not only your words, but also your actions. As you embody these principles, you encourage others to do the same. Over the long term, with intention and resiliency, you invest in understanding and delighting both employees and customers, and in cultivating relationships with other stakeholders in alignment with the Amare Way. The best part: your culture amply rewards those efforts.

Next, we'll build on the Amare Way philosophy by incorporating the ABC practices—Authenticity, Belonging, and Collaboration—that underlie the day-to-day implementation of love-centered business. This will lead us into in Part IV, where we'll recap the dozens of ways—the "Doors"—to bring all the Amare Way practices to life.

WORK
IS
LOVE
MADE
VISIBLE.

–KAHLIL GIBRAN,
FROM *THE PROPHET*

CHAPTER NINE

THE AMARE WAY PRACTICE: EMBODYING THE MOVEMENT THROUGH AUTHENTICITY, BELONGING, AND COLLABORATION

O nce you have the principles of the Amare Way philosophy in place, you are ready to put them into action through what I call the three pillars—or the ABCs—of the Amare Way practice: Authenticity, Belonging, and Collaboration.

Here's a brief overview of the three pillars before we look at each one in detail.

> AUTHENTICITY: Your company's commitment to *amare* is real and put into practice every day—not merely as lip service—which builds trust. Leadership authentically believes in and leads with higher purpose, and everyone in the company is supported to behave authentically and with the energy of love in all business dealings.

BELONGING: Employees, customers, and other stakeholders identify with the company, seeing themselves —and their personal identity—as conjoined with that of the company. There is a feeling of oneness that is based on shared goals and values, and that builds a strong sense of unity as well as deep loyalty.

COLLABORATION: When authenticity and belonging are in place, the Amare Way empowers a spirit of collaboration, one that is active and reciprocal between the company and its employees, suppliers, investors, customers, and community. This grows out of shared interests and leads to mutually beneficial action, allowing for a sense of partnership and joint investment in everyone's success.

BUILDING TRUST AND LOYALTY THROUGH AUTHENTICITY

Authenticity is the first pillar of our Amare Way practice, and it manifests on two levels:

1. On a **personal level**, authenticity is about showing up whole and being true to who you are and your commitment to the company. Outwardly, it is reflected in your words and actions, and in the resonance of your energy— or your "vibe."

2. On a **company level**, authenticity starts with why your company exists—your higher purpose—and is evidenced in how you operate in the business world and in society at large, in line with that purpose.

Put simply, when you are authentic, what you believe, say, and do are consistently aligned. You are not only genuine, honest, reliable, and credible, you make promises you believe in—and you keep those promises. For example, if you tell employees they come first, show it in your decisions. If you tell customers you'll do whatever it takes to delight them, demonstrate it in your actions. If you tell yourself you're always going to be true to your own values at work, deliver on that commitment. These authenticity behaviors—being real, being aligned, and delivering on your promises—all come together to earn trust. In business, earned trust builds loyalty and equity.

A high level of trust is demonstrated in several ways:

- As a business leader, you trust in your expressed vision and in your team's ability and motivation to execute it successfully. If you say it's people before profit, your policies and priorities show it.

- If your values center on kindness and compassion, authenticity means expressing no violence in your language or actions.

- Employees trust that the company authentically sees them, cares for them, and values them, in order for them to fully engage.

- Investors trust that the company will make decisions in accordance with its stated values.

- Suppliers and partners trust that the company does what it says and treats them fairly.

- The communities you serve trust that you will take their interests to heart and deliver on your promises.

- Competitors trust that the company stands by its word. As an Amare Way company, you compete hard and aim to succeed, but you do not dehumanize or seek to destroy your competition.

- Customers trust that the company is who they say they are, that the value proposition is good and equitable, that the products and services are what and how they ought to be, and that they as customers are treated with respect and kindness. How you determine and act on customer requirements, how you shape the customer experience, and how you keep customers happy all demonstrate the authenticity of your caring.

The Authenticity pillar is aligned with the seven principles of the Amare Way philosophy as follows:

When you are authentic about being love-centered in business, you naturally prefer to **treat people well** (*Principle 1*) and be treated well. In doing so, you build trust and **cultivate meaningful connection** with colleagues and customers (*Principle 2*), showing people they matter to you. To be authentically aligned with your company, you must believe in and aspire to its **higher purpose** (*Principle 3*) and ways of doing business, as well as deliver on its promises. You pursue the attainment of financial gain through a **healthy respect for money** (*Principle 4*), not the pursuit of money for its own sake. Authenticity by its nature is rooted in the **energy of love** (*Principle 5*) and requires you to be vulnerable at times too, whereas fear pulls you away from being authentic, and invites in scarcity thinking, greed, incivility, and arrogance. When you **take the long view** (*Principle 6*), it is easier to be authentic and invest your whole self in your work and deeply commit your best. And finally, in order to

prioritize relationships (*Principle 7*), you must show up authentic in each one, thinking in terms of not simply as "me" but as "we."

WINDOW
Authenticity and Telling the Truth

In his book *Principles*, Ray Dalio emphasizes the importance of extreme truth and transparency as keys to success in business, pointing out that while it may not be easy or feel "nice" to be radically open and truthful — either on the giving or the receiving end — harnessing the power of full transparency can be incredibly productive.

An example Dalio gave in a TED Talk concerned an email he received from an employee, in which the employee conveyed how unprepared he believed Dalio was for an internal meeting — and how that negatively affected everyone present. The message was so directly critical that many CEOs would have been personally insulted by it, or even punished the employee for speaking out in this way. But Dalio took a different route: instead of reacting from his ego and becoming defensive, he used the feedback to improve his behavior.

Dalio's response may be a radical departure from how you do business, or even make you cringe. (If you think that he gave his power away to an employee who put him in his place, see Chapter Ten for ways you can embrace vulnerability and make it work to your advantage.) In Dalio's case, he gained a great deal of respect from his staff for accepting accountability for the substandard way he conducted that meeting. In fact, he claimed that this level of openness is precisely what has enabled his company to constantly improve.

On a similar note, in my almost three decades leading my consulting firm, I've made telling the truth our highest value. All in all, we've delivered on it pretty well, yet there have been many times when I personally slipped – not keeping promises to make a decision, complete a task, etc. In those situations, I was inauthentic in that my actions did not match my words about telling the truth. Generally, I could *feel* that something was off, and when I didn't, I had employees courageous enough to point it out. That's a benefit of transparency, and it requires leaders to show vulnerability and not take things personally.

You have the power to embrace that same level of transparency as an authentic leader. When you create an atmosphere in business where things are not hidden, people feel safe expressing their ideas and concerns respectfully, and people genuinely look out for one another, it makes for healthier long-term relationships and better business decisions.

Now, I want to be clear here that being authentic does *not* mean saying and doing whatever you want whenever you want, simply because that is what you are thinking or feeling in that moment. Words and actions must be situationally appropriate and tied to business aims. Herminia Ibarra, leadership expert and organizational behavior professor at London Business School, calls this and other oversimplifications of what authenticity means the Authenticity Paradox. For example, she points out that business leaders cannot simply be utterly and unconditionally transparent and consider that authentic: a new CEO who widely reveals her lack of confidence will immediately lose credibility; a director who makes passes at a team member because it's what he is feeling is being disrespectful, not authentic. In both cases, the situation calls for not acting on one's thoughts and feelings in a vacuum, but rather assessing authenticity in the context of the situation, and of the shared goals and values.

This is likewise true when trying to enhance your brand by attaching to a cause or message that does not fit. Consider when truck manufacturer Ram used a Martin Luther King, Jr. sermon as the voiceover in their 2018 Super Bowl commercial to extol the virtues of service. What resulted? An immediate social media maelstrom of criticism and distaste for using Dr. King's words about the value of service to sell trucks.

The inauthenticity was almost tangible. One ad agency exec was quoted as saying, "We're in a place where we get called out on authenticity and people don't want to be emotionally manipulated."

And therein lies the problem.

Authenticity builds trust. Inauthenticity erodes it.

The Ram ad came across as inauthentic and thereby degraded trust. Why was it inauthentic? Because the attempt to connect MLK's words, images of meaningful acts of service, and Ram trucks did not work. It felt emotionally manipulative. Given the public's reverence for Dr. King, it was also seen as highly inappropriate, especially at a time when intolerance and divisiveness runs so high.

Let's take a look in the mirror to see how authentic you feel your company is, and how authentic you are at work, answering true or false to these ten statements.

MIRROR
How Real Are You?

Is your company authentic?

1. We are sincerely committed to a higher purpose, a greater good.

2. We set priorities and operate based on our stated vision, purpose, and values.

3. We genuinely care about and respect all our employees and customers.

4. We promote honesty and transparency in business dealings.

5. We encourage people to bring their whole selves to work.

Are you authentic at work?

1. I feel comfortable being my whole self at work.

2. What I say and do in business is consistent with my personal beliefs and values.

3. I genuinely care about and respect my company, our employees, and customers.

4. I model authenticity in my company.

5. I always do my best at work.

Before reviewing your answers, let me say congratulations. Answering these questions honestly demonstrates authenticity, and a willingness to be vulnerable — at least with yourself — and that's a good thing!

Think about how your company did on the authenticity statements. Notice any that triggered discomfort as issues that need addressing.

Now, based on your answers to the first set of statements, place your company on the scale below with regard to how it operates —with 1 being completely inauthentically, and 10 being completely authentically.

Next, how did you do on the authenticity statements about you? Based on your answers to the second set of statements, place yourself on the scale below with regard to how you operate at work—with 1 being completely inauthentically, and 10 being completely authentically.

1   2   3   4   5   6   7   8   9   10

If you scored lower on authenticity than you would like, some soul searching may be in order. Is it you, the company, or both? In any case, know that things can usually be improved and that there are small actions you can take. First, simply state your desire to become more authentic. Then, try changing one tangible thing, like cleaning up a misleading communication, altering a policy to be more employee-friendly, or encouraging people to speak up at meetings and without retribution. (That said, if you believe you are not a good fit with your company, see the section in Chapter Ten titled Knowing How and When to Sidestep a Mismatch for further guidance on this topic.) These kinds of actions can move you and your company to be more authentic and inspire others toward a greater sense of *amare*.

Authentically Greedy?

Authenticity requires that the people leading and managing the organization, the people designing and making the products and services, the people doing sales and service, and the support people behind them all need to genuinely buy in and commit to the aims and ways of the company.

So what happens when a company chooses to be driven by greed—embracing fear, incivility, arrogance, and corruption—and its people therefore act in accordance with that intention? Is this being authentic too?

The answer is no, not in the way I propose in this book. Concordance in intent and actions is necessary but not sufficient to constitute authenticity the Amare Way. Goodness is needed too.

To be authentic in an Amare Way company means there must be commitment to a higher good, so that its authenticity will perpetuate goodness, not greed, fear, or evil. Companies steeped in efforts that diminish others rather than uplift them are not authentically aligned with the energy of the universe—or the energy of life. Declaring that one's business culture is subversive and harsh is not a reason for claiming authenticity when carrying out actions from those characteristics. Within the Amare Way, if it's not inherently for the betterment of others, it cannot be considered authentic.

Authenticity and Impostor Syndrome

As a last note, when we gauge whether someone is being authentic or not, we may actually find ourselves misreading discomfort or unfamiliarity as inauthenticity. For example, as Herminia Ibarra describes, a manager who moves from a business group that made decisions based on gentle discussion and rational agreement to one that prefers vigorous debate and persuasive arguments may come across as inauthentic speaking in that manner, when in fact she is simply far out of her comfort zone. Similarly, when an analyst who thrives in the world of numbers, statistics, and spreadsheets is asked to give an inspiring talk from the heart, he may feel that doing so would be inauthentic.

In both cases, going outside one's comfort zone and engaging in something unfamiliar may be easily misconstrued as inauthentic, which is why, Ibarra explains, going against our natural inclinations can make us feel like impostors. In these situations, instead of risking being seen as a person who is fake or disingenuous, you may prefer to remain quiet or stick with what's comfortable. In doing so, you maintain your own authenticity, which is great. Just be certain that your risk aversion is not holding yourself back from growing. And if you're witnessing this behavior from an outside perspective, don't be too quick to judge someone as inauthentic unless you know their full story. They may simply be exuding discomfort, not deception.

Overall, Amare Way companies are authentic about *wanting* to make business love, and their employees are authentic in *delivering* it. As a wonderful byproduct, when people feel a company is authentic, they open up to trusting the company. Barriers go down. Hearts open. Receptivity increases. Happiness expands. Business grows. And with that comes a strong sense of belonging.

FOSTERING HEALTHY BELONGING

The second pillar of the Amare Way practice is belonging, which is a core and fundamental need we all share. As marketing expert Seth Godin says in *Tribes*, "Human beings can't help it: we need to belong."

In business, belonging is fairly straightforward: it happens when your employees, customers, and other stakeholders recognize and embrace desirable similarities between themselves and your company, develop an emotional connection based on those similarities, and feel a sense of kinship, which makes them feel good. In short, people feel a sense of identification with your company or brand. As a result, they genuinely want you to succeed, and they like contributing to your success. (Are you sensing the presence of alignment once again?)

Here is what belonging looks like in Amare Way companies:

- Employee and customer loyalty is off the charts.

- Customers say they are happy you're part of their lives.

- You treat your customers, employees, and suppliers almost like family.

- You hear customers saying that they much prefer to give you their business—and they do.

- There is a palpable sense of connection between management, employees, and customers.

- You enjoy being with your employees, customers, and other stakeholders.

- People proudly proclaim their affinity for you.

An excellent example of this can be seen with Harley David-son devotees. Sarah Robinson, author of the book *Fierce Loyalty*, describes in an interview with *Inc. Online* how the iconic motor-cycle company exemplifies the lasting power of identification and belonging:

> Harley owners don't just ride the bike, they wear the t-shirt, the hat, the tattoo. They understand each other, even if they're meeting for the first time. Being a part of the Harley community is an integral part of how they define themselves. Harley riders won't consider replacing their motorcycle with another brand. Why? Because that would mean giving up their place in the Harley community, and that isn't going to happen. They are just too invested.[55]

From this one illustration, you can see that belonging is not trivial. Harley-Davidson has inarguably created a distinct commu-nity of superloyal followers who deeply identify with them and want to give them their business. This is also true of many sports teams, like the Pittsburgh Steelers, Manchester City, and the

THE AMARE WAY PRACTICE

Golden State Warriors, as well as companies like Apple, Athleta, and Amazon, to name a few. We also see belonging cultivated with countless service providers, including doctors, spiritual leaders, and many other professions.

Now imagine your customers saying they identify and belong with your company the way devoted Harley bikers or Steeler fans or Apple patrons do. Can you picture your customers melding their personal brand with your brand on some level, making it part of how they define themselves?

When customers feel like they belong with you, and you belong to them, you have customer preference, meaning they are loyal and prefer to give you their business above anyone else in your industry. They may even pay more for what you offer, and they are less likely to shop around for better prices because you're not a commodity. What's more, their purchase is not merely a transaction, it's an extension of their being in a relationship with you, and that relationship adds value.

When deep belonging happens, your customers become your ambassadors, praising you to other prospective customers (more on this in the section on Collaboration in this chapter). In getting their needs met through your products or services, they not only feel invited to be part of your company's success, but they *want you to succeed*. In short, when belonging happens, you're no longer just a vendor, you are an integral part of some area of your customers' lives.

The Belonging pillar is aligned with the seven principles of the Amare Way philosophy as follows:

People identify with your company or brand and feel a deep sense of belonging in part because it makes them feel good. After all, why would we choose to belong to something that mainly causes us suffering? To feel good, **people need to be treated well** *(Principle 1)*. The best way to do that is to provide uplifting experiences, which draws on **the energy of love, not fear** *(Principle 5)*. Of course, inherent in belonging is **connection**, one so strong that people meld their personal identity with that of your brand or company *(Principle 2)*. The motivation might be to feed their ego, but it ideally taps into something much deeper than that. Your **higher and shared purpose** gives people that something grander to align and identify with, beyond your products and services *(Principle 3)*, and they inherently sense that your **motivation in making money** is a healthy one *(Principle 4)*, centered on the customers' — not shareholders' or the CEO's — well-being. Lastly, **taking the long view** *(Principle 6)* is essential because belonging is about **relationships**, and people invest more in relationships they believe will last *(Principle 7)*.

Belonging is an invaluable asset. There is, however, a caveat; two forms of belonging can fall far short of how we define it within the Amare Way practice. So let's take a quick look at the kinds of belonging we're *not* striving to achieve.

Two Types of Not-Quite-Belonging

Some forms of belonging in business are a little tricky, because while they may technically be "belonging" in the sense of demonstrating affiliation, that alone is insufficient to characterize what the Belonging pillar is about as an Amare Way practice. The two in particular that fall into this category are "membership belonging" and "forced belonging."

MEMBERSHIP BELONGING requires that customers join a membership program in order to do business with a company or get certain benefits. Some memberships cost money, like joining Costco to shop in their stores or Amazon Prime for fast delivery with no shipping charges. Others are free, such as enrolling in an airline's rewards plan, or signing up for points to get discounts at your local supermarket. The point here is that any of these could be either **transactionally-based** belonging or **relationship-based** belonging. For example, you may think of your Costco membership as simply another card in your wallet you hate paying for (transactionally-based), or you may love Costco and be delighted to be a member (relationship-based). Hence, when emotional connection and desired kinship are *also* in place, membership-based belonging can be love-centered.

FORCED BELONGING connotes that it is not a favorable type of belonging—unless customers *want* to belong with the company that has the monopoly and is the only option. One long-standing industry example is cable companies, which for decades have had regional monopolies. In part because the cable industry was notorious for bad service and for even poorer attitudes, customers felt stuck. They technically belonged, as in being a Spectrum or Cox customer, but they had zero sense of shared identity or desire for affiliation. In other words, the bonding was forced. Worse, any emotional connection was negative; they merely belonged from a lack of choice. This doesn't necessarily mean that every monopoly or situation where there is only one option for a given product or service is bad for customers. But having no competition means having no choice for customers, which leads many companies to decidedly anti-*amare* attitudes, like not caring if customers are happy or if they desire to do business with them. In short, they are far more likely to focus only on making money, and not on actively building a company that makes customers *want* to belong with them.

As you might imagine, mechanisms of transactional belonging don't inherently reflect the deeper personal connection that Amare Way belonging involves. Like everything else transactional, if customer hearts are not involved, and there's no real sense of kinship, the result is a superficial relationship that can be easily lost. However, affiliations based on membership or monopolies *can* go hand in hand with emotional bonding, and they can even strengthen a sense of meaningful identification and belonging.

MIRROR
With Whom Do You Belong?

Think of yourself as a customer in this exercise. Your answers will reveal to you which companies you identify and belong with, and also why.

1. Which companies, large or small, are you most loyal to? Because:

2. With what companies do you feel a positive emotional connection? Because:

3. With what companies do you feel a strong sense of kinship? Because:

4. What companies do you want to go back to again and again? Because:

5. With what companies would you say "I'm a [company name] kind of person." Because:

Now look at your "because" answers. Notice what creates that sense of belonging for you.

Consider these questions too when you think about companies with whom you have a strong sense of belonging:

1. Do you feel uplifted when you do business with them?

2. Do they stand for values you believe in?

3. Do they offer top-quality products and/or services you know you can count on?

4. Do you trust in their ethics and the way they do business?

5. Do they boost your status or self-esteem?

6. Do you feel they genuinely understand and care about you?

I've talked about a few of the big companies that are best known for creating a strong sense of identification and belonging. But smaller companies, without the budget of these big organizations, *can* and *do* create belonging too. For an example, let's look at one of Stacey's favorites, Annmarie Skin Care, a line that has grown from a wife-husband duo when it launched in 2009 into a thriving company today.

By embracing all the qualities Stacey cares most about in choosing skincare—100 percent organic, cruelty-free, non-GMO, and sustainably sourced—Annmarie checks all the boxes. In addition, there is a tremendous amount of love in the language they use, the actions they take, and the service provided by their Customer Care Specialists. It is probably no surprise, then, that Stacey feels a strong sense of belonging with the company. She believes in and personally identifies with the products, loves the product quality, and also loves the people in the company and what they stand for. They consistently listen to what their customers want and need, and provide all kinds of extra perks she values. Because of all this, she feels great about giving them her loyalty, paying for top-quality products, and supporting a company with values she resonates with. She also acts as an ambassador of sorts, gladly sharing how much she loves Annmarie with others. As long as the company remains true to its values, customers like Stacey will actively spread the word and remain loyal to Annmarie Skin Care indefinitely.

Let's do another Mirror activity that converges three persepctives—you, employees, and customers—to help you discover how you can create this level of belonging.

MIRROR
Belonging With Your Company

For each statement, put a ✓ for YES, a ✓✓ for a strong YES, an X for no, or an XX for a strong NO.

YOU

_____ I see myself reflected in my company in positive ways.

_____ There is an emotional connection between me and my company.

_____ I feel a sense of kinship with my company.

_____ I am invested in the well-being of my company.

_____ I am a [company name] kind of person.

_____ I like identifying with the company.

EMPLOYEES

_____ Our employees see themselves reflected in the company in positive ways.

_____ There is an emotional connection between employees and the company.

_____ Employees feel a sense of kinship with the company.

_____ Employees are invested in the well-being of the company.

_____ Most employees would say they are a [company name] kind of person.

_____ Employees like identifying with the company.

CUSTOMERS

_____ Our customers see themselves reflected in the company in positive ways.

_____ There is an emotional connection between customers and the company.

_____ Customers feel a sense of kinship with the company.

_____ Customers are invested in the well-being of the company.

_____ Most customers would say they are a [company name] kind of person.

_____ Customers like identifying with the company.

If most of your answers are positive, continue what you're doing to foster identification and belonging. If not, ask yourself what would foster a greater sense of belonging—and go the extra mile and ask your employees and customers too. Then, start taking steps to act on those insights.

Based on your answers to the YOU statements, place your company on the scale below with regard to the level of belonging it fosters—with 1 being no belonging, and 10 being complete belonging.

Based on your answers to the EMPLOYEES statements, place your company on the scale below with regard to the level of belonging it fosters—with 1 being no belonging, and 10 being complete belonging.

Based on your answers to the CUSTOMERS statements, place your company on the scale below with regard to the level of belonging it fosters—with 1 being no belonging, and 10 being complete belonging.

Once a strong sense of belonging is in place—one that makes your company the kind that you, employees, and customers identify with on a values level, form an emotional connection with, and develop a sense of kinship with—there will be a natural progression toward the third pillar of the Amare Way practice: Collaboration.

TAKING LOYALTY TO THE NEXT LEVEL BY EMBRACING COLLABORATION

As you're likely aware, the word collaboration has become a big buzzword in business. From Slack (software for teams) to Scrums (an Agile methodology) to co-creation (an innovation approach), tools for collaboration abound. From a bigger-picture perspective, the burgeoning "sharing economy" is inherently collaborative, based on a win-win promise.

In the Amare Way, we take collaboration to the next level—elevating it to mean that we're in this together, that we're aligned in uplifting energy and connected in purpose, and that we're actively working toward shared goals and creating greater value jointly.

Here are some of the ways collaboration shows up in Amare Way companies, as a way of thinking and a way of doing:

- Your company mindset is that you are better together and create greater value by collaborating with your multiple stakeholders.

- You acknowledge that you don't know everything, and you actively seek and combine fresh, outside points of view with your inside perspectives to make better decisions.

- You have methods and systems in place that make it easy for people to work together in meaningful ways.

- High levels of employee and customer engagement are the norm and evident to all.

- Collaboration is built into the ways teams work, without overdoing it to the point of burnout.

- You regularly observe and engage customers, and you sincerely pay attention to what they have to say.

- Customers want you to succeed, and they spread the word as raving fans.

- You look for opportunities to work together with competitors toward shared aims that uplift all.

Amare Way collaboration presumes you value and want to satisfy multiple stakeholders, not solely or mainly shareholders. On a basic level, employees are collaborators because they are presumably working toward company goals they believe in, and they receive compensation in return. When customers buy from you, they are in effect collaborating—giving you their business meets their needs as well as yours. Suppliers and investors are, by the nature of the relationship, collaborating with you. So are the communities you exist in. Even competitors can be collaborators, working toward shared policy aims, industry standards, or higher quality deliverables within a shared purpose. In short, when you are love-centered, all your stakeholders want to collaborate with you and help you succeed, making it a win-win-win!

Collaboration is well aligned with the seven principles of the Amare Way philosophy as follows:

Collaboration **treats people well** (Principle 1) by enabling and honoring our fundamental human need to see and be seen, and doing so with the uplifting **energy of love** (Principle 5). Good collaboration is rooted in **inspired connection** (Principle 2) with an intent to add value by working together toward a shared aim that is **on purpose** (Principle 3) and that embraces a **healthy respect for making money** (Principle 4). Lastly, collaboration builds **long-term relationships** (Principle 7), which is part and parcel of **taking the long view** (Principle 6).

In this section, I will break collaboration down into three distinct types:

- collaboration between employees and the company
- collaboration with customers, who become your ambassadors
- collaboration, instead of cutthroat competition, between companies

Let's begin with the first and perhaps most common of the three: collaboration with employees.

Collaboration with Employees

Imagine you're the HR director asking a diverse group of coworkers for input to shape a new employee orientation. Are they enthusiastic in their description of how they feel toward the company? Or are they dissing it and giving you nice-sounding but insincere words to make employee/company relationships seem better than they are?

In Amare Way organizations, strong relationships are always a beneficial outcome of collaboration—and a company's relationship with its employees is one of the most important. While employee engagement is necessary for meaningful and effective collaboration to take hold (see Chapter Six for more on disengagement and engagement), good collaboration allows employees to know that the company authentically sees them, cares for them, and values them —and it takes advantage of the various perspectives and knowledge that people in different roles bring to bear.

I am amazed at how many companies don't leverage what their customer service people and sales reps glean from interacting with customers day in and day out. Their input, when utilized, can often translate into new or modified products and services, improved customer service, and more satisfying customer connections. Collaboration also allows employees to feel more fulfilled, customers to be happier and more committed, and the company to reap financial rewards. Plus, you are tapping into the diverse gifts of your employees, which is a win-win for everyone.

Before we move forward, let's take a look in the mirror to reflect on collaboration within your company.

MIRROR
Utilizing Your Employees' Gifts

---

1. Is meaningful collaboration part of your company culture?
2. Are employees engaged enough to want to collaborate?
3. Is collaboration rewarded in your company?
4. Do people in your company regularly collaborate in an inclusive way?
5. Do you take collaboration too far and wear people out?
6. Do you believe employees have valuable input to offer?
7. Are your collaborative activities generally uplifting?
8. Do your people feel safe enough to be honest in your collaborative efforts?
9. Do you enable "empty" collaboration just to be able to check off a box?
10. Do you believe that collaboration is a good way to empower employees?

Based on your answers to these questions, place yourself on the scale below with regard to how much your company fosters collaboration with employees—with 1 being never, and 10 being frequently.

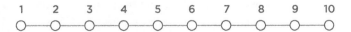

Remember: effective collaboration means that shared goals are in place, and that requires mutual interests. What does that look like for employees? That their everyday work, their ideas, and their contribution to the bigger picture are valued. This could come from developing a business case, brainstorming new product ideas, improving customer complaint management, determining the most meaningful value proposition, identifying partners and investors, generating social media content, strengthening relationships, and a host of other topics. The key is to tie these business applications to the deeper shared goals that underlie effective collaboration.

WINDOW

From Unappreciated Cogs to Valued Collaborators

After a fulfilling eleven-year career with Nordstrom, Stacey moved on to a new chapter as the director of personnel and customer relations for a small, family-owned boutique retail company that consisted of three stores with about twenty employees total – and where collaboration wasn't even on the company's radar.

"The owners of my new company were excellent in their roles as CEO/buyer and CFO, but they admitted to having zero leadership ability. Not one store had its own manager; therefore, there was no sense of pride or accountability. I was appalled to learn that 80 percent employee turnover a year was the norm, and it was clear that employee engagement was pitiful. No one in the company felt any allegiance, and collaboration was nonexistent. So, my first step was to establish a store manager in each location and provide each of them with comprehensive leadership training to become proficient in running their stores largely on their own. With the employees – the majority of whom were students who saw their position as merely a temporary retail job while they were in school – I wanted them to feel much more connection. So I began by simply giving each employee an index card with questions to fill out so that I could get to know each of their interests, favorite snacks and holidays, birthdays and other special events, and the like. Almost immediately, the vibe in the stores began to change. I saw faces light up as they realized someone cared about them as individuals. Engagement deepened as we celebrated each employee's birthday with a card and a cake, and as I regularly checked in with each of them not only about their performance at work, but about their activities outside of work as well.

To foster meaningful collaboration, the store managers and I implemented regular store meetings, using interactive games and calling people out for superb service and positive energy. I also started a monthly company newsletter where I published an inspirational message, employee spotlights, product knowledge, and kudos that employees submitted for each other, among other themes that encouraged employee input. Not only did I hear customers saying how much more attentive and enthusiastic the employees were, but within a year after weeding out all the people who weren't a good match and hiring people who were, we went from losing forty people in a year to only five. The employees on our team came to feel like they were part of something special and were true collaborators the company sincerely cared about and valued. They loved their jobs and were allowed to shine, and they typically left only when they were ready to move on to something bigger. When that day arrived, I could feel proud that the person was going on to her next chapter knowing she deserved to be valued at work, and that she would hopefully seek out opportunities where she could continue to collaborate and lend her gifts to the greater good.

While collaboration with employees clearly has numerous benefits, I want to take a moment to caution you about promoting what is called "empty collaboration." In other words, you want to avoid activities under the heading of teamwork, customer engagement, or collaboration as merely a means to check off a box or complete a task. Why? Because when collaboration is not authentic and meaningful, trust erodes and disengagement happens. As a result, employees tend to become more *me* focused and less *we* focused.

Another thing you want to watch is how much employees are expected to collaborate with each other to achieve a particular goal. Yes, collaborating[56] is part and parcel of being in a company, and for good reason as *The Economist* highlights:

> People can accomplish things together that they could not do on their own. Silos break down, teamwork increases. Diversity of ideas and perspectives adds value. All good, and with the added benefit that participation in collaborative activities is relatively easy to measure.

But, as the article goes on to point out, collaboration can often be overdone, especially in highly visible "knowledge work" technology companies. When collaboration becomes cult-like, people can be pulled into so many collaborative efforts—requiring them to attend meeting after meeting and weigh in on every idea—that they have no time or energy to do the deeper work they need to do with uninterrupted concentration and on their own. This results in what Rob Cross, Reb Rebele, and Adam Grant call "collaboration overload," which can lead even the best collaborators to become disengaged, burnt out, and feel less career satisfaction.

By definition, collaboration overload is depleting, not uplifting. Hence, it is not based in love. Though it's probably obvious to you at this point, I want to be clear that this is not the kind of employee collaboration we are espousing within the Amare Way framework.

Collaboration with Customers

The second type of Amare Way collaboration is with one of your most valued partners: your customers. When you are effectively collaborating with customers, they indeed experience you as a partner rather than merely a vendor selling their newest technologies, novelties, or services. And when this kind of collaboration occurs, it not only lends to a highly effective way of differentiating yourself in competitive markets, but your customers become your best resource for how to continue to understand and meet their needs. When you listen to them, they notice; when you address a new need that arises, they appreciate it. When people know they are understood and cared for through your interactions with them, when they have no doubt you are striving to be the best version of what they desire you to be, they will be more inclined to help you maintain that status—and to grow as well.

WINDOW
Missed Opportunity

As a researcher, I can't tell you how many times I've heard customers lament in focus groups, online panels, and other market research studies that they wished manufacturers and distributors would actively and consistently engage them in understanding and solving problems, and not merely show up to sell. For example, in consulting engagements with medical technology companies, we would often ask a room full of healthcare customers – doctors, nurses, hospital execs – to name one med tech company that truly treated them as a partner. Almost without exception, the customers would be blank; no company came to their minds. They could occasionally name a particular sales rep or customer service person who had been outstanding and established a consultative kind of relationship, but they were hard-pressed to name a company that consistently went beyond the typical transaction-based sales and service to establish and sustain meaningful consultative partnerships. What a missed opportunity.

When we would take these results back to the companies, they would say that of course they wanted to be seen as partners, and to be more collaborative and consultative. I believe they genuinely did want to have deeper and less transactional relationships – the desire was there, the words were there. Unfortunately, the action often did not follow. Why?

Usually, it was because of the pressure to hit monthly or quarterly numbers. Compensation and bonuses encouraged selling, selling, and more selling because top-line revenue ruled. Customer lifetime value – a financial metric well aligned with customer love – was often not even measured. The push to be first to market was another enormous pressure. In effect, these were the things the companies honored. And as you know from our version of Plato's thesis, **what a company honors is what it cultivates**.

Let's do a Mirror activity here to assess your level of collaboration with customers.

MIRROR

Collaborating with Customers

---

1. Do you value collaborating with customers?
2. Is customer collaboration integral to how you do business?

3. When you do collaborate, are you honest about your aims?

4. Do customers see you as a partner or merely a vendor?

5. Do you genuinely value and act on customer feedback?

6. Do you feel you have the answers and don't need much customer input?

7. Are you too busy to actively collaborate with customers?

8. Do you enable your employees to collaborate with customers?

9. Do you mainly think about collaborating when you have new products to sell?

Based on your answers to these questions, place yourself on the scale below with regard to how much you collaborate with customers—with 1 being never, and 10 being frequently.

Because collaboration combines shared interests, goals, and values with action, by having A (authenticity) and B (belonging) in place, it is natural for customers who love you to be in partnership with you on some level. However, I want to once again briefly caution you to be sure you have authentic motives within the partnership. If your primary aim is focused on money but you pretend it's not, or you shroud that aim in nice-sounding language that appeals to customers but is false, you are being neither kind nor respectful, and that violates the fundamental philosophy of business love.

An example that comes to mind is the calls I used to receive once a year from my alma mater. The callers were current college students who would first ask me a few questions about my work and life, and then they would ask for money. When I asked what they did with the answers I provided to the personal questions, they said they didn't know—which translated to me as doing nothing with them, as the true agenda appeared to be fundraising. Every year I told them the same thing: "I won't donate when fundraising is disguised as research that has no real meaning. Separate the two activities, and I will happily donate." Sadly, that never happened.

When you seek customer engagement and input, you must genuinely value it, and you must put that input to use. Inviting customers to collaborate should never be used as a marketing ploy or sales tactic. While you may receive some short-term gains from these kinds of misaligned collaborative efforts, they come at a high cost because the process will lose you trust and allegiance—and when trust and allegiance are lost due to intentional inauthenticity or conscious lying, it is extremely difficult, if not impossible, to win them back. This is why Amare Way collaboration requires both a mindset and a set of behaviors, aligned with the best interests of all parties.

So, what are the best ways to gauge the pulse of customers?

Ongoing research is a powerful way to engage and foster collaboration, and you can do this through focus groups, surveys, usability testing, and online communities. The research can be simple or sophisticated; either way, customers have the opportunity to tell you what they want, as well as what they like and dislike, which may include how they perceive your company, your people, and your offerings. Their input can inform a wide range of business decisions when put to good use.

The key is to remember that the participants giving feedback are human beings who have lives outside your product or service. They are not simply anonymous respondent xyz, or Persona #4, or part of segment N=2,035, and your company is not and should not be their first concern. This recognition affects what you ask them, and what you do with their answers. Bottom line: **You must value that these people are choosing to reveal to you how they think and feel, and what they want and need.** When you circle back to them as valued collaborators, and show them you are taking their input seriously and using it to better serve them, engagement and loyalty skyrocket.

If your interaction is largely in person with customers, simply asking one or two direct and genuine open-ended questions while they are shopping, or in line waiting, or paying a bill can create a meaningful exchange. For example, "How could we make you happier today?" or "What one thing would you like to see different in the store?" (See Chapter Twelve: Getting Started for more ideas on collaborating with customers.)

As we are reminded in a well-circulated quote:

A customer is the most important visitor on our premises. He is not dependent on us. We are dependent on him. He is not an interruption in our work. He is the purpose of it. He is not an outsider in our business. He is part of it. We are not doing him a favor by serving him. He is doing us a favor by giving us an opportunity to do so.
—MAHATMA GANDHI

I've done a lot of business research in my time, and it still astounds me what a privilege it is to have access to the minds and hearts of the numerous customers and others who participate in collaborative efforts, and how eager they often are to share and help. Even when market research and customer studies are done anonymously—where the customer is intentionally not told who the company behind the study is to avoid possible bias—the company can feel a sense of collaboration with customers as they act on the input the customers provided, and customers can feel uplifted knowing they helped businesses they believe in to be and do better.

Amare Way companies are authentic about fostering collaboration with customers for the right reasons, such as to genuinely improve an offering, remove one that's not serving their audience, or create one their customers are requesting. This alignment in shared goals sets the stage for meaningful collaboration. Ideas improve. Relationships get stronger. Business grows.

But what happens when the opposite occurs?

It's imperative to recognize that a company's aim of making more money and maximizing shareholder returns are *not* goals that customers typically care about, since these goals are often not aligned with their best interests. More money and greater shareholder returns may be results of new product innovation and service improvement that come from company–customer collaboration, but they are not the shared goals underpinning that collaboration. The 2008 recession demonstrated how an extreme focus on maximizing revenue and shareholder return—at any cost—can bring down even the biggest companies. Alignment in what companies and customers want and care about are essential for effective collaboration.

Now, you may be wondering, with everyone so busy these days, why customers would want to participate in your company research.

If you're an Amare Way company and ground all of your interactions in love, customers will *want* to help you and your cause, even if they simply enjoy sharing their experience and expressing their opinions. Sure, they may also want the money or points you offer as an incentive, but helping your company is a genuine intrinsic motivator, because customers not only care about you on a personal level, they benefit when you succeed.

Keep in mind that this is far less true for companies that have primarily transactional relationships with customers, in which case collaboration is driven *solely* by extrinsic motivators like money, discounts, or points. This more transactionally-based collaboration may produce short-term benefits but is not an effective long-term strategy, and it is not consistent with the Amare Way philosophical tenet of taking the long view.

One more crucial point to keep top of mind:

While I don't view customer collaboration within the Amare Way expressly as a means to secure fans who enthusiastically praise you, when people are genuinely delighted to be your customers and you are authentic with them, a wonderful byproduct is that they become your devoted ambassadors, or what Ken Blanchard defines as raving fans—"A customer who is so devoted to your products and services that they wouldn't dream of taking their business elsewhere, and will sing from the rooftops about just how good you are." These people rave about you to others not because you've asked them to, but because they sincerely love and trust you, and they want others to have the same experience.

Does this mean that customers are actively thinking they want your company to succeed every time they give you business? Of course not. But we believe that an underlying desire for the other's success is inherent in a love-centered relationship; it does not need to be top of mind or even conscious. Like in a marriage, you're not always thinking about your mate's well-being every time you engage with them, right? But if someone brings it to your awareness by asking you if you care about your spouse, you'd likely say yes. The same is true in business, only with a different kind of love. Once you cultivate raving fans, they become an active part of your tribe, helping with positioning, marketing, and sales. This grassroots form of collaboration is priceless and far more powerful—and often much more authentic—than most paid advertising and public relations campaigns.

So what can *you* do to encourage customers to rave about you?

For one, you can invite them to recommend you through conversations with family and friends, with social media, and with organizations they know. In return, while you can run contests, offer giveaways, or give discounts—you don't need to. It is customers' *intrinsic* motivation to express their commitment to your company and share their excitement with others that is the real prize. Once you earn that motivation, voicing delight with you is your customers' expression of love for you. And an extension of that is that they frequently choose not to shop around—even, to an extent, if your prices are higher—because Amare Way customers are less price-sensitive, which in and of itself is a significant result of running a heart-centered business.

Remember, within the framework of customer love, you are not a commodity. You are a valued relationship. Customers trust you to have their best interests in mind and to treat them well, and saving a little money is not worth diminishing that relationship.

Make no mistake, however: **once you reach the stage of collaborating with your customers, they will be keeping a close eye on you**. The more transparent you are, the more people expect you to remain that way. Think about it: Nobody wants to promote a product from a company whose CEO becomes the latest news scandal. And nobody likes to be made a fool of. So once you achieve this level of connection and loyalty with your customers, be sure you remain authentic and driven by wanting the best for them. This is how an Amare Way company succeeds over the long term.

Collaboration with Competitors

Some of you might be thinking: "Why would I want to collaborate with my competition? It makes no sense to help them!" Stay with me and you'll see how integral it is to riding the Amare Wave.

Most of us have been raised on striving to be number one—in school, in sports, in business—and we've been conditioned to segment everyone into winners and losers. And while there's nothing wrong with winning, the winner/loser mindset does not always lend to treating competitors with respect or to see them as active collaborators.

Make no mistake: the Amare Way values healthy competition; a lack of it can make us lazy, while the presence of it can make us better. In fact, we ought to be grateful to our competitors because they offer opportunities to bring out our best. As Bill Gates declared, "Whether it's Google or Apple or free software, we've got some fantastic competitors and it keeps us on our toes."

WINDOW

Collaborating with Competitors

Business to business collaborations can take many forms, including strategic alliances, joint ventures, and partnerships, all of which can be one-offs or more enduring. Here are three powerful examples.

Many of us have directly experienced Amazon's Marketplace, where it allows third-party sellers – competitors – to seamlessly integrate and sell on their e-commerce platform, which accounted for over half of Amazon's sales in 2018[57] and created a win-win for everyone.

In financial services, Apple Pay and MasterCard[58] are collaborating on e-payments. By teaming up, Apple Pay gets exposure and credibility in merchant services and payment processing, and MasterCard gets cache and first-mover advantage as the first Apple Pay–authorized option, allowing both to benefit from each other's reputation and expertise.

The SmartDeviceLink Consortium has Toyota, Ford, Mazda, and other carmakers collaborating on software alternatives to connect phones to cars, in order to best serve technology companies with products like Apple's CarPlay and Google's Android Auto,[59] allowing all the automakers to benefit.

To reflect the complexities of relationships with competitors, I like to use the phrase "collabetition"[60]—a blend of the words collaboration and competition. A classic example of this comes from the nonprofit world:

> When it comes to attaining gifts from major donors, the American Heart Association (AHA), American Diabetes Association (ADA), and American Cancer Society (ACS) all want to be selected as the charity of choice, and they directly compete for the major donors. However, their ultimate goal is to reduce risk factors common to all three diseases – smoking, poor nutrition, and inadequate physical activity. Hence, the charities collaborate on increasing public awareness about healthy lifestyles, promoting legislation to fund more prevention programs and research, and encouraging screenings for early detection.

Let's take a look at how "collabetive" you are through the following Mirror activity.

MIRROR

Are Your Competitors Sometimes
Your Collaborators?

Which best represents your company's general attitude toward collaborating with your competitors:

a) Over my dead body.

b) Only when we have to.

c) We'd consider it case by case.

d) It's a key strategy for us.

e) We're eager to help competitors.

Now, answer yes or no to the following to indicate your beliefs:

1. When we help competitors, we hurt ourselves.

2. Helping competitors helps our whole industry.

3. We don't trust our competitors enough to collaborate with them.

4. Collaborating with our competition makes us better.

Now, answer yes or no to the following to indicate your actions:

1. We refuse collaboration unless it's forced upon us.

2. We collaborate with competitors on industry-wide initiatives.

3. We share IP and ideas for new products with competitors to accelerate innovation.

4. We refer customers to competitors when their product is better.

Based on your answers to these questions, place yourself on the scale below with regard to how much you collaborate with your competitors—with 1 being never, and 10 being frequently.

In your business, the reality is you may collaborate with your competitors in multiple ways: establishing policies favorable to your industry, sponsoring a trade association, advancing basic research that can fuel innovation for multiple companies, hosting a summit or event that features several providers in your industry, and so on. Further, you may actually refer business to your competitors. This is especially true when you believe that **business is a social enterprise intended to make life better for people**, fostered by a healthy mindset of abundance.

One of the most poignant examples of this generous approach to business is once again demonstrated in the classic film *Miracle on 34th Street*. You'll recall that after years of stiff competition between the two New York City department stores Macy's and Gimbels, Macy's hires a store Santa Claus who begins telling parents where they can find toys if Macy's doesn't carry them or they are too expensive there. Once Mr. Macy finds out, he is outraged that their Santa would send customers away—until customer praise starts to flood in. Though unwillingly at first, the store comes to embrace this "customer first" mentality to such a degree that they maintain a daily book of their competitors' offerings, with staff stationed throughout the store to guide customers to the best source for the items they want. Photos of Mr. Macy and Mr. Gimbel shaking hands in solidarity make the headlines. And, you guessed it, both stores profit, probably more than they would have before they adopted this decidedly *amare* policy. The underlying caring was what made all the difference: Macy's wanted customers to find what they needed for Christmas, and they did everything in their power to help them do it, even if it meant sending them to their staunchest competitor.

Yes, you can actually win more loyalty and "belonging" when you refer customers to competitors. Think about how much more you trust a company that has the courage and honesty to tell you a competitor's product is better. This happened to me recently at REI, when a salesperson advised me to buy a Columbia shirt over the REI brand. In my consulting practice, I routinely advise clients to tell customers when a competitor has a better offering, as in "Buy this medical device from us, but for the disposable supplies that go with it, you can get something just as good from company X for less money this month." And when clients come to us for certain research projects, we routinely tell them that if all they need is data, not strategic insights or recommendations, they can get that for less elsewhere.

The other reason collabetition makes sense is that you likely cannot serve 100 percent of the market, and there is enough to go around (again, an abundance mindset). As Stacey and I were discussing collaboration between companies, she told me about a recent exchange she had with a colleague of hers in the publishing space about a course she was developing for writers.

"I asked Alexa if she would be willing to share my course with her audience, perhaps in one of her mailings or on social media – with the caveat that if she felt it was too close to her own offerings, I would completely understand that it might not be in her best interest to promote mine. Her response to me was, 'Even if we provided the *exact* same thing to writers, I would still gladly promote your course. There are tons of people out there writing books, and they all need great guidance!' The bottom line: there's plenty to go around."

With this type of mentality in mind, you can see that being excellent at what you do and offer—with authenticity at the core —is what counts. In other words, you can still be a market leader without having to dominate the market to the exclusion of competitors who would bring different value to customers. Similar to the nonprofit example with the ADA, AHA, and ACS, rather than putting energy into smearing competitors, you come together with a common goal: to make life better for people. Your focus is on making *your* company the best it can be, authentically caring about the well-being of your customers. When everyone within a single industry embraces that mindset, many more companies can thrive, and society benefits. As John F. Kennedy famously said, "A rising tide lifts all boats."

Hopefully you can see through these examples how collaboration with your competitors can not only be healthy for a company, and how it can grow the overall category, but also how it can increase your customer loyalty in the process. In the same way R.H. Macy in *Miracle on 34th Street* found "collabetition" to endear Macy's customers further to the store, you can find similar avenues for your own business—in partnership with your competition— that will convey loud and clear that customer happiness is your top priority.

WINDOW

Collaboration and Innovation

There are a number of collaborative philosophies and practices that have become popular in the innovation space and are consistent in principle with Amare Way tenets.

> Numerous companies have adopted and institutionalized "open innovation" models, which includes inviting and soliciting ideas from outside the company, and rewarding contributors.

> Agile is a philosophy and set of practices developed in the software world as an alternative to the dominant "command and control" management style. It explicitly and iteratively integrates customer collaboration into the rapid development process.[61]

> Design Thinking, and human-centered design, put people, not products, at the center. As Design Thinking guru Don Norman (my psychology professor a million years ago!) emphasizes in *Emotional Design*[62], these approaches focus on the emotional relationship between products and customers, instead of on the technology. Customers are actively observed and engaged throughout the innovation process, and they are valued as collaborators because they are the experts on themselves, especially what problems they have and what they want to be better.

To bring this segment on collaboration to a close, I offer you an excerpt from Lynne Power's blog post featured in the *Huffington Post*, which nicely summarizes the reality of effective collaboration at work, while tying in several Amare Way ideas:

The reality is that true collaboration is hard – and it doesn't mean compromise or consensus-building. It means giving up control to other people. It means being vulnerable. It means needing to know when to fall on your sword and when to back down. Collaboration is inherently messy. Great ideas need some tension; otherwise they would be easy to make. And ultimately, there needs to be respect – of other people's roles, thoughts, and what they bring to the table. And there also needs to be trust.

In sum, meaningful and effective collaboration happens in the right doses. It may take the form of one employee asking another for feedback on an idea; discrete projects aimed at addressing a particular need; or ongoing and institutionalized programs that engage employees, customers, and others outside the organization, to name a few. But no matter the project, the energy of meaningful collaboration is engaging and uplifting.

It is my hope that after completing this chapter, you can now see how the three pillars of the Amare Way practice bring the seven principles of the philosophy to life, and how you can begin implementing the ABCs in your own business and work.

I also want to remind you to retain a sense of balance. Becoming too extreme can potentially take you off your *amare* path. Take a few of the Amare Way principles as examples: treating one another well does not mean subordinating yourself to others; taking the long view does not mean ignoring today's bills; and getting on purpose does not mean misusing your higher purpose to rationalize bad behavior. The same is true with the ABC pillars: being authentic is not an excuse for having no filters; cultivating belonging is not about creating a cult; and collaboration is not a reason to avoid getting your own work done.

To circle back to our ABC pillars in the simplest way: Amare Way companies are authentic about *wanting* to be love-centered,

and their employees are authentic in *delivering* it. When customers feel a company is **authentic**, they open up to trusting the
company, which leads to a strong sense of **belonging**—feeling desirable similarities, emotional connection, and a sense of kinship.
Once this occurs, it is natural for customers to want to become
collaborators and raving fans—and for a company to *want* to collaborate with them in return, as well as with their employees,
partners, and even competitors. Taken together, these three pillars
are powerful ingredients for making business love, as put forward
in the manifesto that follows. Feel free to use it in your company!

THE AMARE WAY
MANIFESTO

We are dedicated to the principles and practices
of the Amare Way. We believe that love belongs in our
organization and makes us happier and more successful.
We always strive to do good and promise to do no evil.

Our work is driven by a higher and shared purpose.
We are committed to succeed financially while achieving our
purpose, without being predatory or greedy.

We are not afraid and do not let fear drive our business.
We reject warlike thinking, language, and behaviors in our
organization. Instead, we choose to be kind and compassionate
in our beliefs, words, and actions.

We value and respect all our stakeholders, first and foremost
our employees. We are not at war with our competitors; we
treat them with respect, and we want them to succeed as well.

We love our customers and want them to love us. We do not
act like we own customers. We do not think of customers as
prey or targets or kill. We are honored to serve them and
grateful for their loyalty.

We recognize love as the uplifting energy that connects us all
and binds us together. We are proud to be in this powerful
movement that is bringing love and humanity back into
business, where it belongs.

PART FOUR

SETTING YOURSELF UP
FOR SUCCESS

Be the change you wish to see in the world.
—GANDHI

NO MATTER
HOW LONG
YOU HAVE
TRAVELED
IN THE
WRONG
DIRECTION,
YOU CAN
ALWAYS
TURN
AROUND.

CHAPTER TEN

HARNESSING ADVANTAGE: TURNING FIVE COMMON TRAPS INTO STEPPING STONES

n Part II of this book, we discussed several unsavory characteristics and habits that often influence us and our companies
in less than favorable ways—and how we can turn those traits
around. In this chapter, I want to bring to light five additional
hangups that I have seen over and over again lead business leaders
down a rocky path. These common traps are: a scarcity mindset,
being attached to outcomes, fear of veering away from the status
quo, being entrenched in a mismatch with your company, and
embracing money as a god.

In bringing these into your awareness, I hope you'll be equipped
to either steer clear of these traps, or use them as stepping stones
to find your way to greener grass for you and your business.

SAYING YES TO AN ABUNDANCE MINDSET AND NO TO A SCARCITY MINDSET

A key responsibility for business leaders is to set the tone for the company by establishing its fundamental mindset, which may either be rooted in scarcity, or in an optimistic belief in abundance. Here's what I mean.

An abundance mentality resides in the idea of endless possibilities, with trust that life will provide for our needs when we are in alignment, and that there is plenty for everyone we share the planet with. A scarcity mentality, in contrast, is derived from a belief in "lack" and the presumption that life is a zero-sum game, or rather, "if *they* have a lot, there won't be enough for *us*." Abundance is love-based. Lack is fear-based. Guess which mentality helps power the Amare Wave?

Stephen Covey is credited for coining the terms "scarcity mentality" and "abundance mentality" in his bestselling book *The 7 Habits of Highly Effective People*. According to Covey, when we have scarcity thinking, we focus on what we *don't* have. When we have abundance thinking, we focus on what we *can* and *do* have. This is important because in large part—in business as in life—our mindset creates our reality, or as author and metaphysical teacher Mike Dooley puts it, *thoughts become things*. With this in mind, consider why you would choose a mindset that causes suffering when you can choose one that doesn't.

Case in point:

Innovation expert Christopher Hawker calls this belief in lack a *not-enough attitude* and describes people with this mindset as "the ones who typically complain about not having enough time, money, energy or resources to achieve their goals. Typically, they frame their challenges through what they lack. As a result, their businesses and those around them focus on the wrong priorities: preservation rather than growth, familiar surroundings instead of new frontiers, and complacency over challenges."[63] What's more, scarcity-based leaders narrowly accept things for how they currently *are*—resigning themselves to existing limitations—instead of considering how they *could* be. They can also make the common mistake of conflating a scarcity mindset with what they deem a "realistic" mindset, which is often based in fear.

For example, if you're having a hard time making ends meet, you might buy into a scarcity mindset because at the present time, your reality is that there isn't enough. However, when you shift your mindset to "there is plenty for everyone," you activate the "thoughts become things" magic, which breaks you out of scarcity mindset and into abundance mindset. Will your money situation instantly change? Probably not. But the active belief that there is more than enough for you and everyone else in the world *does* change what's possible for you. In sum, if you believe you'll never have enough, you more than likely won't; if you sincerely believe prosperity is available to you (which it is!)—and you know there's no cause to trample anyone to get it—prosperity will more likely come your way.

As you might imagine, a scarcity mentality sucks up a lot of your productive energy in business because you are constantly worried you will never have enough. As a result, it's easy for the acquisition of money—through whatever means necessary—to become your highest priority. This is fed by the illusion that getting more money will pacify the scarcity mindset. But in reality, however much you acquire is never quite satisfying; the scarcity mindset persists. It also goes back to what we discussed about the power of skewed relativity in Chapter Four: when making money is your guiding factor, it's easy to rationalize your actions and ratchet down your judgments of how "bad" certain behavior really is. This can occur especially when you embody a fear-based scarcity mindset.

When we adopt a scarcity mentality and, as we have been strongly conditioned to do in business, harbor a lack of trust, we often find ourselves grasping onto short-term thinking. This causes us to get caught up in micromanagement and turf issues, feel disconnected, hyperfocus on protection of self—and, above all, work within a highly limiting narrow-mindedness.

If you look at what you have in life, you'll always have more.
If you look at what you don't have in life, you'll never have enough.

—OPRAH WINFREY

When you adopt a love-based abundance mindset, you are freed up from the heaviness of negative thinking and from obsessing about what isn't working. Instead, you recognize what *is* working and what might be possible to achieve, which lets you envision and often accomplish incredible things. In *Abundance: The Future Is Better Than You Think,* Peter Diamandis and Steven Kotler present strong evidence that with new technologies, abundance for all can happen. To paraphrase Bill Clinton, there are positive trend lines that counter the dark pessimism in today's headlines. This expansiveness of abundance thinking is what leads to world-changing innovations—or what Jim Collins and Jerry Porras call BHAGs (big, hairy, audacious goals)—that provide incredible value to society, such as:

HENRY FORD'S DREAM: A car in every driveway to give all Americans freedom to go places like never before

JFK's MOON CHALLENGE: Getting a man on the moon and home safely within a decade

MICROSOFT'S AIM: A computer on every desk and in every home

GOOGLE'S AMBITION: Organizing all the world's information and making it accessible and useful to all

Now, you might challenge me and say these goals were actually about money or prestige, and it's certainly possible that those factors were significant drivers of these aims. But even if that is true, the fact is they are all imbued with a powerful and compelling spirit of possibility and openness, unrestricted by notions of lack or scarcity.

When you let go of a belief in lack and replace it with a belief in abundance, you cultivate win-win situations where you, your employees, your suppliers, your customers—everyone—is pleased with what they receive. This is a far better mindset than the one that underlies win-lose scenarios: relentlessly pressuring employees to do more with less, trying to squeeze as much as possible from suppliers, maximizing how much customers will pay regardless of the situation, and the list goes on.

Even more beneficial is the gratitude you feel when the tone of your business is rooted in abundance. This attitude of gratitude is as profound as it is contagious. In fact, almost no feeling is more powerful than being grateful for all you have and can do.

MIRROR
Abundance Mindset or Scarcity Mindset:
Where Are You?

Using the table on the following page, ask yourself which side you are closer to, using some of the comparisons described by entrepreneur Caroline Castrillon.[64]

Abundance Mindset	Scarcity Mindset
Focus on opportunities	Focus on limitations
Thinks big and embraces risk	Thinks small and fears risk
Long-term focus	Short-term focus
Willing to share knowledge	Stingy with knowledge
Investment with a return	Cost control
Trust the process	Attached to the outcome
Focus on the customer	Focus on the competition

Based on your responses, place yourself on the scale below with regard to how much you embrace an abundance mindset—with 1 being never, and 10 being on a regular basis.

If you're honest with yourself, you instinctively know from this exercise that the negativity of a scarcity mindset is not healthy or uplifting. But I also recognize that some people are raised with this thinking, and therefore never truly realize they embrace scarcity over abundance, or that it's a defeating practice. If this is the first time you're seeing this tendency in yourself, don't despair. Breaking out of a scarcity mindset is a process, one I offer the following tips to overcome.

DOOR

- Adopt a daily affirmation. Do this to reinforce your belief and remind yourself that the world is abundant in nature—because indeed it is. This may sound like:

  "There is enough for everyone" or "I naturally attract prosperity" or "My company abundantly creates and receives." For more, search "abundance affirmations" or explore the work of Louise Hay, an early and prolific proponent of abundance thinking. (And if these sound too "woo-woo" for you, feel free to come up with your own.)

  Repeat your positive statements every day. This may be during a five-minute break, a walk around the block, in the shower, etc. The idea is to create a habitual time that you affirm your belief in abundance out loud. Also, repeat it whenever you notice scarcity thinking is triggered. You may be surprised how this simple repetitive act begins to shift your mentality, which is the first step in the Law of Attraction.

- Replace jealousy with gratitude. Instead of being envious of others' success or material wealth, celebrate it and be happy for them. Learn from their success. Remember, it's not all about you (this is not breaking news, right?) and there is plenty to go around. Envy is unnecessary and self-defeating.

- Envision what your abundant life looks like for you and for your company. Close your eyes and imagine every detail, as if you're watching a movie. Write specifics of what you desire in a journal, and don't be afraid to dream big. Create a vision board or slideshow to make it more real. Pay particular attention to the feeling—the inner state—you want to have. The more exact you can be, the better.

- Share it with others. Look for opportunities with friends and colleagues to express your abundance mindset—in casual conversation, in business meetings, in presentations, etc. Keep it simple and real, such as by saying, "We can both do well" when discussing a key competitor. Or after acknowledging disappointment or frustration when your team doesn't win a bid, you might say ,"One door closes, another opens."

ATTACHING FULFILLMENT TO THE WORK, NOT THE OUTCOMES

If there's anything you could point out where I was a little different, it was the fact that I never mentioned winning.

—UCLA COACH JOHN WOODEN, WINNER OF THE MOST NATIONAL COLLEGE BASKETBALL CHAMPIONSHIPS IN HISTORY

The second trap people often fall into is how attached we are to outcomes, how that attachment drives decisions we might not otherwise make, and how it can ultimately harm us in the end. We'll call Attachment to Outcomes A2O for short.

In a lot of companies, decisions come down to the financial bottom line. This makes people very attached to their numbers—whatever the marker is: P&L (profit and loss), market cap, company valuation, EBITDA margin (assessment of a firm's operating profitability as a percentage of its total revenue), etc.

Now, before we go any further, I want to clarify here that outcomes in business are very important. I'm not saying companies shouldn't set measurable goals. They should. I'm also not saying that companies shouldn't tie key decisions to business objectives, or tie compensation to performance. Again, there is good reason to do so. Further, I'm not saying that outcomes, results, and performance don't matter in business. They absolutely do. What I *am* saying is to not be *attached* to the outcomes, which is very different from them not mattering at all.

Allow me to explain.

In a business as love paradigm, you most definitely want to achieve results, financial and otherwise; Amare Way companies possess an inherent desire to prosper. The difference is that you are not attached to whether you do or not.

I realize this may sound counterintuitive. It took quite a long time for me to accept this, and I still struggle with it sometimes. You've likely heard the saying, "It doesn't matter whether you win or lose, it's how you play the game." Sounds nice, sure, but how do you live up to it when big money is attached to winning? More generally, how can you run a successful business and not be attached to results? The answer encompasses three factors.

The first factor—**results**—is that your work is not as good when your main focus is on the outcome. Therefore, and ironically, when you are attached to outcomes, results suffer. Why? Because attachment to the outcome actually becomes a distraction that takes you out of the present and away from the doing. In contrast, when your focus is solely on your work, or the doing, you can be all in, without the intrusion of expectations or self-conscious judgment. You are in the zone—or as author Mihály Csíkszentmihályi calls it in his book *Flow: The Psychology of Optimal Experience*, "flow state"—so fully absorbed in what you're doing that time and space seem to disappear. In other words, everything is here and now, in the work in front of you.

You've been in flow, at least on occasion; we all have. It is not hyperfocus, it is simply focused presence, which is a highly enjoyable and productive state to be in.

The second factor—**the emotional cost**—is that being attached to outcomes will almost always cause you distress. You know the feeling of being attached to an outcome, right? It often feels as if your happiness and sense of self depends on achieving that outcome. As a result, you try to control everything and everyone associated with that achievement, hence your focus is on the results more than on your work. When this happens, you become smaller in your vision, your awareness, your freedom, and your enjoyment. This is because the outcomes or results take control of what you think, how you react, and what you do. In short, they define you . . . at least until the next project comes along with its objectives and outcomes. And, perhaps even worse, you may make decisions that are in conflict with your values because achieving the outcome is all that matters.

The third factor—**self-definition**—is a reflection of how you see *yourself* in these outcomes. Again, not being attached doesn't mean you don't desire results or care about outcomes; of course you do. You want to achieve your business objectives, be recognized for your contributions, be well-paid, come up with solutions, improve SOPs, be first to market, gain market share, increase your company's valuation, and so on. You want your work to make a meaningful difference in people's lives—and you want personal outcomes like inner peace and financial security too. But the achievement of these business and personal outcomes need not *define* you as a person. In other words, *what* you achieve does not determine your happiness, value, or self-worth.

This is actually a central teaching of the *Bhagavad Gita*—and perhaps its most puzzling lesson. The ancient Indian scripture petitions us to be responsible for our work, *not* for the fruits of our labor. The fruits will be what they will be. But how can we focus on doing the work as best we can without worrying about the outcomes?

Results—in life and in business—are almost always determined by multiple factors, of which *your* action, *your* work, is only one. When you are attached to your expectations of outcomes, and they don't come to be, it's easy to become angry, bitter, resentful, or disenchanted. The negative energy of these emotional states becomes a tremendous impediment to your success.

A powerful piece in the *Gita* depicts the god and teacher Krishna saying to the confused warrior and student Arjuna, "Let go of the outcome. Be alike in success and defeat."

Think about this for a minute. Can you imagine, as a CEO or leader in your company, being the same whether your company fails or succeeds? It's a powerful and in many ways liberating idea.

To illustrate this further, let's look at a quote from monk and author Chaitanya Charan:

> When we become attached to the result, we set ourselves up for illusion in both success and failure – in success, we become proud thinking that we are so great that we have achieved the result. In failure, we become dejected thinking that the failure reflects our ineptitude and worthlessness, thus eroding our self-esteem. But instead if we understand that our part is as one cause, then we can do our part diligently without becoming distracted or disheartened.

But, you may be asking, how can I possibly be successful in business without desiring success, when that desire is what motivates me, pushes me forward, and drives my actions? And how can I desire specific outcomes without being attached to them?

Stephen Cope beautifully answers these questions in *The Great Work of Your Life*, his application of the *Bhagavad Gita* to living one's purpose. Over many centuries, he explains, and many failed efforts to eradicate desire by willing it away, yogis have discerned there are two aspects to desire: One is **grasping and craving**, which takes you out of the present and inevitably leads to suffering. The other is **aspiration**, which is the salutary aspect of desire that comes from our highest selves—meaning we aspire with resolve and determination to achieve what is good and noble.

Both kinds of desire can be highly energizing, but in different ways. The energy of *grasping* is stirred up, restless, tunnel-visioned, and separating, while the energy of *aspiring* is at ease, with inner calm, quiet determination, and unity.

In business, we experience a lot of grasping and clinging, which is not good. Cope says:

> Clinging to outcomes has a pernicious effect on performance. Clinging (or grasping) of any kind disturbs the mind. And this disturbed mind, then, is not really fully present to the task at hand. It is forever leaning into the next moment – grabbing. And, not being present for the moment, it cannot fully devote its powers to the job at hand.

In other words, grasping interferes with being mindful, with being present. The benefits of mindfulness for business are well documented, and include greater emotional intelligence, improved focus, and greater productivity, to name a few. The bottom line? We give up these benefits when we are grasping for results.

WINDOW
My A2O Experience with Money, Growth, and Acquisition

When I was 20+ years into my consulting practice, I started to explore the possibility of selling my firm, ResearchWorks. At the time, I had a small staff of excellent employees. We were doing good work with clients we loved, grossing a modest $1 to $1.5 million annually. The combination provided professional gratification as well as a decent living. After doing some research, I found that the sweet spot for consulting firms like mine being acquired was annual revenues between 10 and 15 million, so that became the outcome I wanted.

I explicitly set an aggressive goal of doubling our revenues every 18 months. My math told me that would increase our annual revenues to about 12 million in under five years, a perfect time for acquisition – and with that, financial freedom. I had also looked into which factors affected business valuations, but instead of systematically addressing them, I kept reminding myself of the financial goal: double every 18 months, double every 18 months, double every 18 months.

I remember the feelings that accompanied this goal. On one hand, I felt an unsettled "stirring up" about the idea of rapid growth leading to successful acquisition. But the stirred-up sensation that I labeled as excitement (social science research tells us that we can assign different emotional labels for the same state of physiological arousal) felt like a tightness inside me – a constricting of energy and narrowing of possibilities, not an openness or expansion. My attitude was simply: this outcome will happen because I want it to be so.

Over time, our business strategy changed. We stopped pursuing smaller projects and focused most of our attention on winning the most profitable gigs with bigger clients who had greater needs and more money. This in and of itself was not bad; it was the grasping energy of desire that went with it that was problematic. In short, I let financial considerations override many other decision criteria. Before long, my business resembled a roller-coaster. Our staffing became shaky and misaligned with our financial goals. Morale was affected. I was becoming less productive and happy and was hard-pressed to provide inspired leadership. The quality of my work suffered too, which was not good for my team or our clients.

Though I was diligently meditating every day as I have been for decades, and was trying to be mindful and honest, I ignored the fundamental unease I felt in my gut toward this financial goal. *I have to have this outcome*, I thought, so that meant I couldn't question it. What about the fact that deep inside I knew I was operating out of alignment with what the universe had in store? I simply pretended I didn't know what I knew and ignored signals to the contrary. And I continued to cling to that financial outcome intensely, even as it became apparent that we were not on course to achieve it.

After a couple years of this, it was – ironically – our disappointing financials that propelled me to yield and let go of the grasping and clinging attachment to my desire, to accept that a different goal, a different energy, and a different direction was needed. It was a painful and powerful lesson in the costs of being attached to outcomes in business. And it led to making good money in a different way and me writing the book you are reading right now.

Returning to the *Bhagavad Gita*, Krishna points out that when someone is motivated only by their desire for results—for the fruits of their actions—they become constantly anxious about generating those results. This kind of grasping desire produces attachment, which leads to suffering.

In contrast, aspirational desire begins with being *unattached to outcomes.*

Cope says, "It's not about being unattached to your actions, or being dispassionate in your work, or being disconnected from your purpose. To the contrary." What occurs is that when your mind is not obsessed with the desire of grasping and clinging, it is free, clear, resolute, and at ease. In this state, you can be totally absorbed in what you're doing, completely and authentically engaged, and fully aligned with your higher purpose.

To be clear, goals or outcomes per se are not the problem. As Csíkszentmihályi explains, "The pursuit of a goal brings order into awareness because a person must concentrate attention on the task at hand and momentarily forget everything else." The key point here is to use the desired outcome to direct all your energy into the work, which can take you into an optimal state of consciousness. This is where happiness comes from, and this is why Krishna advises Arjuna to *solely* focus on doing the best job he can, and not be concerned about the results.

MIRROR
Is Your A2O Bringing You Down?

Consider these questions about yourself as they pertain to attachment to outcomes.

1. How often do goals or desired outcomes distract you from doing your best work?

2. How often do you feel "in the flow" in business?

3. Have you experienced the connection between being fully absorbed in your work and the results you generate?

4. To what extent is your self-esteem tied to making money or achieving other results?

5. Can you imagine simply aspiring to goals without clinging or grasping toward them?

6. Can you think about business without hyperfocusing on outcomes?

Based on your answers to these questions, place yourself on the scale below with regard to how much you're attached to outcomes—with 1 being all the time, and 10 being never.

Now consider the following questions with regard to your company.

1. Does your company prioritize achieving outcomes at all costs?

2. How are employees treated when they do their best and still fall short of expectations?

3. Can you envision your company aspiring toward specific goals without being obsessed by them?

Based on your answers to these questions, place your company on the scale below with regard to how much it's attached to outcomes—with 1 being all the time, and 10 being never.

The bottom line is, even if your company is only about results, you can still choose to be unattached. Is it easy to be unattached to outcomes? No. People practice mindfulness, meditation, compassion, etc. for decades and still slip up. Grasping and aspiring can also easily be confused, especially when our egos get involved. Knowing and managing our egos, our desires, and our attachments is a lifetime project. But when we let go of these long-held habits, particularly in business, and become more mindful and less attached to outcomes, we return to our natural state of being uplifted and connected—the energy of love. And when we're able to return to the energy of love, there is greater compassion, fulfillment, and unity—and less greed, separateness, and suffering.

DOOR

The following tips will help you become aware if you're steeped in "grasping" and bring you back to "aspiring."

- Learn what attachment feels like in your body and mind by concentrating your attention on something you feel a "grasping" attachment to—a production milestone, a sales goal, a raise, etc.

- Do an honest self-assessment of what outcomes in your work you are attached to, then imagine not achieving those outcomes and mentally play out what might happen. Then shrug it off.

- Notice, without judgment, whenever you feel the clinging and grasping kind of desire. Now actively choose to let it go and refocus on your work.

- Introduce the idea of non-attachment into your company and suggest a one-week "awareness" experiment to try it out with no risk.

- Surround yourself with people who support you in having aspirational desires and in not getting so wrapped up in outcomes.

- Be present and practice mindfulness. When you drift off, gently bring yourself back to full focus on the task at hand.

- Meditate, every day. Start with sixty seconds, eight breaths in and out through the nose. Occupy your mind by saying to yourself "I am breathing in" with each inhale, and "I am breathing out" with each exhale.[65]

WELCOMING CHANGE INSTEAD OF SUCCUMBING TO THE STATUS QUO BIAS

Catching the Amare Wave naturally involves change, yet many of us are resistant to it, and because of that, we sometimes sabotage our best interests. For a variety of reasons, we default into sticking with the way things are. From our resistance to move from horses to cars a century ago (and for some, to autonomous self-driving cars today), to voting familiar politicians back into office—even when they've done virtually nothing to effect positive change—to eating "comfort" foods we know don't promote health, we are a species that tends to feel most comfortable doing what we've always done, even when it doesn't bring us the results we wish for. This is called the **status quo bias**, a well-studied phenomenon, particularly in the field of behavioral economics.

If you are not aware of how this dynamic of resistance to change works, it could easily throw you off course in catching and riding the Amare Wave. This section, however, will help you avoid that.

In business today, we see numerous places where we resist change and stay with the status quo:

- As leaders, we may keep with an innovation approach, HR plan, or sales strategy even though it's not working.

- We may keep the same policies and procedures in place even when they cause unnecessary bottlenecks.

- We may retain people who don't do a good job, despite multiple efforts to improve.

- We may stay in roles that are not a good fit and suffer from the mismatch as a result.

Why do we do this? One major reason is fear: fear of a loss of status or security; fear of possible failure; fear of criticism and rejection; fear of the unknown. But there are also external forces, such as peer pressure, a climate of mistrust, organizational politics, or compensation dynamics. And we all know how powerful culture is in business—it is designed to maintain things as they are.

And it's not only those of us who lead businesses. Customers, too, often resist change. A classic example comes from the soft drink industry. Back in 1985, and with much fanfare, Coca Cola brought "New Coke" to market to replace its original Coke formulation. Blind taste tests had shown that many Coke drinkers preferred its sweeter taste over the original Coke flavor. But the switch garnered a great deal of highly publicized derision, mainly from people upset that the company had taken away what they were used to—or rather, the status quo. The problem was not about taste, per se; it was that the company underestimated customer reactions to what they perceived as a loss. After seventy-nine days, the original Coke formula was brought back, and eventually the new flavor was put to rest.

What happened here? The relevant lessons in this example are threefold and can be applied to a variety of products and services:

1. **Customers want to be able to count on you.** For example, we frequent the same restaurants and coffee houses in multiple cities because we reliably know what we'll get.

2. **Loyalty runs deep.** Research shows that people attach value to what they are used to, simply because they are used to it. In a sense, it is "theirs." Taking that away feels like an affront to their loyalty and a devaluing of the relationship.

3. **Customer research needs to be nuanced to reveal loyalties and the biases they induce.** Coke had clues from their qualitative research, but they ignored them in favor of taste test results that supported the outcome they wanted.

So, if I'm encouraging you to break away from the status quo, why am I painting a bleak picture of how unwilling people are to change and how resistant your customers might be to it? Because I want to acknowledge that resistance to change for most people is a constant challenge; it frequently seems easier and even safer to stick with what we have.

The movie *Moneyball* depicts a great example of this in the big business of professional baseball.

Early on, Oakland Athletics' General Manager Billy Beane needs to put together a winning team, but he has a relatively measly budget and just lost three of his star players to rival teams, including a five-time All-Star and MVP. Billy pleads with his boss for more money but gets a clear *no*, coupled with advice to do what they always do to get the players they need.

The most revealing scene is a meeting between manager Billy Beane and the team's professional and seasoned scouts, discussing which players to bring on to fill the big holes they have. Billy recognizes they are trying to do what they've always done, with the traditional approach of replacing the players they lost with those who have similar skills – and Billy also knows this won't work, especially with their limited and non-competitive budget. Instead, he tells them that they need to think of how to get to the World Series with less money and no superstars, describing alternative ways to scout players and build a winning team. He pushes for doing things differently, and ultimately rejects the status quo approach because he knows it won't work for their situation.

In the end, however, the scouts are adamant about maintaining the status quo, despite the fact that there isn't evidence that their traditional approach works, and that they don't have enough money to recruit superstars. In pursuing "what they know," they simply do what is comfortable and safe. As a result, they avoid taking risks and opening themselves (being vulnerable) to criticism and potential failure from doing something different.

Without giving away the ending, I'll just say that Billy goes with his gut and bravely rejects the status quo. He takes a big risk with a very different and novel approach, and the team does well. Even better? The approach he uses becomes the new status quo in the major leagues. Nice Hollywood ending for a true story.

As I watched that movie, it reminded me of what an almost client once told me: "I think your group is the best fit and can really help us. But it's riskier to engage your boutique firm. No one ever gets fired for hiring McKinsey or Boston Consulting Group. That's a safer bet with my Board." And that's what they did.

Behavioral economics research gives us a lot of explanations for the status quo bias: loss avoidance, choice overload, regret avoidance, risk aversion, etc. You have probably experienced that in business, "sunk costs"—or the fear of trying something new and being wrong—often keep companies doing what is clearly not working. They are so invested in what they've been doing, it seems impossible to them to change.

Now, I am not advocating always choosing change over the status quo. At times, it is actually counterproductive to do so. The status quo bias does, in fact, have its benefits: it lets us avoid the downside risk of choosing something that's "not as good" as what we had before, and it can save us from going through a lot of work to evaluate options and make a decision. Because of this, in some business situations, maintaining the status quo can be the better choice—especially if we don't necessarily need or benefit from "new and improved."

But a business should never get too stuck that they don't grow and innovate with the times. They should frequently entertain fresh perspectives that may change their trajectory, make tweaks to a product or service offering, and let go of patterns and traditions that simply aren't working any longer. And they should consider these changes keeping in mind the desires of their customers (this is where customer collaboration is key!) and recognizing that it may indeed be necessary to lose some customers as they make positive leaps forward. It all depends on the objective of the initiative.

Let's see what this Mirror activity reveals to you about how often you tend to get stuck in the status quo.

MIRROR
Are You Status Quo or Status No?

Consider the following with regard to yourself in business.

1. Do you typically resist doing things differently at work?

2. Under what business circumstances do you avoid risk?

3. Do you jump on the change bandwagon because you are drawn to excitement?

4. Under what business circumstances do you seek out or welcome risk?

5. Are you the change agent or the naysayer in your company?

Based on your answers to these questions, place yourself on the scale below with regard to how often you tend to stay with the status quo—with 1 being all the time, and 10 being never.

Note here that the bias toward the status quo becomes a problem when it shuts us down and actually *costs us the upside benefit* of something better. In short, the trap is that the more you sink into the status quo, the more you will continue to sink into the status quo.

So, what to do? Here are a few concrete actions you can take.

DOOR

- When you are facing possible change, you need to determine if maintaining the status quo makes sense, or if the bias is leading you to make sub-optimal decisions and avoid change. You can do this by first noticing if you feel resistance — a restricting of your breathing, narrowing of your thinking, or hardening of your beliefs. Notice, too, your cognitive machinations that may support the status quo. Simply becoming aware of resistance and your accompanying thought process can help you make a more considered and even-handed decision.

- Sometimes the mere prospect of change can induce an acute stress response — and not just fight or flight, but also freeze or faint (i.e., resignation or collapse). When you find that happening, the instant antidote is to move your body in a specific way (in an appropriate place). For example, per Dr. Katie Hendricks's "fear melters," sway to counter a fight response, and shake (like dogs do!) to counter a freeze response.

- To habituate yourself to change (excuse the oxymoron!), try little things with virtually zero risk. For example, if you cross your left leg over your right in meetings, do the opposite. Same with how you fold your hands. Or try sitting in a different chair. (It amazes me, when I teach graduate courses, how many students sit in the same seat week after week, as though they own it!) Take a different route when you drive to work. Eat something new for lunch. Type in a different font. Get a new coffee mug. In short, mix it up!

Many of the exercises I've shared throughout the book center on knowing yourself, being honest and vulnerable about what is influencing you, and being in alignment with yourself and your company's vision and purpose. All of these will also help you recognize and, when appropriate, dismiss the status quo bias.

KNOWING HOW AND WHEN TO SIDESTEP A MISMATCH

What happens when your business objective and desired overall work environment is not aligned with your company's vision, culture, or modus operandi? What if you want your company to be more love-like, but that is not the way it operates, nor is it their vision? We all know that entrenched habits are hard to change.

As a business leader, you may be in a position to advocate, influence, or make the beneficial changes we've discussed throughout this book. Of course, part of that depends on your role, connections, and power; and part depends on external forces, like timing, corporate legacy, and other mitigating circumstances. Perhaps you can facilitate change at an overall corporate level, or maybe you can make incremental change within a business unit or department. Or maybe you're in a position where you feel your voice doesn't count much at all.

In Chapter Seven, I had you do three different Mirror segments that focused on assessing alignment—within your company, with yourself, and between you and your company. Please refer back to those now on pages 116 and 120–22. If your assessment of your company's alignment, and of the alignment between you and your company, were low or moderate, the following sections will be critical in helping you determine your next steps if indeed you have a mismatch. And if you didn't complete those Mirror activities, here are the pertinent segments again so that you can complete them now.

Alignment Within Your Company

Consider how aligned you are—or aren't—with your company by noting your level of agreement with the following statements on a scale of 1 to 5, with 1 being not aligned, and 5 being completely aligned.

_____ There is consistency and integrity across my company's corporate vision, strategy, and execution.

_____ There is consistency and integrity across my company's purpose, values, and brand identity.

_____ There is consistency and integrity across my company's value proposition and the value it delivers.

_____ What my company believes, says, and does all match.

_____ There is consistency and integrity in how my company behaves behind the scenes, when doing business, and in society at large.

Based on your ratings to these questions, rate your company's overall alignment—with 1 being completely out of alignment, and 10 being completely in alignment.

1	2	3	4	5	6	7	8	9	10
O	O	O	O	O	O	O	O	O	O

Being in Alignment

Consider how aligned you are—or aren't—by noting your level of agreement with the following statements on a scale of 1 to 5, with 1 being not aligned, and 5 being completely aligned.

_____ I generally feel in alignment with myself in business.

_____ I stay true to my core values and beliefs at work.

_____ I feel genuine and authentic as a business leader.

_____ I feel connected with something bigger than myself.

_____ I feel uplifted—and uplifting—in my leadership role.

___ I feel I am on my right path for now.

___ I know how my body feels when I'm true to myself.

___ I know how my body feels when I'm not true to myself.

Based on your answers to these questions, place yourself on the scale below with regard to how in alignment you are with yourself —with 1 being completely out of alignment, and 10 being completely in alignment.

| 1 | 2 | 3 | 4 | 5 | 6 | 7 | 8 | 9 | 10 |

I would suggest that if you scored five or lower on either of these assessments, you may need to seriously evaluate if you are indeed in the right career or workplace. I know it can be very disheartening, but if you determine that alignment is lacking either *within* your company or *between* you and your company, you *can* and *should* make a conscious choice.

CHOICE #1. Acknowledge the mismatch for what it is, yet choose to stay with the company and put up with the lack of alignment. You may choose this less than favorable option for numerous reasons: money, job security, health insurance, future pension, resume-building, lack of other jobs in your area, high unemployment rates, low self-confidence, fear of change, feeling stuck, commitment to the cause, cherished coworkers or customers, the list goes on. By knowing precisely why you are staying and feeling the reasons are justified, it may trouble you less because you are being as authentic as you can be while sticking with the company. Even though this choice isn't ideal, making an informed and conscious choice may give you a sense of empowerment.

If this is your choice, however, I strongly recommend that you develop and use targeted coping mechanisms so that self-criticism and regret don't plague you, and so that you don't grow to harbor anger and resentment toward your colleagues and company. An example of what I mean is illustrated in the following brief story.

A good friend of mine, a well-respected physician-executive, chose to stay with a prominent healthcare system for an additional five years under its new leadership, even though the culture became all about money, and their values were the antithesis of his. He was miserable and hated being at work, yet he believed in the institution's purpose and knew his presence would keep them on a better track. He also knew he would fully achieve his retirement goals and enable his wife to retire per her plan if he stuck it out a few more years.

To counter the negativity at work, he dove deeply into his yoga and meditation practice, bought a small parcel of land and a house in the country, and became a "gentlemen farmer" (and tractor driver!). He also made sure to devote more time to being with his wife, kids, and grandkids.

While his work life wasn't as fulfilling, these other pursuits were fully aligned with his values and his own higher purpose, providing him with feelings of connection and of being uplifted. By taking care of himself in these ways, he could consciously keep working at the healthcare organization—even with the fundamental mismatch in values and goals—and have the wherewithal to continue making the biggest difference there he possibly could.

CHOICE #2. Stay in your job, but try to influence your company toward a more love-like way of operating. If the culture is so strongly entrenched in warlike thinking, or leadership is so desperate about making payroll, that there seems to be no space for love, it may be difficult to propose changes or approach leadership with suggestions without jeopardizing your job. But if you believe in the power of love in business and want to move the company in that direction, here are a few things you can do.

DOOR

- Approach the powers that be and offer respectful suggestions for making room for different thinking that can reduce frustration, make people happier, and achieve better results. Note that you'll need to come in with a strong business case supported by relevant anecdotes, data, and success stories to back your request — especially in an entrenched culture or during desperate times.

- Simply start conducting your work activities with the energy of love and see what happens. Begin with behavior, and let beliefs follow. Doing little things like smiling more, thanking people, telling stories of customer happiness, or mentioning your shared higher purpose has the potential to influence others in a positive way.

- Consider going counter-culture. My colleague and former client Natalie Neelan wrote **Rebel at Work: How to Innovate and Drive Results When You Aren't the Boss** to address this specific conundrum. In the book, she bluntly shares techniques for becoming what she dubs a smuggler, a rebel "smuggling" in value, collaborative spirit, and good ideas in toxic work environments. This approach can be risky, as you could lose your job or become further disenfranchised, but it can also be highly rewarding in that you are taking appropriate action aligned with who you are and what you believe is best for the company and its customers.

CHOICE #3. Bravely recognize that you cannot or will not work at a company that does not share your values. Staying would mean that the misalignment between company values and your values would require you to make too many compromises, which in turn would pull you out of alignment with yourself and sap your energy (perhaps it already has). In this case, you would start creating or looking for a new position more in line with your values and desired work environment, give the proper notice, and leave when you were able.

EMBRACING MONEY AS A GIFT, NOT A GOD

In Chapter Two, we talked about the positive role of money within the Amare Wave movement, so you already know that financial gain is integral to being an Amare Way company and that love-centered companies are highly profitable. There's no doubt that money is an important and necessary concern of most successful people and companies; it is the emotional baggage we attach to it that creates problems.

From an Amare Way perspective, we value money for all the good it can do. As the main medium of economic exchange around the world, money simplifies things because it is measurable and comparable. Money is thereby something companies can easily organize around—but this ease becomes a downside when money is the *primary* component they organize around.

As I described in Chapter Four, maximizing profit, or shareholder return, has been the main objective for many businesses for a long time. Money—within numerous companies—has thereby become like a god and worshipped as such. The seemingly righteous goal of amassing money has come to justify the means—any means—of getting it, which frequently leads us to ignore our ethics, compromise our values, and cause tremendous suffering to other people and our planet. Within warlike business, and certainly within politics as well, there are countless examples of almost unfathomable acts, where the idolization of money is used to vindicate the damage done in its wake.

From reading this book—and perhaps by simply being the person you are—you intuitively know that money is a false god, like the biblical golden calf. As such, it is never the *reason* to be in business; *higher purpose* is. Recall the company profiles I shared with you in Chapter Two—Trader Joe's, USAA, Southwest Airlines, REI, Costco, and TOMS. They are all hugely successful from a financial standpoint, and they are also 100 percent committed to their higher purpose. Monetary returns are a gift for them, not a god. Their profits not only allow these companies to compensate all members of the company well, but the funds are used to provide excellent employee benefits, establish nonprofits devoted to the greater good, advocate for environmental causes, lend to animal and planetary welfare, uphold sustainability practices, bring desired items into the marketplace, better the lives of the disenfranchised, support military families, and more. And all of those profits are earned through ethical business practices focused on making life better for people.

In short, the desire for money is not inherently good or bad. In our culture, making money is critical to companies and people— and there's nothing wrong with that, **as long as we don't let the desire for money override our other values or cloud our perceptions and priorities**.

To give you another perspective on why "money as god" is so destructive on a deep level, I ask you to consider this:

When a group kills innocent citizens in order to wipe out what they consider evil, or follow their religious convictions, or worship their "god," we call it terrorism. We cannot understand how people could do that. We abhor it. We repudiate it with laws and policies. We judge and punish it harshly, all while the killers justify their actions as the will of God.

Yet when a company hurts innocent citizens in order to wipe out competition, or follow their growth strategy, or worship their god (money), we call it business. We not only understand how a company could do that, we often accept and even admire it. Worse, we enable it with laws and policies, and we even judge and reward it generously. In concert, the company justifies its actions as the way of business.

Kind of bizarre when you see the two perspectives juxtaposed like that, isn't it?

Let's take a minute here to do a Mirror activity to assess how you view money. Remember, be honest with yourself. This can be a touchy topic for a lot of people, but it's worth acknowledging where you truly stand.

MIRROR
The Buck Stops . . . Where?

---

1. How do you view the role of money in your life?

2. Do you worship money?

3. Does the desire for money rule you?

4. Do you believe money buys happiness?

5. Do you dislike money?

6. Do you feel undeserving of prosperity?

7. Do you believe that people are wrong if they desire a lot of money?

8. What is more important to you than money?

9. What would you be willing to do for money? In business? In your personal life?

10. What would you absolutely not do for money? In business? In your personal life?

When you compare your answers to the last two questions, are you surprised by the gap between what you would do and what you wouldn't do? Is there a definitive line for you?

Based on your answers to all of the questions, place yourself on the scale below with regard to what degree you view money as a god—with 1 being the ruling element of your life and your decisions, whether ethical or not, and 10 being a vital part of existence but never one you would compromise your ethics, values, or the well-being of others to obtain.

Look, I get it: in business, the things that constitute your higher purpose are more difficult to measure than money. They do not directly buy you things or pay your bills—money does. But while money is definitely something to aspire to make, to share, and to enjoy, it is not worthy of worship. The sacrifice is too great. Once again, if there is something to be "worshipped" in business, it is our higher purpose. And when money flows from doing work that provides value to society, alleviates suffering, and improves lives, it truly is a gift that can be used to afford you an abundant life, both for your family and for the causes you choose to support.

DOOR

I return to Chapter Two once again, where I provided a list of guidelines to help you make decisions that uphold a respect for money. These same statements, reworded slightly, will also help you to avoid allowing money to rule your life as a god.

If your money-making action . . .

- deceives anyone, you don't pursue it.

- harms anyone, you don't pursue it.

- requires you to bend your ethics, you don't pursue it.

- is not aligned with your core values, you don't pursue it.

- unsettles anyone on the decision-making team, you listen and are open to re-evaluation.

- would damage or destroy your reputation should it become public or its motives were revealed, you don't pursue it.

- would require a cover-up, you don't pursue it.

Do not value money for any more nor any less than it's worth;
it is a good servant but a bad master.

—ALEXANDER DUMAS

Ready to make some changes?

These final two chapters are intended
to help you move successfully from
awareness to action as an Amare Way
company.

The compilation of the 22 Mirror
exercises, along with dozens of Key
Takeaways and Action Steps, will
serve as an easy-to-follow self-
assessment guide and action plan.
(And if you're not quite ready to take
that leap, that's okay too. You can
skip for now to the Conclusion on
page 319 and come back to these
chapters later.)

I can't wait to see you
riding the Wave!

TAKE A
GOOD LOOK
AT YOURSELF
BEFORE
YOU CRITICIZE
ANOTHER,
FOR WHAT
YOU SEE WRONG
IN THEM
WILL ALSO BE
A LESSON
FOR YOU.

CHAPTER ELEVEN

ONE MORE LOOK AT YOURSELF AND YOUR COMPANY: THE MIRROR ACTIVITIES AND ASSESSMENTS AT A GLANCE

While you may have completed the Mirror activities chapter by chapter, I realize that you also may have skipped some or all of them in favor of taking in all of the content first. Either way, I want to give you an opportunity to easily access all of the Mirror activities in one place, organized by chapter.

If you have already completed all the Mirror activities, you can skip to the "Big Picture" section on page 263. Once there, I recommend that you go back in the book to the assessment bars you filled in at the end of each Mirror (page numbers are provided) and fill them in here as well. That way, you can see them all in one place for a more holistic view and use them as a benchmark as you set priorities and strive to score higher in the various categories. Note that all of the assessment bars are designed such that the higher the score, the more aligned you are with *amare* beliefs and actions.

If you haven't yet completed the Mirror Activities, I strongly suggest you take the time to do so now. Reflecting on the various questions and answering them truthfully will allow you to have a clear view of where your strengths and opportunities lie, and you'll be able to focus on improving through the suggestions I've given you in the Door segments, as well as the Getting Started Action Steps I offer you in Chapter Twelve.

Let's take a look in the Mirror (again)!

Chapter Four

A SHORT IN THE HARDWIRING:
HOW WE'VE ADOPTED A BUSINESS AS WAR MENTALITY

MIRROR
Measuring Your
"Business as War" Beliefs

The wording of the questions in this mirror exercise is one-sided by design to help you expose your beliefs to yourself. Be honest, even if you don't like what comes out. Respond to each on a 1 to 5 scale, with 1 being Strongly Disagree and 5 being Strongly Agree.

- Business is war.
- We need to fight to win in business.
- The world is here for us.
- Greed is good in business.
- Making money trumps everything.
- Competitors are enemies to be destroyed.
- Customers are prey to be captured.
- Employees are commodities.
- Business is "us" vs. "them."

Based on your answers to these questions, place yourself on the scale below with regard to how you view business as war—with 1 seeing business completely as war, and 10 not seeing business as war at all.

> ## MIRROR
> ### How "Good" Are You in Business?

1. Is your company ethically good? Under what conditions?

2. Does your company compromise its values? Under what conditions?

3. Is your company generally warlike?

Based on your answers to these questions, place your company on the scale below with regard to how "good" you are in business —with 1 ranking low, and 10 ranking best.

> ## MIRROR
> ### How Predatory Is Your Language?

1. Have you noticed the violence in the language of business?

2. When you think about how pervasive it is in business, does it bother you?

3. Is violent or predatory language commonly used in your company?

4. Do you tend to use warlike euphemisms in your work?

5. Do you believe business needs this kind of language in order to motivate people?

6. Do the words you use in business match your values and beliefs?

7. Can you imagine eliminating violence-laden language in your company?

8. Do you believe business can be highly profitable without resorting to warlike language?

9. Will you commit to replacing predatory words with more compassionate language?

Based on your answers to these questions, place yourself on the scale below with regard to how prevalent predatory language is in your work world—with 1 being highly prevalent and 10 being nonexistent.

Chapter Five

IF YOUR BUSINESS IS MISSING LOVE, ARE **YOU** MISSING LOVE?

MIRROR
How Vulnerable Are You at Work?

1. Do you believe vulnerability is good for business?

2. Do you believe vulnerability is more a sign of weakness or strength?

3. Do you know how to be vulnerable at work?

4. Under what conditions do you show vulnerability at work?

5. Do you hide things about yourself or your actions for fear of criticism or rejection?

6. Do you sometimes feel fearful or insecure in business and are afraid to show it?

7. Do you know what it feels like to be vulnerable and accepted at work?

8. Do you trust others at work enough to show your vulnerabilities?

9. Do others at work trust you enough to show you their vulnerabilities?

10. Do you demonstrate to others that it is okay to be vulnerable at work?

Based on your answers to these questions, place yourself on the scale below with regard to how willing you are to be vulnerable at work—with 1 being not at all willing, and 10 being fully willing.

MIRROR
How Incivil Are You at Work?

---

1. Do you act rudely to your coworkers?

2. Do you make hostile or condescending comments?

3. Do you ignore or exclude people in your workplace?

4. Do you make jokes at other people's expense?

5. Do you ever resort to bullying and meanness in your interactions?

6. Do your words or actions make others uncomfortable?

7. Do you smile or say hello to coworkers?

8. Do you acknowledge coworkers when you walk by each other?

9. Do you say thank you when someone does something kind for you?

10. Do you put your phone away during meetings?

11. Do you speak up when you witness incivility?

Based on your answers to these questions, place yourself on the scale below with regard to how incivil you tend to be toward others—with 1 being all the time, and 10 being never.

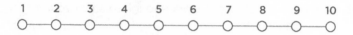

MIRROR
How Arrogant Are You at Work?

1. Do you generally believe you know better than everyone else?

2. Do you ever become overbearing or threatening in your dealings with others?

3. Do you find yourself contemptuous of others?

4. Do you criticize others in a threatening or hostile way?

5. Do you find it difficult or even unbearable to honestly consider others' perspectives?

6. Do you find it a waste of time to explain your decisions to others?

7. Do you get defensive when your opinions are challenged?

8. Do you equate arrogance with confidence or strength of character?

9. Do you use arrogance to try to bolster your self-esteem?

Based on your answers to these questions, place yourself on the scale below with regard to how arrogant you tend to be toward others—with 1 being all the time, and 10 being never.

Chapter Six

IS FEAR ENERGY RULING YOUR BUSINESS?

MIRROR
Fear/Ego Responses vs.
Love/Heart Responses

1. You pitch a new idea that isn't well received. Your response is:

2. You make a mistake that costs your company a lot of money or some degree of embarrassment. Your response is:

3. You get laid off during an economic downturn or other restructuring within the company. Your response is:

4. A bully at work flies off the handle at you. Your response is:

5. Your company's stock value drops precipitously. Your response is:

6. Your performance is evaluated and you don't believe it reflects the work you've been putting in. Your response is:

7. A customer says something nasty, but true, about your company. Your response is:

Based on your responses to these questions, place yourself on the scale below with regard to how often you tend to react from fear vs. how often you react from love—with 1 being always from fear, and 10 being always from love.

| 1 | 2 | 3 | 4 | 5 | 6 | 7 | 8 | 9 | 10 |

MIRROR
Gauging Customer Hatred

1. Does your company hate, disdain, or dislike its customers?

   If you answered yes:

2. In what ways is that conveyed to employees?

3. In what ways is that conveyed to customers?

4. Hate is fueled by fear. Does your company operate out of fear?

   If you answered yes:

5. How do you see it manifested toward employees?

6. How do you see it manifested toward customers?

Based on your answers to these questions, place yourself on the scale below with regard to how your company feels about its customers—with 1 being hateful toward them all of the time, and 10 being loving toward them all of the time.

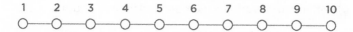

MIRROR
Where Do You Fall on the Engaged-O-Meter?

Place a checkmark next to all the statements that merit a yes.

o   I feel engaged in my work most days.

o   I believe in the company mission.

o   I feel motivated to do my best.

○   I feel seen and heard at work.

○   I want to be there.

○   I feel valued.

○   I believe what I do at work is important.

○   I feel connected to the people at my company.

○   I feel uplifted by my work.

Based on your responses to these questions, place yourself on the scale below with regard to how engaged you feel at work—with 1 being not engaged at all, and 10 being wholly engaged.

| 1 | 2 | 3 | 4 | 5 | 6 | 7 | 8 | 9 | 10 |

Chapter Seven

TO THINE OWN SELF—AND BUSINESS—BE TRUE: THE IMPORTANCE OF ALIGNMENT

MIRROR

Is Your Company in Alignment?

Consider how aligned your company is—or isn't—by noting your level of agreement with the following statements on a scale of 1 to 5, with 1 being not aligned, and 5 being completely aligned.

____ There is consistency and integrity across your corporate vision, strategy, and execution.

____ There is consistency and integrity across your purpose, values, and brand identity.

____ There is consistency and integrity across and your value proposition and the value you deliver.

____ What you as a company believe, say, and do all match.

____ There is consistency and integrity in how your company behaves behind the scenes, when doing business, and in society at large.

____ All the ways you show up are situationally appropriate and in sync.

Based on your ratings to these questions, place yourself on the scale below with regard to how in alignment your company is overall—with 1 being completely out of alignment, and 10 being completely in alignment.

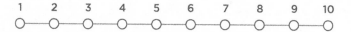

> # MIRROR
> ## Being in Alignment; Staying in Alignment

Consider how aligned you are—or aren't—by noting your level of agreement with the following statements on a scale of 1 to 5, with 1 being not aligned, and 5 being completely aligned.

Being in Alignment

____ I generally feel in alignment with myself in business.

____ I stay true to my core values and beliefs at work.

____ I feel genuine and authentic as a business leader.

____ I feel connected with something bigger than myself.

____ I feel uplifted—and uplifting—in my leadership role.

____ I feel I am on my right path for now.

____ I know how my body feels when I'm true to myself.

____ I know how my body feels when I'm not true to myself.

Based on your answers to these questions, place yourself on the scale below with regard to how in alignment you are with yourself —with 1 being completely out of alignment, and 10 being completely in alignment.

Staying in Alignment with Yourself

1. What business situations or people tend to strengthen your alignment?

2. What business situations or people tend to pull you out of alignment?

3. What do you do in the moment when you feel yourself being pulled out of alignment?

4. What do you do in the moment when you notice you are not aligned with yourself?

5. How do you enable yourself to stay out of alignment with yourself?

6. What do you do to prevent being pulled out of alignment with yourself?

7. What do you do to get yourself back into alignment with yourself?

8. What do you do to overcome your own resistance to getting yourself back into alignment?

9. What do you do when you notice you are back into alignment?

Based on your answers to these questions, place yourself on the scale below with regard to how you keep yourself in alignment— with 1 being not so good at staying in alignment, and 10 being excellent at staying in alignment.

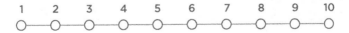

Chapter Eight

THE AMARE WAY PHILOSOPHY: GROUNDING YOUR BUSINESS
IN SEVEN FOUNDATIONAL PRINCIPLES

MIRROR
The Amare Way Philosophy and Your Company At-A-Glance

For each principle, rate your company on all three criteria. In each box, put in a ✓ for YES, a ✓✓ for a strong YES, an X for no, or an XX for a strong NO.

	We believe this	We practice this	We reward this
Treat one another well			
Inspire connection			
Get on purpose			
Respect money			
Choose love over fear			
Take the long view			
Prioritize relationships			

Now, go down the "We believe this" column and notice which of the principles you do and don't believe and to what extent. Then look across each row to see how aligned and consistent your beliefs and actions are, and how well you reward what you believe in and do. Consider what enables and impedes your Amare Way beliefs, actions, and rewards.

If you're feeling the positive energy (internal feeling of expansion) of adopting the Amare Way philosophy within your company, consider the following options:

- You can go all in with the seven principles and make them your own to fit your culture.

- You can choose with your team a few high-priority principles and integrate those immediately, with an eye toward consistency across beliefs, actions, and rewards. Then you can work toward integrating the other principles within an appropriate timeframe.

- You can also start slow with investing your energy, particularly if you feel you are light years away from a love-centered philosophy.

  For example, if the "We believe this" is filled with Xs, then it will be a heavy lift to fully adopt the Amare Way philosophy. It can be done, especially if you are doing a corporate reboot of sorts, but it will require incredible fortitude and sufficient resources to keep it going in the face of what may be strong resistance. In this case, consider choosing one principle and invest your efforts there. You'll find that the results will flow over into the other principles, making it easier to incorporate them. Remember, too, that sometimes it's easier to change behaviors than it is beliefs—as in, "try it, you'll like it."

Now, based on your results in the summary chart, rate your company on the scale below with regard to how aligned it is with the Amare Way philosophy—with 1 being totally unaligned, and 10 being in line with all of the principles.

Chapter Nine

THE AMARE WAY PRACTICE:
EMBODYING THE MOVEMENT THROUGH AUTHENTICITY,
BELONGING, AND COLLABORATION

MIRROR
How Real Are You?

Answer true or false to these ten statements.

Is your company authentic?

1. We are sincerely committed to a higher purpose, a greater good.

2. We set priorities and operate based on our stated vision, purpose, and values.

3. We genuinely care about and respect all our employees and customers.

4. We promote honesty and transparency in business dealings.

5. We encourage people to bring their whole selves to work.

Are you authentic at work?

1. I feel comfortable being my whole self at work.

2. What I say and do in business is consistent with my personal beliefs and values.

3. I genuinely care about and respect my company, our employees, and customers.

4. I model authenticity in my company.

5. I always do my best at work.

Before reviewing your answers, let me say congratulations. Answering these questions honestly demonstrates authenticity, and a willingness to be vulnerable—at least with yourself—and that's a good thing!

Think about how your company did on the authenticity statements. Notice any that triggered discomfort as issues that need addressing. Now, based on your answers to the first set of statements, place your company on the scale below with regard to how authentically it operates—with 1 being completely inauthentically, and 10 being completely authentically.

Next, how did you do on the statements about you? Based on your answers to the second set of statements, place yourself on the scale below with regard to how authentically you operate at work—with 1 being completely inauthentically, and 10 being completely authentically.

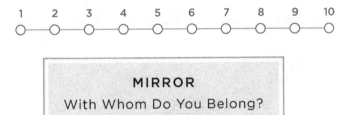

MIRROR
With Whom Do You Belong?

Think of yourself as a customer in this exercise. Your answers will reveal to you which companies you identify and belong with, and also why.

1. Which companies, large or small, are you most loyal to? Because:

2. With what companies do you feel a positive emotional connection? Because:

3. With what companies do you feel a strong sense of kinship? Because:

4. What companies do you want to go back to again and again? Because:

5. With what companies would you say "I'm a _____ kind of person." Because:

Now look at your "because" answers. Notice specifically what creates that sense of belonging for you.

Consider these questions too:

1. Do you feel uplifted when you do business with them?

2. Do they stand for values you believe in?

3. Do they offer top-quality products and/or services you know you can count on?

4. Do you trust in their ethics and the way they do business?

5. Do they boost your status or self-esteem?

6. Do you feel they genuinely understand and care about you?

MIRROR
Belonging With Your Company

For each statement, put a ✓ for YES, a ✓✓ for a strong YES, an X for no, or an XX for a strong NO.

YOU

_____ I see myself reflected in my company in positive ways.

_____ There is an emotional connection between me and my company.

_____ I feel a sense of kinship with my company.

_____ I am invested in the well-being of my company.

_____ I am a [company name] kind of person.

_____ I like identifying with my company.

EMPLOYEES

_____ Our employees see themselves reflected in the company in positive ways.

_____ There is an emotional connection between employees and the company.

_____ Employees feel a sense of kinship with the company.

_____ Employees are invested in the well-being of the company.

_____ Most employees would say they are a [company name] kind of person.

_____ Employees like identifying with my company.

CUSTOMERS

_____ Our customers see themselves reflected in the company in positive ways.

_____ There is an emotional connection between customers and the company.

_____ Customers feel a sense of kinship with the company.

_____ Customers are invested in the well-being of the company.

_____ Most customers would say they are a [company name] kind of person.

_____ Customers like identifying with the company.

If most of your answers are positive, continue what you're doing to foster identification and belonging. If not, ask yourself what would foster a greater sense of belonging—and go the extra mile and ask your employees and customers too. Then, start taking steps to act on those insights.

Based on your answers to the YOU questions, place your company on the scale below with regard to the level of belonging it fosters—with 1 being no belonging, and 10 being complete belonging.

1   2   3   4   5   6   7   8   9   10

Based on your answers to the EMPLOYEES questions, place your company on the scale below with regard to the level of belonging it fosters—with 1 being no belonging, and 10 being complete belonging.

Based on your answers to the CUSTOMERS questions, place your company on the scale below with regard to the level of belonging it fosters—with 1 being no belonging, and 10 being complete belonging.

MIRROR
Utilizing Your Employees' Gifts

1. Is meaningful collaboration part of your company culture?

2. Are employees engaged enough to want to collaborate?

3. Is collaboration rewarded in your company?

4. Do people in your company regularly collaborate in an inclusive way?

5. Do you take collaboration too far and wear people out?

6. Do you believe employees have valuable input to offer?

7. Are your collaborative activities generally uplifting?

8. Do your people feel safe enough to be honest in your collaborative efforts?

9. Do you enable "empty" collaboration just to be able to check off a box?

10. Do you believe that collaboration is a good way to empower employees?

Based on your answers to these questions, place yourself on the scale below with regard to how much your company fosters collaboration with employees—with 1 being never, and 10 being frequently.

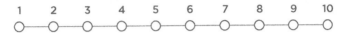

| 1 | 2 | 3 | 4 | 5 | 6 | 7 | 8 | 9 | 10 |

MIRROR
Collaborating with Customers

---

1. Do you value collaborating with customers?

2. Is customer collaboration integral to how you do business?

3. When you do collaborate, are you honest about your aims?

4. Do customers see you as a partner or merely a vendor?

5. Do you genuinely value and act on customer feedback?

6. Do you feel you have the answers and don't need much customer input?

7. Are you too busy to actively collaborate with customers?

8. Do you enable your employees to collaborate with customers?

9. Do you mainly think about collaborating when you have new products to sell?

Based on your answers to these questions, place yourself on the scale below with regard to how much you collaborate with customers—with 1 being never, and 10 being frequently.

| 1 | 2 | 3 | 4 | 5 | 6 | 7 | 8 | 9 | 10 |

MIRROR

Are Your Competitors Sometimes
Your Collaborators?

Which best represents your company's general attitude toward collaborating with your competitors:

a) Over my dead body.

b) Only when we have to.

c) We'd consider it case by case.

d) It's a key strategy for us.

e) We're eager to help competitors.

Now, answer yes or no to the following to indicate your beliefs:

1. When we help competitors, we hurt ourselves.

2. Helping competitors helps our whole industry.

3. We don't trust our competitors enough to collaborate with them.

4. Collaborating with our competition makes us better.

Now, answer yes or no to the following to indicate your actions:

1. We refuse collaboration unless it's forced upon us.

2. We collaborate with competitors on industry-wide initiatives.

3. We share IP and ideas for new products with competitors to accelerate innovation.

4. We refer customers to competitors when their product is better.

Based on your answers to these questions, place yourself on the scale below with regard to how much you collaborate with your competitors—with 1 being never, and 10 being frequently.

Chapter Ten

HARNESSING ADVANTAGE: TURNING FIVE COMMON TRAPS INTO STEPPING STONES

MIRROR

Abundance Mindset or Scarcity Mindset:
Where Are You?

Using the following table, ask yourself which mindset you are closer to, using some of the comparisons described by entrepreneur Caroline Castrillon.

Abundance Mindset	Scarcity Mindset
Focus on opportunities	Focus on limitations
Thinks big and embraces risk	Thinks small and fears risk
Long-term focus	Short-term focus
Willing to share knowledge	Stingy with knowledge
Investment with a return	Cost control
Trust the process	Attached to the outcome
Focus on the customer	Focus on the competition

Based on your responses, place yourself on the scale below with regard to how much you embrace an abundance mindset—with 1 being never, and 10 being on a regular basis.

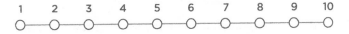

> ## MIRROR
> ### Is Your A2O Bringing You Down?

Consider these questions about yourself, as they pertain to attachment to outcomes.

1. How often do goals or desired outcomes distract you from doing your best work?

2. How often do you feel "in the flow" in business?

3. Have you experienced the connection between being fully absorbed in your work and the results you generate?

4. To what extent is your self-esteem tied to making money or achieving other results?

5. Can you imagine simply aspiring to goals without clinging or grasping toward them?

6. Can you think about the enterprise of business without hyper-focusing on outcomes?

Based on your answers to these questions, place yourself on the scale below with regard to how much you're attached to outcomes—with 1 being all the time, and 10 being never.

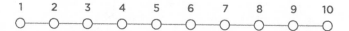

Now consider the following questions with regard to your company.

1. Does your company prioritize achieving outcomes at all costs?

2. How are employees treated when they do their best and still fall short of expectations?

3. Can you envision your company aspiring toward specific goals without being obsessed by them?

Based on your answers to these questions, place your company on the scale below with regard to how much it's attached to outcomes—with 1 being all the time, and 10 being never.

> # MIRROR
> ## Are You Status Quo or Status No?

Consider the following with regard to yourself in business.

1. Do you typically resist doing things differently at work?

2. Under what business circumstances do you avoid risk?

3. Do you jump on the change bandwagon because you are drawn to excitement?

4. Under what business circumstances do you seek out or welcome risk?

5. Are you the change agent in your company or the naysayer?

Based on your answers to these questions, place yourself on the scale below with regard to how often you tend to stay with the status quo—with 1 being all the time, and 10 being never.

> # MIRROR
> ## The Buck Stops . . . Where?

1. How do you view the role of money in your life?

2. Do you worship money?

3. Does the desire for money rule you?

4. Do you believe money buys happiness?

5. Do you dislike money?

6. Do you feel undeserving of prosperity?

7. Do you believe that people are wrong if they desire a lot of money?

8. What is more important to you than money?

9. What would you be willing to do for money? In business? In your personal life?

10. What would you absolutely not do for money? In business? In your personal life?

When you compare your answers to the last two questions, are you surprised by the gap between what you would do and what you wouldn't do? Is there a definitive line for you?

Based on your answers to all of the questions, place yourself on the scale below with regard to what degree you view money as a god—with 1 being the ruling element of your life and your decisions, whether ethical or not, and 10 being a vital part of existence but never one you would compromise your ethics, values, or the well-being of others to obtain.

THE BIG PICTURE

Now that you've completed all the Mirror activities and assessed where you are in each category, you will find it helpful to have a "big picture" version, with each theme and assessment bar here in one place. I encourage you to go back to each assessment bar, either within the chapters where you completed them, or in this chapter if you completed them here, and fill in the number for each category. This way, you can see at a glance where your strongest, and where you might want to focus first on improvement.

Measuring Your
"Business as War" Beliefs
page 49 / 242

How "Good" Are You in Business?
page 59 / 243

How Predatory Is Your Language?
page 65 / 243

How Vulnerable Are You at Work?
page 72 / 244

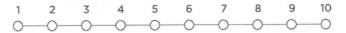

How Incivil Are You at Work?
page 77 / 245

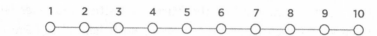

How Arrogant Are You at Work?
page 81 / 246

Fear/Ego Responses vs. Love/Heart Responses
page 95 / 247

Gauging Customer Hatred
page 103 / 248

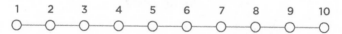

Where Do You Fall on the Engaged-O-Meter?
page 108 / 248

Is Your Company in Alignment?
page 116 / 249

Being in Alignment; Staying in Alignment
page 120 / 250

1 2 3 4 5 6 7 8 9 10

The Amare Way Philosophy and Your Company At-A-Glance
page 154 / 252

1 2 3 4 5 6 7 8 9 10

How Real Are You?
page 165 / 254

1 2 3 4 5 6 7 8 9 10

With Whom Do You Belong?
page 174 / 255

1 2 3 4 5 6 7 8 9 10

Belonging With Your Company
page 176 / 256

1 2 3 4 5 6 7 8 9 10

Utilizing Your Employees' Gifts
page 181 / 258

1 2 3 4 5 6 7 8 9 10

Collaborating with Customers
page 186 / 259

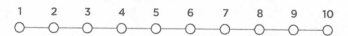

Are Your Competitors Sometimes Your Collaborators?
page 194 / 260

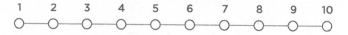

Abundance Mindset or Scarcity Mindset:
Where Are You?
page 209 / 261

Is Your A2O Bringing You Down?
page 219 / 262

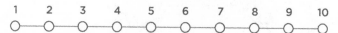

Are You Status Quo or Status No?
page 226 / 263

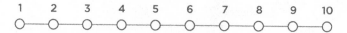

The Buck Stops . . . Where?
page 235 / 263

After sharing the core ideas of this book with a
Tanzanian LYFT driver in Washington DC, and asking his
opinion on what it means to "make business love,"
he briefly pondered how it mattered to business people,
and then said this to me:

"It brings them blessing."

May it bring you blessing too.

THE
WAY TO
GET
STARTED
IS TO
QUIT
TALKING
AND
BEGIN
DOING.

—WALT DISNEY

CHAPTER TWELVE

GETTING STARTED:
KEY TAKEAWAYS AND ACTION STEPS FOR
BECOMING A CULTIVATOR OF LOVE AND
JUMPING ONTO THE AMARE WAVE

Now that you have reached this point in the book, I recognize that you've taken in a great deal of content and worked through a lot of reflective exercises. I want to thank you for opening yourself to new possibilities and for being so honest with yourself about where you and your company can make some improvements. That, by itself, is an admirable first step! If you're ready to take it even further and are eager to start implementing some changes, I want to make the process as useful for you as possible.

I know that moving in a new, and possibly quite foreign direction might feel a bit overwhelming, so in this chapter, I've made it easy for you to approach adopting the Amare Way—and therefore taking a leap onto the growing Amare Wave—by compiling each theme of the book, beginning with those in Chapter Four, into two easy-to-digest sections: Key Takeaways, and Getting Started Action Steps. This way, you can quickly remind yourself of the pertinent parts of each theme, and then choose one or more action steps where you feel most compelled to make some incremental change.

But before you do that, my recommendation is to start here:

Ask yourself and your colleagues two bold and simple questions:

1. As a company, do we love our customers?

2. Do they love us?

Consider your answers a telling baseline that you can come back to as you grow into being a more love-centered business.

Now, determine which of the following four paths is most appropriate to move you forward.

1. Assess your needs: Look at the summary of your mirror scores on pages 263 to 266. Choose an area you want to improve and find the corresponding action steps in this chapter.

2. Be systematic: Read this chapter section by section, circle or mark takeaways that most resonate, then decide where to focus with action steps.

3. Tune in: Close your eyes, take a few deep breaths, and ask, "What next step would serve me best to become more love-centered in business?" Do whatever comes up.

4. If none of the three ways above work for you, turn to the Alignment section on page 281. Starting there will generate guidance for what to do next.

Whichever path you choose, keep in mind the three main factors that affect behavior change efforts:

- MOTIVATION – Is it something you desire?
- ABILITY – Do you have the requisite skills, tools, and knowledge?
- OPPORTUNITY – Do you have time, space, and permission to take the action?

All of the steps are meant to feel doable, no matter where you are in relation to where you want to be—and I encourage you to try whichever ones are applicable to your growth. You can even copy certain key takeaways to utilize as motivational tools you post, use in meetings, or decorate office space! Taking even small steps by choosing just one action, and then another, will go a long way in lifting you onto the current of the Amare Wave, one I can't wait to see you ride!

Ready to become a more love-centered business? The rest of this chapter will give you the tools you need to do just that.

DITCH PREDATORY LANGUAGE FOR LOVE-LIKE LANGUAGE

Key Takeaways

Most of us use some predatory language in everyday business conversation and don't even notice it as such, but the fact that it is ubiquitous in our culture and common in business does not make it right or acceptable.

The basis of Amare Way language is eschewing warlike terminology and instead choosing thoughtful, compassionate, and uplifting communication.

When it comes to the words we choose, warlike words might motivate people to get the job done, but compassionate words can also inspire people to get the job done—without the hostility and suffering the combative terms often incite.

We have reached a time when there is no longer space for a violence-based paradigm that uses predatory language in relating to customers or competitors. In using love-like language in its place, we not only perpetuate a positive mindset and lift people up, we genuinely serve employees, meet customer needs, and sustain healthy relationships—all of which has the power to greatly increase profitability over the long haul.

Getting Started Action Steps

1. Search out hostile words in your meeting agendas, presentations to staff, or appointments with clients, and make a conscious effort to substitute those words with more uplifting ones. Here are a few examples:

   How do we **hunt down** our target customers?

   Becomes: How do we **find and make welcome** our target customers?

   What market niches can we **exploit** with our solutions?

   Becomes: What market niches can we **benefit** with our solutions?

   What's our **plan of attack** to **capture** these business partners?

   Becomes: What's our **plan of action** to **serve** these business partners?

2. Once you begin using new language, set a standard for it within your company. You may find it helpful to make a chart of words and phrases you don't use in your company and post it in a central place, inviting the staff to make additions.

3. Make a game out of "catching" people using warlike words, as well as catching people using kind substitutions. You may very well get the whole company on board with using loving language as its default.

4. Work to eliminate violent idioms from your vernacular, such as "Kill two birds with one stone," "There's more than one way to skin a cat," or "I want so and so's head on a platter." We often say these things without thinking, but when you realize what you're actually saying, it's clear that these phrases don't embody ideas worth repeating.

MAKE VULNERABILITY AN ASSET

Key Takeaways

Being vulnerable does not mean you are weak or submissive; rather, it means you have the courage to be yourself and the willingness to deeply connect with others, even when it's difficult.

People who embrace vulnerability are wholehearted. They feel worthy of love, belonging, and connecting, and they believe what makes them vulnerable makes them beautiful and special.

Wholehearted people view vulnerability not as uncomfortable or excruciating, but simply as necessary.

Vulnerability is at the root of social connection.

In a business culture that embraces vulnerability, not only can you can show up as you, but customers feel seen and valued as they are too.

Getting Started Action Steps

1. Humbly own and admit your mistakes—out loud. You may be surprised just how much respect people will have for you when you do this.

2. Reject being a know-it-all. No one likes being around a person who thinks they're smarter than everyone else.

3. Embrace that everyone has feelings of vulnerability on some level, whether they're hiding them or not. Be unafraid of showing yours so that others feel comfortable showing theirs.

USHER IN CIVILITY WITH KINDNESS

Key Takeaways

Besides being a good practice for its own sake, civility has a heavy influence on how your team interacts with your customers, suppliers, and others important in the running of your business.

*

When a company operates with kindness, and civility is the standard among the leaders and staff, it is much more common for all team members to extend courtesy to the people you serve—and for those people to forge stronger loyalty to your products or services.

*

Kindness is action driven by concern for others, not for self— and involves not merely thinking, believing, or intending, but doing.

*

PwC's survey of CEOs found that within companies, kindness increases employee commitment, improves communication, minimizes negative competition internally, and strengthens relationships with business partners and investors.

Getting Started Action Steps

1. Set the expectation that civility is required in your company and that incivility will not be tolerated, at any level. Provide examples to clarify exactly what is and is not acceptable.

2. Model civility in all of your interactions—even the small ones. Have good manners, use kind words ("please" and "thank you" still go a long way!), refill the coffee pot . . . you get the idea.

3. When people speak to you, listen—without busying yourself doing something else, looking in another direction, or displaying body language that conveys you don't care or would rather not be bothered.

4. Employ the "ten-foot rule"—smile and make eye contact when you are within ten feet of a coworker or customer.

5. Establish specific expectations in the workplace, and provide appropriate rewards/consequences for both civil and uncivil behaviors.

6. Offer enlivened training with fun role modeling to improve civility in the workplace—demonstrate the incivil version, then flip it into the kind version for impact on how to treat employees, suppliers, and customers.

7. Be the one to set an uplifting tone that the company embraces as a whole.

REPLACE ARROGANCE WITH HUMILITY

Key Takeaways

Arrogance often emerges when egos override emotional intelligence, or when a person is fearful or insecure and doesn't want to show it—like in the classic bully syndrome, or as an unintended consequence of efforts to build self-esteem.

~

Arrogance is not confidence, and is not necessary for business success; in fact, it hurts productivity in numerous ways.

~

Arrogance in no way demonstrates strength of character and is not a necessary or even desirable ingredient for success.

🙦

What typifies the most successful business leaders, and arguably our greatest world leaders too, is humility.

🙦

Research shows that companies with humble CEOs have reduced turnover and experience increased employee engagement.

🙦

Having an authentic sense of mission, and aligning with a higher purpose beyond financial profit, helps temper arrogance and is part of what I hope The Amare Wave inspires in you.

Getting Started Action Steps

1. Recognize the need to take care of your culture, your people, your customers, and your balance sheet—as well as take care of yourself.

2. Demonstrate that you are not only for yourself but that you are part of a much larger ecosystem.

3. Value authentic humility and resist rewarding arrogance. Create your version of the "No Asshole Rule," which sets a clear standard for what is and is not tolerated.

4. Remember why you exist: to carry out your higher purpose, not solely to feed your ego and to make money.

5. Humbly view your purpose as sacred and your employees and customers as worthy of love, which is what leads team members, investors, partners, and customers to support the company too.

OPERATE WITH LOVE ENERGY

Key Takeaways

Fear energy, with its denigrating and separating nature, confines you to a limited realm of possibility.

꙳

Shifting your responses away from the ego and making decisions more from an aligned place allows you to transmute fear into an opportunity for growth—while making you more conscious of **you**.

꙳

It is easier to stay grounded in the spirit of **amare** when you keep top of mind that most businesses were conceived out of a desire to improve something for others, which serves as a reminder that business as an enterprise can be the greatest agent for awakening us to the power of love.

꙳

Every situation can elicit a fear/ego response and an **amare** response. Be aware of how the fear response feels constricting inside, while the **amare** response—even if not immediately natural for you—feels expansive.

When companies love their customers, the customers know it —and the company's staff knows it.

When the leaders of a company operate from a place of fear, they embrace fighting energy, treat business as war, lack a higher purpose, become greedy, lose their way, and don't foster uplifting experiences or meaningful connection between people, which leads to disengagement, where people just plain stop caring. However, when the leaders of a company operate from a place of love, it promotes meaningful engagement, where the energy is uplifting and connecting, engaging us deeply as human beings and as workers, opening us to opportunity, and leaning toward growth and expansion.

Business as a social and economic enterprise ideally operates from a place of love, and is how companies like yours can stand out and dare to prosper differently.

Getting Started Action Steps

1. Understand that everything is energy, expressed in frequency and vibration (a central tenet of quantum physics), and that love energy is always higher in its vibration than fear energy.

2. When you feel yourself becoming filled with fear energy, observe your feeling without judging it, then consciously move yourself out of the constriction of fear energy and toward the expansiveness of love energy. The following modes of interruption can be helpful for shifting this state:

- take a deep breath
- change your cognition to a positive thought
- say to yourself, "Stop!"
- wash your face
- swig some water
- physically move your body
- any other interruption that works for you

3. Be encouraged and motivated by the fact that love as a leadership strategy or management tool has the following beneficial effects:

   - trust is increased
   - people feel valued and become more secure about their jobs
   - a healthy sense of cohesiveness is promoted
   - self-esteem flourishes
   - Creativity, open-mindedness, and the willingness to critically challenge each other's ideas increases

4. Make a conscious effort to come from **amare**, especially during times you may not naturally do so, so that you are able to focus on a more nourishing response, whether toward yourself or toward others.

5. Study the Ego Response/Amare Response scenarios again on pages 96–98 to get a feel for the difference, then apply those techniques to your own situation.

6. Keep top of mind that love is not in opposition to power; it does not impede action, achievement, or growth. Being an energy that uplifts and connects, love actually inspires and fuels action—inspired action—which then naturally directs power toward achievement and growth, which leads to inspired results . . . and the cycle continues.

7. Love yourself.

GET ALIGNED, STAY ALIGNED

Key Takeaways

Alignment is critical because it provides a common ground for connection, commitment, and love between your company, employees, customers, investors, and other stakeholders, based on shared goals and values.

Alignment encompasses the following:

- Consistency and integrity across your corporate vision, strategy, and execution; your purpose, values, and brand identity; and your value proposition and the value you deliver.

- What you as a company believe, say, and do all match.

- How your company behaves behind the scenes, when out front doing business, and in society at large are situationally appropriate, in sync, and in line with the promises you make.

Within the Amare Way framework, the priorities you set, decisions you make, things you say, and actions you take are all attuned to and express the same positive energy and vibrational frequency.

Everyone in every role in the company needs to genuinely buy in and commit to the beliefs, aims, and ways of the company—

and for that buy-in and commitment to be fully authentic, there must also be consistency between personal goals and values and corporate goals and values.

Higher purpose is the starting point for getting into alignment, which is much stronger when your higher purpose is something your stakeholders believe in and care about too.

When you are in alignment, your sense of yourself and your role in your business are consistent and healthy, in line with your core values and beliefs. There is less ego and angst, as well as less uncertainty. You have more flow and ease in your life, and you feel more internal guidance, as though you are operating from a higher place, in sync with a larger whole.

Truly knowing yourself, as a precursor to alignment, means you are honest about who and what you are, what you value, what uplifts you, and what de-energizes you.

Being in alignment with yourself and loving yourself go hand in hand. When you love yourself and how you present yourself to the world, it feels good to be you—and you are a more effective leader when you love yourself in a healthy way.

Getting Started Action Steps

1. Get to know yourself. Start by completing all the Mirror activities—one at a time—if you haven't already. If you resist doing that, get to know that part of yourself too.

2. Review a typical workday. Notice when you tighten up. Imagine what would need to change to eliminate that feeling and bring you into better alignment.

3. List your core values. Compare them with your company's core values. Assess the fit.

4. Do a daily check-in with yourself, like executive coach Marshall Goldsmith does every day, to see if you are living in line with your priorities and values, and doing what you said you would do.

5. Ask trusted colleagues if and under what conditions your words and actions match and don't match.

6. Do one thing for one minute every day—stepping outside, drawing on a white board, looking at happy photos of people you love—whatever it is that quickly helps you feel more aligned.

7. Talk to customers to determine if your desires and goals are aligned with their goals and desires. Have your sales force do the same thing.

8. Conduct a company audit and assess consistency and integrity across your vision, strategy, and execution; your purpose, values, and brand identity; and your value proposition and the value you deliver.

GROUND YOUR BUSINESS
IN THE AMARE WAY PHILOSOPHY

PRINCIPLE 1: TREAT ONE ANOTHER WELL
Key Takeaways

In business as in life, we are all human beings. And regardless of title, station in life, culture, ethnicity, or age, we all desire love and kindness, respect and understanding.

*

"Treating others well" ideally expands from "Don't do to others what you wouldn't want done to you" to offering sincere empathy and compassion—empathy being what allows us to "get" the other's perspective, on both a thinking and feeling level; and compassion being the understanding, connection, and feeling of caring we have for the suffering of others.

*

Based on the law of reciprocity and the science of human behavior (or the notion of karma), you will reap benefits from treating others well—because when you are good to others, they are more likely to be good to you.

Getting Started Action Steps

1. Put yourself in others' shoes: Ask yourself how you would react if what you did or said to a colleague or customer was being done or said to you—if you were in their position.

2. Filter your words: Before you speak, submit your words to what some call the three gates of speech. Is it true? Is it kind? Is it necessary?

3. Slow down: In tough situations, take a breath—actually stop long enough to breathe in and breathe out—before you react, to help ground yourself and find compassion.

4. Tune in: If you sense misalignment, harshness, incivility, or lack of respect for others, acknowledge it, apologize if appropriate, and reframe things to better honor the other person's humanity.

5. Offer compassion: If a colleague or customer is going through a rough time, rather than merely seeing their problem as a disruptor to business, show them you care by asking what's going on, expressing kind words, or offering some one-on-one time.

6. Seek to empathize with another person's pain or angst: First, simply listen and be present with them. Then, if you have wise or comforting words to offer, do so. Being empathic goes hand in hand with offering compassion, which in turn sets the stage for offering kindness.

7. When you're tempted to jump to a frustrated or angry conclusion based on someone's actions or words, take a breath first and consider if they might be going through a difficult time, or simply having a bad day, then respond with kindness. This may sound like, "Is everything okay? You seem pretty upset about this." Or, "Are you all right? You're not usually [late, behind on a project, so heated about something like this, this negative, etc.]" Or with a customer, you might say, "I know you must be really [disappointed, frustrated, angry, etc.] right now. How can I turn that around for you?"

8. Keep top of mind the meaning of **amare** that is "being grounded in a desire to better each other's well-being." This prepares you to treat others well in business and life.

PRINCIPLE 2: INSPIRE CONNECTION
Key Takeaways

Recognizing that we are all interconnected, for connection is the nature of our being and is fundamental to being human within a society, enables us to see and appreciate each other and our shared goals and values.

Business provides numerous opportunities for connection; every point of contact, every interaction, is a chance to inspire meaningful connection.

Business is personal. We don't shut down our "person-ness" or leave our humanity behind when we go to work, or to the doctor, or out to eat, or shopping. We are always human beings, and the Amare Way nurtures and values our humanity by encouraging authentic connection within the space of business.

While the Amare Way is not a religious belief, a type of dogma, or tied to any particular tradition, the notion of us all being somehow connected as part of a greater whole is common to many wisdom traditions and spiritual practices, and is central to the Amare Way philosophy.

From a quantum physics perspective, we recognize that what connects us beyond our shared goals and values, our desire to be treated well, and to love and be loved is a unifying and uplifting energy that is neither static nor fixed. It is an ecosystem of universal energy that we affect, are affected by, and exchange with one another through our intentions, interactions, and experiences.

The Amare Way helps generate, focus, and amplify the energy of love—call it God, Spirit, the Force, Higher Consciousness, Source, Nature, or simply "energy"—to create meaningful connection within the context of business and commerce.

Getting Started Action Steps

1. Smile genuinely when you meet someone's eye. A sincere smile acknowledges the other person's presence and sparks a feeling of connection on a soul level, whether you know each other well or not.

2. Pay attention to how people respond. When you ask a customer or coworker how they are, regardless of their status, sincerely listen with your mind and heart.

3. Suspend judgment. Challenge yourself to interact with coworkers, customers, and critics without judging them or taking things personally.

4. Be genuinely interested in others. Don't just act interested, be interested.

5. Ask questions that inspire sincere and respectful conversation. Instead of regularly asserting your opinion as if it's the "right one" or the only one that matters, or

dominating the conversation, show that you are genuinely interested in connecting, not merely sharing your side of things, particularly when you may have opposing opinions.

6. Actively look for aspects that unite. Make it a point of relating to coworkers, customers, and other contributors within your business on an interest, background, life situation, event, talent, or goal you share.

7. Be mindful of norms for physical contact as well as cultural differences. People in American cultures, for example, tend to prefer high-arousal positive affective states, like excitement and enthusiasm, and are generally comfortable with handshakes and pats on the back. People in East-Asian cultures, on the other hand, typically favor low-arousal positive affective states, such as calm and peacefulness, and favor bows over physical contact.[66]

8. Recognize the humanity in each other. Listen attentively with eye contact when others speak, seek to see things from others' points of view, and respect that every human being is here for a reason at this time in history to contribute something of value.

PRINCIPLE 3: GET ON PURPOSE
Key Takeaways

People naturally align with purpose, and not only are employees more attracted and devoted to companies when they believe in the company's higher purpose, so too are customers and investors.

Companies with a higher purpose do better financially than those without one, all else being equal.

Having a higher purpose not only adds meaning and motivation to your business, but it keeps leaders on focus, employees staying on task during hard times, and customers coming back.

Don't mistake "maximizing shareholder value" as a higher purpose. It is an important goal, but it is not a higher purpose.

In determining your higher purpose, look for one that resonates with your people and your customers—one that is shared, explicit, and generates decisions and actions that are in alignment.

Getting Started Action Steps

1. Be honest about whether the purpose that drives your business is a shared and higher purpose, If it's not, brainstorm how to make it so.

2. Have your executive team individually answer management guru Peter Drucker's famous "first question": What business are you in? If the answer is about what you make or sell, go back to the drawing board.

3. Clarify your shared, higher purpose with the "so that" technique[67], as in "We do _____ so that_____ so that _____ so that_____, etc. Somewhere in that benefits chain is your higher purpose.

4. Recognize and celebrate the positive impact your company has on people's lives and society at large.

5. Communicate your higher purpose within your company and to the outside world explicitly and proudly. Make the connection clear between what your people do, your products and services, and that purpose.

6. Enable, encourage, and reward actions that are tied to advancing your higher purpose.

7. Give your people paid time off to support efforts connected to your higher purpose.

PRINCIPLE 4: RESPECT MONEY
Key Takeaways

The desire for money is perfectly healthy. The more you have, the more good you can do in the world, and the more you're able to create a comfortable life for you and your loved ones.

Financial abundance is fully aligned with catching the Amare Wave and in running an Amare Way business.

Succeeding financially is—and should be—a must for a new love-based paradigm in business to take hold.

Money isn't inherently bad; it's the behaviors we often justify in pursuit of money that give it the bad rap.

People who run Amare Way companies indeed pursue financial abundance and the reward of profits, but they do it with their customers' and employees' best interests at heart.

Business exists to make life better for people. When care and thought—and love—is at the heart of delivering on that goal, money, on some level, typically comes.

Love alone doesn't achieve profits, but it is the guiding force that propels all decisions that influence the company's success —and having a healthy respect for money is a vital piece of that alignment.

Getting Started Action Steps

1. Assess your policies and procedures to make sure they keep money in its proper perspective.

2. Ask your team if what you say about money and what you do about money are consistent and aligned.

3. Enjoy your prosperity without flaunting it or becoming greedy.

4. Consider how much you can pay your people, not how little.

5. Commit to the following guidelines when making business decisions that involve money:

   - Will this money-making action deceive anyone? If so, we won't pursue it.

   - Will this money-making action harm anyone? If so, we won't pursue it.

   - Will this money-making action manipulate anyone? If so, we won't pursue it.

- Will this money-making action not be aligned with our core values? If so, we won't pursue it.

- Will this money-making action damage or destroy our reputation should it become public or its motives be revealed? If so, we won't pursue it.

- Will this money-making action require us to violate our ethics? If so, we won't pursue it.

PRINCIPLE 5: CHOOSE LOVE OVER FEAR
Key Takeaways

Integrating love into business requires us as professionals to not let fear drive us.

*

You can operate out of fear and greed with your more primitive brain, a capacity designed for dangerous and threatening situations; or you can operate out of love and compassion with your higher, more evolved brain, your natural and aligned state. The choice is always yours.

*

Both love and fear can be linked to productivity gains in business under certain conditions, but Amare Way companies recognize that gains motivated by fear are short term and come at a significant cost.

*

In the long term, love works better. And at the end of the day, love feels better than fear.

*

Being love-centered influences how you treat each other well, how you generate interconnection, and how you stay attuned to your company's higher purpose.

Getting Started Action Steps

1. Take an honest look at the energy that drives your company. If fear is a big part, resolve to fix it. If love is, celebrate it.

2. Aim to uplift, not to intimidate.

3. Practice noticing and letting go of fear when it shows up.

4. Examine your internal communications and notice how much you use fear as a motivator and how much you use love.

5. Remember that you know how to win in business without fighting or diminishing others, and with the intention of elevating yourself and others.

6. Make it a point to use words that engender love-like language.

7. Recognize that greed and arrogance have no place in your business or life.

8. Show up whole. Do not in any way diminish or hide from your own power or enable others to do so.

9. Set expectations of being love-centered (using other labels if you prefer) with all your stakeholders.

10. Build the positive energy of love into the continuum of employee milestones—from new employee orientations to retirement celebrations.

11. Support other companies who are also love-centered and ethical—even competitors—knowing that when we all work toward a greater good, everybody wins.

PRINCIPLE 6: TAKE THE LONG VIEW
Key Takeaways

A commitment to **amare** means thinking, planning, and making decisions with the long term in mind.

In today's business environment, leaders who embody resilience, perseverance, and vision are those who successfully take the long view, invest in lasting relationships, and gainfully ride the Amare Wave for the duration.

A business culture that makes maximizing shareholder return its main objective frequently leads management to myopically zero in on short-term profits and stock prices, often putting the company's long-term viability at risk.

Short-term needs are important and cannot be ignored, but they cannot be allowed to override everything else.

Shared goals and values, as well as authenticity and transparency, set the stage for establishing trust in relationships, and for cultivating an enduring sense of belonging and collaboration—all of which are germane to taking the long view.

Within the Amare Way, the goal is to not become attached to short-term outcomes such that you diminish your organization's long-term viability, compromise your guiding values and higher purpose, or shut down your humanity.

Getting Started Action Steps

1. Explicitly set and reinforce expectations that your decisions will be based on long-term viability.

2. Let all your stakeholders know what it means to them that you are taking a long-term view, e.g., slower and steadier growth for investors, knowing it will not appeal to everyone.

3. Make sure your KPIs and internal reward system are aligned with your long-term focus, not merely hitting quarterly numbers.

4. Prepare whatever you need to stand up to pressure to conform to Wall Street–like expectations.

5. Pay your people well and invest in sustaining healthy relationships with all your stakeholders.

PRINCIPLE 7: PRIORITIZE RELATIONSHIPS
Key Takeaways

The most valuable equity a company has is its relationships.

When the quality of the relationship with your leaders, employees, distributors, suppliers, customers, and even colleagues is the priority, arrogance, incivility, and ego become replaced with empathy, compassion, and kindness— perspectives that are tremendously beneficial for ourselves, even as we offer them to others.

With customers, it's often less about the product quality, the refund, or the wait time than it is about the health of the relationship and the surrounding feelings.

When valuing and maintaining strong relationships is paramount, all the other pieces of your business fall more easily into place.

The best way to stand out and succeed in a competitive market is through meaningful relationships grounded in love that meet shared goals. When this is your guiding light, the Amare Way will powerfully differentiate your company, and can even become the heart of your culture, brand definition, and value proposition.

Getting Started Action Steps

1. Think in terms of "we" not just "me"—and mean it.

2. Put people before products and profits. Being clear and explicit when and how you do so helps others in your company do the same.

3. Regularly ask yourself: How will this decision or this action affect the relationship? Then, make choices that favor sustaining healthy relationships. This applies to everyone:

employees, customers, investors, suppliers—all your stakeholders.

4. When you say or do something hurtful to others at work, own up to it—don't merely apologize. Make amends and tell them how you will avoid that hurtful behavior in the future.

5. Feature your commitment to relationships in your messaging to attract employees, and in the customer experience you promise. Deliver day in and day out on putting employees and customers first.

6. Make it easy for customers to be delighted—through your guarantees, your return policies, your customer service process, and your people. Ensure every part of the experience you provide honors the relationship.

7. Make changes to any policies and procedures you currently have that are filled with empty words, by altering them to be meaningful and strengthen relationships.

TRANSFORM YOUR BUSINESS BY EMBODYING THE AMARE WAY PILLARS

AUTHENTICITY

Key Takeaways

Authenticity means that your company's commitment to **amare** is real and put into practice every day—not merely as lip service—which builds trust. Leadership authentically believes in and leads with higher purpose, and everyone in the company is supported to behave authentically and with the energy of love in all business dealings.

On a personal level, authenticity is about showing up whole, and being true to who you are and in your commitment to the company. This is reflected outwardly in your words and actions, and in the resonance of your energy—or your "vibe."

On a company level, authenticity starts with why your company exists—your higher purpose—and is evidenced in how your company operates in the business world and in society at large, in line with that purpose.

When you are authentic, what you believe, say, and do are consistently aligned. You are not only genuine, honest, reliable, and credible; you make promises you believe in—and you keep those promises.

As an authentic leader, when you create an atmosphere in business where things are not hidden, where people feel safe expressing their ideas and concerns respectfully, and where people genuinely look out for one another, it makes for healthier long-term relationships and better business decisions.

Authenticity builds trust. Inauthenticity erodes it.

A company cannot choose to be driven by greed, or to embrace fear, incivility, arrogance, and corruption, and consider themselves authentic.

To be authentic in an Amare Way company means there must be commitment to a higher good; if it's not inherently for the betterment of others, it cannot be considered authentic.

Amare Way companies are authentic about wanting to make business love, and their employees are authentic in delivering it.

Getting Started Action Steps

1. Ask yourself before every action, "Am I being real?"

2. Trust in your expressed vision and in your team's ability and motivation to execute it successfully.

3. Make sure your words and actions match—if you say it's people before profit, your policies and priorities must show it.

4. Center your values on kindness and compassion, and ban any expression of violence in your language or actions.

5. Ensure that your company authentically sees your employees, cares for them, and values them, so that they can fully engage.

6. Make decisions in accordance with your company's stated values so that investors trust you.

7. Ensure that your company does what it says and treats suppliers and partners fairly.

8. Take your community's interests to heart and deliver on your promises.

9. Aim to succeed, but not by dehumanizing or seeking to destroy your competition.

10. Engender trust with your customers by being who you say you are, by having a value proposition that is good and equitable, by ensuring your products and services are what and how they ought to be, and by treating customers with respect and kindness.

BELONGING

Key Takeaways

Belonging happens in business when people feel a sense of identification with your company or brand; and when your employees, customers, and other stakeholders recognize and embrace desirable similarities between themselves and your company, develop an emotional connection based on those similarities, and feel a sense of kinship, which makes them feel good. As a result, they genuinely want you to succeed, and they like contributing to your success.

When customers feel like they belong with you, and you belong with them, you have customer preference, meaning they are loyal and prefer to give you their business above anyone else in your industry. They may even pay more for what you offer, and they are less likely to shop around for better prices, because you're not a commodity.

Purchases by loyal customers are not merely a transaction; they are an extension of their being in a relationship with you, and that relationship adds value.

"Membership belonging" and "forced belonging" don't inherently reflect the deeper personal connection that Amare Way belonging involves—if customer hearts are not involved, and there's no real sense of kinship, the result is a superficial relationship that can be easily lost.

When customers' needs are met through your products or services, they not only feel invited to be part of your company's success, but they want you to succeed, even becoming your ambassadors and praising you to other prospective customers.

Getting Started Action Steps

1. Identify one simple thing you can do to create a meaningful sense of belonging with all your stakeholders— employees, customers, investors, partners, suppliers, and the community at large.

2. Invest in knowing and understanding your customers' hearts—their desires, values, and aspirations.

3. Empower your customer-facing people to take time to connect with customers on a deeper level.

4. Track and publicize employee and customer praise that shows a strong sense of identification and kinship.

5. Invest in, measure, and reward employee and customer loyalty.

6. Give customers easy ways to share their stories and proudly proclaim their affinity for you.

7. Treat your customers, employees, and suppliers almost like family (assuming you have healthy family relationships!).

8. Genuinely thank customers for choosing to give you their business.

9. Make sure your employees like being with your customers and other stakeholders, and if they don't, fix it.

COLLABORATION

Key Takeaways

The Amare Way views collaboration as being "in this together," aligned in uplifting energy and connected in purpose, actively working toward a shared goal and creating greater value jointly.

Amare Way collaboration presumes you value and want to satisfy multiple stakeholders, not only shareholders.

When you are love-centered, all your stakeholders want to collaborate with you and help you succeed, making it a win-win!

Collaboration with Employees

Good collaboration allows employees to know that the company authentically sees them, cares for them, and values them—and it takes advantage of the various perspectives and knowledge that people in different roles bring to bear.

Be careful not to engage employees in empty collaboration or collaboration overload, both of which deplete rather than uplift.

*

Effective collaboration means that shared goals are in place, and that requires mutual interests and engagement. For employees, that means being valued—for their everyday work, their ideas, and their contribution to the bigger picture.

Collaboration with Customers

When you are effectively collaborating with customers, they experience you as a partner rather than merely a vendor selling their newest technologies, novelties, or services. When this kind of collaboration occurs, it not only lends to a highly effective way of differentiating yourself in competitive markets, but your customers become your best resource for knowing how to continue to meet their needs.

*

When you seek customer engagement and input, you must genuinely value it, and you must put that input to use. While you may receive some short-term gains from misaligned collaborative efforts, such as inviting customers to collaborate as a marketing ploy or sales tactic, they come at a high cost because the process will lose you trust and allegiance—and when trust and allegiance are lost due to intentional inauthenticity or conscious lying, it is extremely difficult, if not impossible, to win them back.

*

Gauging the pulse of customers through ongoing research is a powerful way to engage and foster collaboration—whether through focus groups, surveys, usability testing, online communities, informal interactions, or other means.

✎

Amare Way companies are authentic about fostering collaboration with customers for the right reasons, such as to genuinely improve an offering, remove one that's not serving their audience, or create one their customers are requesting.

✎

When people are genuinely delighted to be your customers and you are authentic with them, a wonderful byproduct is that they become your devoted ambassadors—or raving fans —which is a grassroots form of collaboration that is priceless and far more powerful, and often much more authentic, than most paid advertising and public relations campaigns.

✎

The more transparent you are, the more people expect you to remain that way, so once you achieve this level of connection and loyalty with your customers, be sure you remain authentic and driven by wanting the best for them.

Collaboration with Competitors

To reflect the complexities of relationships with competitors, consider the phrase "collabetition"—a blend of the words collaboration and competition.

✎

When you sincerely believe that business is a social enterprise intended to make life better for people, fostered by a healthy mindset of abundance, collaboration with your competitors can take several forms: establishing policies favorable to your industry, sponsoring a trade association, advancing basic research that can fuel innovation for multiple companies, hosting a summit or event that features several providers in your industry, and so on.

⚓

You can actually win more loyalty and "belonging" when you refer customers to competitors for the right reasons.

⚓

Collabetition makes sense in part because you likely cannot serve 100 percent of your particular market anyway.

⚓

You can still be a market leader without having to dominate the market to the exclusion of competitors who would bring different value to customers. Rather than putting energy into smearing competitors, you come together with a common goal: to make life better for people through your offerings.

Getting Started Action Steps

1. Set the expectation inside your company that you are better together and create greater value by collaborating with your multiple stakeholders.

2. Explicitly acknowledge that you don't know everything, and actively combine fresh, outside points of view with your inside perspectives to make better decisions.

3. Listen, listen, and listen some more—set up ongoing research to track engagement and invite real collaboration on a regular basis.

4. Put simple methods and systems in place—such as idea walls, online sharing, daily huddles—that make it easy for your people to collaborate in meaningful ways.

5. Engineer collaboration into team meetings, customer interactions, and other appropriate activities, without overdoing it to the point of burnout.

6. Welcome and encourage the idea that everyone deserves to realize and contribute their gifts toward the greater good of the company.

7. Invest in fostering high levels of employee and customer engagement, and celebrate it!

8. Regularly observe and engage with customers, and sincerely pay attention to what they have to say.

9. Make it easy for customers to spread the word as raving fans.

10. Look for opportunities to work together with competitors toward shared aims that uplift all.

TURN FIVE COMMON TRAPS INTO STEPPING STONES

SAY YES TO AN ABUNDANCE MINDSET AND NO TO A SCARCITY MINDSET

Key Takeaways

A key responsibility for business leaders is to set the tone for the company by establishing its fundamental mindset, which may either be rooted in fear and scarcity, or in an optimistic belief in abundance.

An abundance mentality resides in the idea of endless possibilities, with trust that life will provide for our needs when we are in alignment, and that there is plenty for everyone we share the planet with; while a scarcity mentality is derived from a belief in "lack" and the presumption that life is a zero-sum game.

When we have abundance thinking, we focus on what we can and do have. This is important, because in large part—in business as in life—our mindset creates much of our reality.

A scarcity mentality sucks up a lot of your productive energy in business because you are constantly worried you will never have enough. But when you adopt a love-based abundance mindset, you recognize what is working and what might be possible to achieve, which lets you envision and often accomplish incredible things.

When you let go of a belief in lack and replace it with a belief in abundance, you cultivate win-win situations where you, your employees, your suppliers, your customers—everyone—is more pleased with what they receive.

The gratitude you feel when the tone of your business is rooted in abundance is as profound as it is contagious. In fact, almost no feeling is more powerful than being grateful for all you have and can do.

Getting Started Action Steps

1. Choose to believe that there is enough to go around, and have faith that life conspires to support us all.

2. Adopt a daily affirmation that you repeat throughout your day, such as:

   "There is enough for everyone."

   "I naturally attract prosperity." Or

   "My company abundantly creates and receives."

   Choose an activity during which you repeat your affirmation as many times as you can. This may be during a five-minute break, a walk around the block, in the shower, etc. The idea is to create a habitual time that you affirm your belief in abundance out loud. Also, repeat it whenever you notice scarcity thinking is triggered.

3. Replace jealousy with gratitude. Instead of being envious of others' success or material wealth, celebrate it, be happy for them, and learn from their success.

4. Envision what your abundant life looks like for you and for your company. Close your eyes and imagine every detail, as if you're watching a movie. Write specifics of what you desire in a journal, and don't be afraid to dream big. Create a vision board or slideshow to make it more real. Pay particular attention to the feeling—the inner state— you want to have. The more exact you can be, the better.

5. Share your abundance mindset with others. Look for opportunities with friends and colleagues to express it—in casual conversation, in business meetings, in presentations, etc.

6. Say thank you one hundred times in a row, every day.

ATTACH FULFILLMENT TO THE WORK, NOT THE OUTCOMES

Key Takeaways

Outcomes, results, and performance absolutely matter in business. The goal is to not be attached to the outcomes, which is very different from them not mattering at all.

When you are attached to outcomes, results suffer, because attachment to the outcome actually becomes a distraction that takes you out of the present, and away from the doing. But when your focus is solely on your work, or the doing, you can be all in, without the intrusion of expectations or self-conscious judgment.

Attachment to outcomes has an emotional cost, in that it will almost always cause you distress, because it is as if your happiness and sense of self depends on achieving that outcome.

You want your work to make a meaningful difference in people's lives—and you want personal outcomes like inner peace and financial security too. But the achievement of these business and personal outcomes need not define you as a person, meaning what you achieve does not determine your happiness, value, or self-worth.

Results—in life and in business—are almost always determined by multiple factors, of which your action, your work, is only one.

There are two aspects to desire: One is **grasping and craving**, which takes you out of the present and inevitably leads to suffering; the other is **aspiration**, which is the salutary aspect of desire that comes from our highest selves, where we aspire with resolve and determination to achieve what is good and noble.

The benefits of mindfulness for business are well documented; they include greater emotional intelligence, improved focus, and greater productivity, to name a few.

When your mind is not obsessed with the desire of grasping and clinging, it is free, clear, resolute, and at ease. In this state, you can be totally absorbed in what you're doing, completely and authentically engaged, and fully aligned with your higher purpose.

Getting Started Action Steps

1. Learn what attachment feels like in your body and mind by concentrating your attention on something you feel a "grasping" attachment to—a production milestone, a sales goal, a raise, etc.

2. Do an honest self-assessment of what outcomes in your work you are attached to. Then, imagine not achieving those outcomes and mentally play out what might happen. Then shrug it off.

3. Notice, without judgment, whenever you feel the clinging and grasping kind of desire. Now actively choose to let it go and refocus on your work.

4. Introduce the idea of non-attachment into your company and suggest a one-week "awareness" experiment to try it out with no risk.

5. Surround yourself with people who support you in having aspirational desires and in not getting so wrapped up in outcomes.

6. Be present and practice mindfulness. When you drift off, gently bring yourself back to full focus on the task at hand.

7. Meditate, every day. Start with sixty seconds, eight breaths in and out through the nose. Occupy your mind by saying to yourself, "I am breathing in" with each inhale, and "I am breathing out" with each exhale.

WELCOME CHANGE INSTEAD OF SUCCUMBING TO THE STATUS QUO BIAS

Key Takeaways

The status quo bias reflects that we feel most comfortable doing what we've always done because it is familiar, even when it doesn't bring us the results we desire.

Multiple factors keep us in the status quo: fear of a loss of status or security; fear of possible failure; fear of criticism and rejection; fear of the unknown; as well as external forces such as peer pressure, a climate of mistrust, organizational politics, compensation dynamics, and our entrenched business culture.

Innovating, exploring fresh perspectives that move your business forward, tweaking elements of your product or service offering, and letting go of patterns and traditions that simply aren't working any longer, are keys to embracing change and letting go of the status quo bias.

The status quo can be effective to maintain at times. It becomes a problem when it shuts you down and actually costs you the upside benefit of something better.

Getting Started Action Steps

1. Become aware of resistance when you are facing possible change—restriction of your breathing, narrowing of your thinking, hardening of your beliefs, or cognitive machinations that may support the status quo—as you weigh if maintaining the status quo makes sense, or if the bias is leading you to make suboptimal decisions and avoid change.

2. When you find the mere prospect of change inducing an acute stress response, move your body in a specific way, such as swaying to counter a fight response, shaking (like dogs do!) to counter a freeze response, or doing a quick jog in place to shift your energy.

3. Try little things with virtually zero risk, like sitting in a different chair, taking a different route when you drive to work, eating something new for lunch, typing in a different font, drinking from a new coffee mug, etc.

KNOW HOW AND WHEN TO SIDESTEP A MISMATCH
Key Takeaways

If you determine that alignment is lacking within your company or between you and your company, you can and should make a conscious choice:

- #1: Acknowledge the mismatch for what it is, but choose to stay with the company and find ways to cope with the lack of alignment.

- #2: Stay in your job, but try to influence your company toward a more love-like way of operating.

- #3: Recognize that you cannot or will not work at a company that does not share your values.

Getting Started Action Steps

1. If you choose to stay with your company, engage in targeted coping mechanisms—take up a hobby outside of work; enjoy a home improvement project; indulge in a daily self-care or mindfulness ritual; spend time reading or writing; walk, hike, or bike regularly as weather permits— so that self-criticism and regret don't plague you, and so that you don't grow to harbor anger and resentment toward your colleagues and company.

2. If you choose to stay and try to influence your company toward a more love-like way of operating:

   - Approach the powers that be and offer respectful suggestions—with a strong business case supported by relevant anecdotes and success stories to back your request—for making room for different thinking that can reduce frustration, make people happier, and achieve better results.

- Simply start conducting your work activities with the energy of love—smile more, thank people, tell stories of customer happiness, or mention your shared higher purpose.

- Consider going counter-culture by being a rebel "smuggling" in value, collaborative spirit, and innovative ideas.

3. If you realize the misalignment is too severe and will cause you to make too many personal value compromises if you stay with your company, start creating or looking for a new position more in line with your values and desired work environment, give the proper notice, and leave when you are able.

EMBRACE MONEY AS A GIFT, NOT A GOD
Key Takeaways

Money is an important and necessary concern of most successful people and companies; it is the emotional baggage we attach to it that creates problems.

Organizing a business around money makes for a measurable metric, but it becomes a downside when money is the primary thing you organize around.

Money is not inherently good or bad. In our culture, making money is critical to companies and people—and there's nothing wrong with that, as long as you don't let desire for money override your other values or cloud your perceptions and priorities.

While money is definitely something to aspire to make, to share, and to enjoy, it is not worthy of worship.

When money flows from doing work that provides value to society, alleviates suffering, and improves lives, it truly is a gift that can be used to afford you an abundant life, both for your family and for the causes you choose to support.

Getting Started Action Steps

1. Get yourself on track when it comes to how you view the acquisition of money in business by using the guidelines I suggested for all of your financially related decisions in Principle 4—Respect Money:

   If your money-making action . . .

   - deceives anyone, you don't pursue it.

   - harms anyone, you don't pursue it.

   - requires you to bend your ethics, you don't pursue it.

   - is not aligned with your core values, you don't pursue it.

   - unsettles anyone on the decision-making team, you listen and are open to re-evaluation.

   - would damage or destroy your reputation should it become public or its motives were revealed, you don't pursue it.

   - would require a cover-up, you don't pursue it.

I hope you are now feeling energized to take steps toward launching your company onto the growing Amare Wave! As you do, you will no doubt discover additional methods and hatch ideas that are specific to your particular company's growth. I would love to hear about your progress and what tools you used to make the leap. Please share your challenges and success stories at:

amarestories@theamarewave.com

Your story may very well be featured on the Amare Wave website, or in a future installment of the Amare Way series of books. Remember, every company who jumps onto the wave strengthens its momentum. I look forward to seeing your company at the peak!

CONCLUSION

A CALL TO MAKE BUSINESS LOVE

The Amare Wave is real. It is happening. It is now. And it has the capacity to diminish decades of pain and suffering and bring astounding happiness and prosperity to business and society—that is the power of love and business coming together.

Let us resolve that the wave will only grow in momentum and influence . . . that we will not be deterred by the inevitable detractors or by the resistance that change naturally attracts . . . that we will ride the Amare Wave with confidence, humility, and enthusiasm . . . that together, we will be strong in making love in business the new normal.

"We" of course, involves *you*. By choosing this book and reading it, you have crossed a threshold in your awareness. You know that business exists to make people's lives better and to uplift society. You know business is not war and that a warlike approach causes suffering. You know that business is missing love, and how the energy of love can transform business. You know business can be the greatest agent for awakening us to the power of love, which our world greatly needs now. You cannot ever unknow these things. They are a part of you.

What you *can* do is choose—choose what you will do with that greater awareness, that awakening, that quickening of purpose you feel deep inside. This is about you, my friend: your work, your company, your world. Will you be complacent and let things be as they are? Will you be complicit in the business as war paradigm? Or will you reject those old ways that no longer serve, despite their long tenure and deep roots? Will you say YES to putting love to work, even taking one tiny step at a time? Will you even go all in and fully align yourself and your company with the uplifting and connecting energy of love?

Know that you can do this. You already have inside you what you need to move forward. To quote a magician I saw when my kids were little, "We all have magic within us." Where you are right now is exactly where you need to be. It is your launching pad to what is next for you. I invite you to make that "next" a channel for bringing the energy of love into business and making our world a little better.

We are indeed sitting on the cusp of a major paradigm shift in business and society. Yes, we can do this. You can do this. Take the chance. I promise it will be at times exhilarating, scary, sensible, crazy, wondrous—and more than anything, deeply healing. The world needs all of us to do our part, as much as we possibly can.

So, let's do this! With authenticity, belonging, and collaboration, we can make the Amare Way *the* way of twenty-first-century business and beyond. Further, you can make this magnificent transformation in our society part of *your* personal legacy of greatness.

I offer my profound thanks to you for investing your time and energy into *The Amare Wave*. To you all, I say, namaste: The divine light in me bows to the divine light in you. Please share your experiences with our growing community of people putting love to work and choosing to be a force for good.

I wish you courage, brilliance, and fortitude as you tap into your power to move yourself, your company, and the world of business into the transformative energy of love.

APPENDIX

TWO INSPIRING STORIES:
A SNEAK PEEK INTO THE NEXT BOOK IN THE AMARE WAY SERIES

As more and more companies join the Amare Wave movement, we are thrilled to share their stories and inspire even more companies to do the same. Here, we offer the love-centered transformational stories of two distinct types of business leaders—one that led to the profound and sometimes painful reinvention of a very sweet company, and one that inspired a huge online community through complete authenticity and raw vulnerability.

These stories offer a preview of what's to come in the next installment of the Amare Way series. We hope you find them as motivating as we did, and that you'll be eager to read about more leaders who build and run companies with the uplifting and connecting energy of love. Maybe your story will be included too.

Stay tuned for our future publication, *Riding the Amare Wave: Inspired Stories of Leading with Love*, that will feature the transformative and uplifting profiles of leaders of large and small companies alike—established corporations and startups, nonprofits and B Corps, government agencies and NGOs—all kinds of organizations that are successfully putting *amare* to work in their organizations.

Here's to the Wave!

CHUAO CHOCOLATIER

Reinventing a Company with Love

Chuao Chocolatier is a love-centered business if there ever was one. High-energy, optimistic, and enthusiastic co-founder and leader Michael Antonorsi sees his business as a way to spread joy. In fact, his official title is Chief Joy Activator, and his default email signature is "With Love and Gratitude." Spreading joy is why Chuao Chocolatier exists, and that is their intention in all they do.

Yet, that goal hasn't always been easy.

Early on, the co-founders had conflicting visions and values that on many levels were costly to resolve, and there were challenges in achieving brand awareness to support their distribution aims. The decision to buy their building instead of rent kept the long view in mind, but it made the short term harder because it diverted operating capital. For nine years, Chuao was merely a transactional company that was chasing its tail and losing money. But after deep personal work, Michael became clear that what they did was not just sell chocolate; they provided an opportunity to experience joy *through* chocolate.

After a brand makeover based on a rich understanding of how chocolate can generate joy in people, the company embarked on a deep cultural renewal. The transformation took the revitalized company in its first year to a breakeven point, grew the company by 127 percent the second year, and after only three years, fully recovered the losses of the prior nine years.

Today, at the top level, three words guide the organization: honesty, willingness, and gratitude. Michael encourages his people to live and work with honesty about themselves and their actions, to be willing to grow from that honesty, and to be grateful for that growth. He also consistently invites them to go beyond their comfort zone. In front of their building is a huge wooden sculpture of the word JOY, and throughout their facility are framed sayings like, "The privilege of a lifetime is to become who you truly are" by Carl Jung. And "It is not joy that makes us grateful; it is gratitude that makes us joyful" by Brother David Steindl-Rast. The fact that his product is chocolate—"the food of the gods" as Michael says with delight—makes it easier for the company to deliver on their purpose. Every chocolate bar even says "crafted with joy" on the label.

Chuao also embraces four values: self-discovery, brave honesty, grateful giving, and creative wow. When the first three are happening, creativity is unleashed, and . . . wow happens! In addition, they abide by an organizational code of conduct, based on *The 4 Agreements* by shaman and healer Don Miguel Ruiz. They are: Be impeccable with your word, don't take anything personally, don't make assumptions, and always do your best. Michael acknowledges that these are aspirational—it's hard to always be impeccable with your word, as we all know. But when someone isn't, it's an opportunity for self-discovery and brave honesty to kick in.

Honoring these values and living up to their code of conduct requires self-realization, vulnerability, and honesty. To foster these traits, Michael offers every employee the opportunity to do a (paid!) ten-day meditation course called Vipassana, a transformational program he envisions as the core of employee training at Chuao Chocolatier.

As a leader, Michael also walks his talk. Cruising his production line, he jokes with employees who are carefully placing marshmallows and nuts into not-yet-hardened chocolate bars moving by, enthusiastically reminding them of their purpose: to put joy into every bar.

YOGA GIRL

Personal Transformation That Inspired
the Creation of a Community

Rachel Brathen grew up with the idea that it was her job to save everybody. After putting herself in the role of having to fix everything or make everything better for others, she never actually knew what it was to put herself first. At eighteen, she found herself deeply depressed, drinking seven days a week, and smoking a pack of cigarettes a day—until she enrolled in a meditation retreat that completely changed her life.

A Swedish native, Rachel traveled to Costa Rica after graduating from school in Stockholm and found the joy of incorporating yoga into her everyday life. Deepening her yoga practice, she moved to Central America where she spent years exploring the intricate studies of yoga and spirituality, then moved to Aruba in early 2010 where she started teaching yoga full time.

In 2012, Rachel began sharing her experiences with yoga on Instagram. By 2014—a year of profound loss for her, of which she shared details with her followers—she began receiving an overwhelming response from people who were also going through difficult times, asking her for help. That's when Rachel turned to crowdfunding to meet her audience's needs, raising half a million dollars and becoming the most successful crowdfunded yoga project to date. Bridging the gap between social media and receiving actual support—what she calls "kind of like Netflix for yoga"—she launched oneOeight, which is made up of a vast community of dedicated practitioners from all over the world looking to cultivate balance, create space for inner healing, and deepen their yoga practice. With an amazing team of experienced guides and teachers, oneOeight offers heart-centered classes designed to fit the always evolving needs of body, mind, and soul. "It's become this beautiful little community of really heartfelt offerings," says Rachel.

Though her classes integrate alignment, core work, and breathing techniques with basic poses and creative sequencing, that is only a small piece of the work she does. She also incorporates holistic therapeutic tools like sharing, active listening, and journaling in every session, and there is a deep level of heart healing at the center of every class, aimed to deepen not only an inner connection, but one with the people around us.

In 2016, she and her husband Dennis opened Island Yoga—the largest yoga studio in the Caribbean—boasting three shalas, a boutique, an organic café, and offices for their team. She is also now a successful published author. Her first book, *Yoga Girl*, was a *New York Times* bestseller, and her second book, *To Love and Let Go* was released in September, 2019.

Giving back to the community has always been at the center of all of Rachel's initiatives. With the help of an outstanding staff and volunteers, she runs two nonprofit organizations in addition to oneOeight: Sgt Pepper's Friends, an animal rescue foundation based in Aruba; and Yoga Girl® Foundation, benefiting women and children in need.

Rachel admits that business and yoga for a lot of people don't go well together; it's common for people in the yoga industry to get completely taken advantage of because of the idea that it's almost shameful to make money out of something you love—and something so sacred. But a podcast episode she did with Deepak Chopra where they spoke about capitalism, yoga, and meditation crystalized her perspective. "I don't think anyone is in yoga to make millions of dollars," she says. "We all want to help other people find tools to heal. I think as long as that intention is there, you're going to end up in a good place." She adds, "In that way, through capitalism, the world will heal."

ENDNOTES

Chapter One

CATCHING THE AMARE WAVE: WHY LOVE? WHY NOW?

[1] A new playbook for this kind of values-based workplace mentoring is titled *Wisdom at Work*, by entrepreneur Chip Conley.

Chapter Two

THE POSITIVE ROLE OF MONEY WITHIN THE MOVEMENT

[2] Lutz, Ashley. "How Trader Joe's Sells Twice as Much as Whole Foods." businessinsider.com. https://www.businessinsider.com/trader-joes-sales-strategy-2014-10 (accessed July 17, 2019).

[3] Supermarket News. Trader Joe's Co. www.supermarketnews.com. https://www.supermarketnews.com/data-table/trader-joes-co-0 (accessed August 12, 2019).

[4] Statista. "Projected sales of Trader Joe's in the U.S. 2015–2021." https://www.statista.com/statistics/562981/projected-sales-of-trader-joes-in-the-us/ (accessed September 2, 2019).

[5] Gajsek, Dejan. "Trader Joe's Growth Study – Building a Grocery Store with Cult-Like Fans." dgajsek.com. https://dgajsek.com/trader-joes-growth-study/ (accessed July 17, 2019).

[6] Wack, Kevin. "Bank of the Year: USAA." americanbanker.com. https://www.americanbanker.com/news/bank-of-the-year-award (accessed July 17, 2019).

[7] USAA. "Get to Know USAA History." usaa.com. https://www.usaa.com/inet/wc/about_usaa_corporate_overview_history?akredirect=true (accessed September 29, 2019).

[8] Mosbrucker, Kristen. "USAA Profits Rebound Amid Notable Natural Disasters." bizjournals.com. https://www.bizjournals.com/sanantonio/news/2018/04/23/usaa-profits-rebound-amid-notable-natural.html (accessed July 17, 2019).

[9] Because I so admire what Southwest Airlines has done for decades and am a devoted customer, I add this comment with some reluctance. Note that the information on how the airline is changing is my perspective and mostly anecdotal at this point.

Over forty years, a beautiful, love-based culture was established that made Southwest Airlines highly successful on all measures. However, with the new leadership of recent years, that long-standing *amare* culture may be at risk. As one longtime SWA mechanic told me, "Employees aren't treated so great any more, like we used to be. It's all about money now. Shareholders come first, not employees." He added with obvious pain that, on the inside, SWA people characterize it this way: "It took forty years for the other airlines to start to be like us. It took just six years for us to become like them."

This sentiment was corroborated in a 2014 Motley Fool report that stated: "Meanwhile, as Southwest has become more like the legacy carriers, it has given up its edge in operational performance. While Southwest Airlines still positions itself as a disruptive innovator in the airline industry, its superiority over competitors is much less certain now." [source] https://www.fool.com/investing/general/2014/04/09/is-southwest-airlines-co-losing-its-edge.aspx

My own experience, and that of several friends and colleagues, is that the happiness is gone—most flights used to be joyful with lots of jokes and laughter among the flight attendants and passengers. It still happens, but now it's unfortunately more the exception than the rule—probably because employees have less happiness to share.

The conundrum is that Southwest's stock value has soared to new heights—more than tripling in value since the new CEO took the helm—so shareholders are happy. But what happens when SWA's main differentiator, outstanding customer service from committed and happy employees, erodes to a point where it becomes a liability?

I believe the love-based culture of Southwest Airlines is being deeply challenged, and will continue to be as many of the old-timers start to retire. Many Southwest people, though, are still very devoted and striving to hold to the old values and ways of being, which will protect the airline for awhile—but it won't last forever. They will eventually get depleted without the infusions of loving energy they once thrived on, and competitors will likely seize the opening and become what SWA was.

It's not too late, however. SWA is certainly capable of recovering their original culture and legendary customer service, and not only can their people be happy again, but they can get back to setting new performance records and regain their fun-loving personality—not only in words, but in action.

[10] Macrotrends. "Southwest Airlines Revenue 2006–2019 | LUV." macrotrends.net. https://www.macrotrends.net/stocks/charts/LUV/south-west-airlines/revenue (accessed July 17, 2019).

[11] Southwest. "Southwest Airlines Co. 2018 Annual Report to Shareholders." investors.southwest.com. http://investors.southwest.com/~/media/Files/S/

Southwest-IR/LUV_2018_Annual percent20Report.pdf (accessed July 17, 2019).

12 Southwest. "Southwest Airlines Reports Fourth Quarter and Annual Profit; 46th Consecutive Year of Profitability." investors.southwest.com. http://investors.southwest.com/news-and-events/news-releases/2019/01-24-2019-113106440 (accessed July 17, 2019).

13 McCoy, Sean. "REI Posts Record Revenues for 15th Straight Year." gearjunkie.com. https://gearjunkie.com/rei-2018-revenue-stewardship (accessed July 17, 2019).

14 REI Co-Op. "2018 Stewardship Report." rei.com. https://www.rei.com/stewardship (accessed July 17, 2019).

15 REI Co-Op. "In Its 80th Year, REI Co-Op Turned Record Sales into Record Impact." newsroom.rei.com. https://newsroom.rei.com/news/corporate/in-its-80th-year-rei-co-op-turned-record-sales-into-record-impact.htm (accessed July 17, 2019).

16 Levine-Weinberg, Adam. "Costco Wholesale Corporation Ends Fiscal 2018 with Another Month of Incredible Sales." fool.com. https://www.fool.com/investing/2018/09/10/costco-wholesale-corporation-end-fiscal-2018-sales.aspx (accessed July 17, 2019).

17 Kalogeropoulos, Demitrios. "Why Costco Is Up 27 percent in 2018." fool.com. https://www.fool.com/investing/2018/11/11/why-costco-is-up-27-in-2018.aspx (accessed July 17, 2019).

18 American Customer Satisfaction Index (ACSI) Retail and Consumer Shipping Report 2018–2019.

19 Mainwaring, Simon. "Purpose at Work: Lessons from TOMS on How to Lead with Purpose." forbes.com. https://www.forbes.com/sites/simonmainwaring/2018/12/13/purpose-at-work-lessons-from-toms-on-how-to-lead-with-purpose/#40696393e81b (accessed July 17, 2019).

20 FourWeekMBA. "How Does TOMS Shoes Make Money? The One-for-One Business Model Explained." fourweekmba.com. https://fourweekmba.com/toms-one-for-one-business-model/ (accessed July 17, 2019).

21 Nielsen. "Consumer-Goods' Brands That Demonstrate Commitment to Sustainability Outperform Those That Don't." nielsen.com. https://www.nielsen.com/us/en/press-room/2015/consumer-goods-brands-that-demonstrate-commitment-to-sustainability-outperform.html (accessed July 17, 2019).

22 Conscious Capitalism. "Conscious Capitalist Credo." consciouscapitalism.org. https://www.consciouscapitalism.org/credo (accessed July 17, 2019).

23 I want to be clear that in drawing on this research, I am positing that the companies they identify as "firms of endearment" are sufficiently *amare*-like to justify the application here.

24 The same FoE companies also outperformed the set of "great" companies described in the very influential book *Good to Great* by Jim Collins, by 3 to 1 over a ten-year period. Interestingly, in *Good to Great*, the "great" companies were categorized as such based exclusively on their financial performance over many years relative to competitors. This contrasts with the FoE companies that were identified as such based on a more holistic and humanistic perspective, which in fact excluded profitability.

25 Outlined in Frederic Laloux's excellent book *Reinventing Organizations*.

Chapter Three

BUSINESS AND THE EVOLUTION OF CONSCIOUSNESS

26 Thesis, antithesis, and synthesis are a triad of terms often used to describe the work of the German philosopher Hegel.

Chapter Four

A SHORT IN THE HARDWIRING:
HOW WE'VE ADOPTED A BUSINESS AS WAR MENTALITY

27 Appelbaum, Binyamin. *The Economists' Hour: False Prophets, Free Markets, and the Fracture of Society.* New York: Little, Brown and Company, 2019.

28 Interestingly, during natural disasters, price gouging is severely frowned upon, derided, and often punished, as though in these circumstances people come before profit. In most states, price gouging during times of emergency is illegal (which also means price gouging is permitted the rest of the time!).

29 Ross, Lee, and Richard Nisbett. *The Person and the Situation: Perspectives of Social Psychology.* Great Britain: Pinter & Martin Ltd, 2011.

30 Bilotkach, Volodymyr. "Boeing 737 MAX: How Much Could the Grounded Fleet Cost the Company?" theconversation.com. http://theconversation.com/boeing-737-max-how-much-could-the-grounded-fleet-cost-the-company-114863 (accessed July 17, 2019).

31 *The New York Times* reported that more than 200,000 Americans have died of overdoses related to prescription opioids since OxyContin came on the market.

32 This example was cited in the book *Pre-suasion* by persuasion expert Dr. Robert Cialdini.

33 O'Neil, Tim. "Sr. Mary Jean Ryan Led the Health Industry in Efforts to Continuously Improve Patient Saftey." chausa.org. https://www.chausa.org/publications/catholic-health-world/assembly-2018-coverage/sr-mary-jean-ryan-led-the-health-industry-in-efforts-to-continuously-improve-patient-safety (accessed July 17, 2019).

34 Herwick III, Edgar B. "How Gun Culture Permeates Our Everyday Language." pri.org. https://www.pri.org/stories/2016-06-15/how-gun-culture-permeates-our-everyday-language (accessed July 17, 2019).

Chapter Five

IF YOUR BUSINESS IS MISSING LOVE, ARE **YOU** MISSING LOVE?

35 Now you might be wondering, what about jerks? Do we really want a business paradigm that encourages jerks to "be themselves?" We address this in the Arrogance section of this chapter.

36 Kambouris, Angela. "Being Vulnerable Is the Boldest Act of Business Leadership." entrepreneur.com. https://www.entrepreneur.com/article/309784 (accessed July 17, 2019).

37 Porath, Christine. "How Rudeness Stops People from Working Together." hbr.org. https://hbr.org/2017/01/how-rudeness-stops-people-from-working-together (accessed July 17, 2019).

38 ELI. "About ELI: Our Approach." eliinc.com. https://www.eliinc.com/about-eli/our-approach/ (accessed July 17, 2019).

39 Mielach, David. "Bosses, Employees Agree Humble Leadership is Most Effective." businessnewsdaily.com. https://www.businessnewsdaily.com/1768-humble-bosses.html?_ga=2.165123071.1534003424.1556831018-1686567645.1556831018 (accessed July 17, 2019).

40 Stontell, Alyson. "Why 'Arrogant Jerks' Become Rich and Successful in Silicon Valley." businessinsider.com. www.businessinsider.com/asshole-ceos-startup-founders-and-success-2014-11 (accessed July 17, 2019).

41 Several of these questions are variations of items in the validated Workplace Arrogance Scale (aptly nicknamed WARS) developed by Stanley Silverman and colleagues at the University of Akron and Michigan State University.

42 Zlotowicz, Meir. *Ethics of the Fathers: Pirkei Avos.* Mesorah Publication, 1984.

Chapter Six

IS FEAR ENERGY RULING YOUR BUSINESS?

[43] Gladwell, Malcolm. *Outliers: The Story of Success.* Back Bay Books, 2011.

[44] Juline, Kathy. "Creating a New Earth Together." eckharttolletv.com. http://www.eckharttolletv.com/article/Awakening-Your-Spiritual-Lifes-Purpose (accessed July 17, 2019).

[45] Quote Investigator. https://quoteinvestigator.com/2018/02/18/response/ (accessed July 17, 2019).

[46] Bolden-Barrett, Valerie. "Study: Disengaged Employees Can Cost Companies Up to $550B a Year." hrdive.com. https://www.hrdive.com/news/study-disengaged-employees-can-cost-companies-up-to-550b-a-year/437606/ (accessed July 17, 2019).

[47] Gallup. "State of the American Workplace Report." news.gallup.com. https://news.gallup.com/reports/199961/7.aspx (accessed July 17, 2019).

[48] Crabtree, Steve. "Worldwide, 13 percent of Employees Are Engaged at Work." news.gallup.com. https://news.gallup.com/poll/165269/worldwide-employees-engaged-work.aspx (accessed July 17, 2019).

Chapter Seven

TO THINE OWN SELF—AND BUSINESS—BE TRUE: THE IMPORTANCE OF ALIGNMENT

[49] Be. "Know Thyself." arkintime.com. https://arkintime.com/know-thyself/

Chapter Eight

THE AMARE WAY PHILOSOPHY: GROUNDING YOUR BUSINESS IN SEVEN FOUNDATIONAL PRINCIPLES

[50] NPR. "Modern Lessons from Hillel." npr.org. https://www.npr.org/templates/story/story.php?storyId=129706379 (accessed July 17, 2019).

[51] Wieseke, Jan, Anja Geigenmüller, and Florian Kraus. "On the role of empathy in customer-employee interactions. db-thueringen.de. https://www.db-

thueringen.de/servlets/MCRFileNodeServlet/dbt_derivate_00030486/ ilm1-2014210187.pdf (accessed July 17, 2019).

52 Strecher, Vic. "6 Quick Steps for Finding Your Company's Authentic Purpose." huffpost.com. https://www.huffpost.com/entry/6-quick-steps-for-finding_b_9558032 (accessed July 17, 2019).

53 Bonchek, Mark. "Purpose Is Good. Shared Purpose Is Better." hbr.org. https://hbr.org/2013/03/purpose-is-good-shared-purpose (accessed July 17, 2019).

54 Bezos, Jeffrey P. Letter to Shareowners. ir.aboutamazon.com. https:// ir.aboutamazon.com/static-files/1bfd8929-81a0-46d7-a378-6aff9a203093 (accessed July 17, 2019).

Chapter Nine

THE AMARE WAY PRACTICE:
EMBODYING THE MOVEMENT THROUGH AUTHENTICITY,
BELONGING, AND COLLABORATION

55 McKeown, Les. "How to Get Fiercely Loyal Customers." inc.com. https:// www.inc.com/les-mckeown/how-to-get-loyal-customers.html (accessed July 17, 2019).

56 How is *collaboration* different from *cooperation*? While the etymologies are quite similar, collaboration has a connotation of being more active than cooperation and with a stronger commitment to shared goals. Collaboration also has more of a "we're in this together" sensibility to it, while cooperation has an inference of division of labor in order to achieve an aim. In these respects, collaboration ties more strongly than cooperation to the Amare Way framework. That said, both are beneficial, and done right, both can be uplifting and energizing to everyone involved, as well as effective at improving outcomes.

57 Statista. "Percentage of Paid Units Sold by Third-Party Sellers on Amazon Platform as of 1st Quarter 2019." statista.com. https://www.statista.com/ statistics/259782/third-party-seller-share-of-amazon-platform/ (accessed July 17, 2019).

58 Leonard, Kimberlee. "Examples of Successful Strategic Alliances." small-business.chron.com. https://smallbusiness.chron.com/examples-successful-strategic-alliances-13859.html (accessed July 17, 2019).

59 Bloomberg. "Ford, Toyota Form Telematics Bloc to Stymie Google and Apple." industryweek.com. https://www.industryweek.com/technology/ford-toyota-form-telematics-bloc-stymie-google-and-apple (accessed July 17, 2019).

60 I am grateful to whomever coined the term "collabetition." Co-opetition is another portmanteau used to describe competitors working together.

61 The online *Harvard Business Review* article "Embracing Agile" offers a useful synopsis of the strategy with a nice range of examples of successes.

62 Norman, Don. "Emotional Design: Why We Love (Or Hate) Everyday Things." nngroup.com. https://www.nngroup.com/books/emotional-design/ (accessed July 17, 2019).

Chapter Ten

HARNESSING ADVANTAGE:
TURNING FIVE COMMON TRAPS INTO STEPPING STONES

63 Hawker, Christopher. "Lead with Thoughts of Abundance, Not Scarcity." Entrepreneur.com. https://www.entrepreneur.com/article/252840 (accessed September 30, 2019).

64 Castrillon, Caroline. "How to Shift from a Scarcity Mindset to an Abundance Mindset." Thrive Global. www.thriveglobal.com. https://thriveglobal.com/stories/how-to-shift-from-a-scarcity-to-an-abundance-mindset-3/ (accessed August 5, 2019).

65 I learned the 60-second technique from meditation expert Davidji, and the way to occupy the mind from *True Love* by Thich Nhat Hanh.

Chapter Twelve

GETTING STARTED:
KEY TAKEAWAYS AND ACTION STEPS FOR BECOMING A
CULTIVATOR OF LOVE AND JUMPING ONTO THE AMARE WAVE

66 Tsai, Jeanne L. "Ideal Affect in Daily Life: Implications for Affective Experience, Health, and Social Behavior." ScienceDirect. sciencedirect.com. https://www.sciencedirect.com/science/article/pii/S2352250X1730132X?via%3Dihub (accessed September 30, 2019).

67 I am grateful to Marty Goodman for sharing this technique with me when I was designing a workshop for San Diego Social Venture Partners.

RECOMMENDED READING

Business, Leadership & Love

Blanchard, Kenneth, and Colleen Barrett. *Lead with LUV: A Different Way to Create Real Success.* Upper Saddle River, N.J.: FT Press, 2011.

De Haaff, Brian. *Lovability: How to Build a Business That People Love and Be Happy Doing It.* Austin, Texas: Greenleaf Book Group Press, 2017.

Farber, Steve. *Love Is Just Damn Good Business: Do What You Love in the Service of People Who Love What You Do.* New York: McGraw-Hill, 2019.

Laloux, Frédéric. *Reinventing Organizations: A Guide to Creating Organizations Inspired by the Next Stage of Human Consciousness.* Brussels, Belgium: Nelson Parker, 2014.

Roberts, Kevin. *Lovemarks: The Future Beyond Brands.* New York: PowerHouse, 2007.

Sanders, Tim. *Love Is the Killer App: How to Win Business and Influence Friends.* New York: Three Rivers Press, 2002.

Sisodia, Raj, Jag Sheth, and David Wolfe. *Firms of Endearment: How World-Class Companies Profit from Passion and Purpose*, 2nd Ed. Hoboken: Pearson FT Press, 2014.

The Business of Emotions

Brown, Brené. *Daring Greatly: How the Courage to Be Vulnerable Transforms the Way We Live, Love, Parent, and Lead.* New York: Random House, 2018.

Conley, Chip. *Emotional Equations: Simple Steps for Creating Happiness + Success in Business + Life.* New York: Simon & Schuster, 2012.

Fredrickson, Barbara. *Love 2.0: How Our Supreme Emotion Affects Everything We Feel, Think, Do, and Become.* New York: Gildan Media Corp., 2013.

Goleman, Daniel, Annie McKee, Bill George, and Herminia Ibarra, et. al. *HBR Emotional Intelligence Series: How to Be Human at Work.* Boston: Harvard Business Publishing, 2018.

Norman, Donald. *Emotional Design: Why We Love (or Hate) Everyday Things.* New York: Basic Books, 2004.

Porath, Christine. *Mastering Civility: A Manifesto for the Workplace.* New York: Grand Central Publishing, 2016.

Psychology, Business & Life

Ariely, Dan. *Predictably Irrational: The Hidden Forces That Shape Our Decisions.* New York: HarperCollins Publishers, 2008.

Csíkszentmihályi, Mihály. *Flow: The Psychology of Optimal Experience.* New York: Harper Perennial, 2008.

Dalio, Ray. *Principles: Life and Work.* New York: Simon & Schuster, 2012.

Diamandis, Peter, and Steven Kotler. *Abundance: The Future Is Better Than You Think.* New York: Simon & Schuster, 2015.

Gladwell, Malcolm. *The Tipping Point: How Little Things Can Make a Big Difference.* New York: Little, Brown and Company, 2000.

Pink, Daniel. *Drive: The Surprising Truth About What Motivates Us.* New York: Riverhead Books, 2009.

Ross, Lee, and Richard Nisbett. *The Person and the Situation: Perspectives of Social Psychology*, 2nd Ed. London: Pinter & Martin, Ltd. 2011.

Spirituality for Business and Life

Cope, Stephen. *The Great Work of Your Life: A Guide for the Journey to Your True Calling.* New York: Random House, 2015.

Easwaran, Eknath, ed., trans. *The Bhagavad Gita*, 2nd Edition. *Easwaran's Classics of Indian Spirituality.* Tomales, CA: Nilgiri Press, 2007.

Hanh, Thich Nhat. *True Love: A Practice for Awakening the Heart.* Sherab Chodzin Kohn, trans. Shambala, 2011.

Ruiz, Don Miguel. *The 4 Agreements: A Toltec Wisdom Book.* San Rafael: Amber-Allen Publishing, 1997.

Tsu, Lao. *Tao Te Ching: A New Translation and Commentary*, 3rd Ed. Ralph Alan Dale, Trans. Barnes & Noble Press, 2004.

ACKNOWLEDGMENTS

I am deeply grateful to so many people who provided support to me in a myriad of ways. From the beginning, my wife Dana believed in me and this book, and our path together. My mother, my sisters and their husbands, my kids, my nieces and nephews, and my extended family saw its importance and encouraged me to get it done. Mimi, Rozy, Sheri, and Marcy provided valuable design input. Alyssa, Guillermo, Jessa, Austin, Benj, Arielle, Eli, Benny, Osama, Jake, Peter, Kevin, Bobby, Ginger, Jeff, Susie, Ed, Liz, Monte, and Nancy shared helpful perspectives and stories. And my little dog Zoey, often by my feet, was a constant source of unconditional love.

There are a few colleagues I want to call out for the depth and richness of their assistance. I want to thank consultant Gunter Wessels for his generous and invaluable thought partnership and co-presentations in the early days of this book's development. Much gratitude to my dear friend and energy guru Jim Case for keeping me honest and providing vital perspective throughout. Furkan Cavus-Ismail was a very helpful and dedicated research assistant while earning his MBA. Steve Stegman provided an ongoing litmus test of how practical my ideas were. David Berke fed me numerous articles and resources that informed my thinking. Neville Billimoria generously shared his knowledge and insights at the intersection of spirituality and business. I thank Rick Kleine for his constructively critical eye and decades of encouragement to write my book. Teresa Sanchez helped me expand my thinking about the predatory language of business, and Jim McKenzie gave me great insight into what happens when a company's relationships with its customers sour. Doug Solomon and Jim Tenuto buoyed my spirits with their wit and wisdom. Carlos Figueroa provided his usual stellar design expertise for my initial presentations. A big thank you too to colleagues at HITMC, HATA, 10X, San Diego Cause Conference, and UCSD Rady School for inviting me to present early iterations of these ideas at their meetings.

This book greatly benefited from hundreds of interviews and deep conversations with a wide range of kind and smart people who provided insight, encouragement, and ideas along the way. I am so grateful to you all. Though I did not keep track of all the individuals by name, and I apologize to those not listed here, I do want to acknowledge Landis White, Lucas Reeve, Corey Salka, Jayme Rubenstein, Gene Barduson, Ted Simendinger, Teri Sun, Michael Johnson, Neil Treister, Debbie Newport, Robin McCoy, Elizabeth Riordan, Karma Bass, Paul Kurtin, Sherry Sidoti, Jim Torti, David Sleet, Peter Levesque, Mike Pietranka, Gioia Messinger, Steve Winton, Tim McMullen, Sherri Dumford, Shahid Shah, John Lynn, Stephen Friedman, John Adler, Steve Scheier, Mas Vidal, Rob Kenney, Ivy Gordon, Christine Brittle, Kezya Arum, Peter Coughlan, Michael Antonorsi, Joseph Reid, Howard Sharfstein, Michael Lurie, Michelle Musgrove, Julie Mackinnon, Betsy Kirkland, Deborah Jordan, Rahul Dubey, Tony Little, Brian my neighbor, Mareo McCracken, Josh Weeks, Lynn Reaser, Chris Koepke, Jack Fyock, Brett Hazuka, Joe Hage, Martin Eichholz, Gary Fly, Tara Williams, Eric Klein, Eric Kaufmann, Rifat Nasi, Jeff Grad, Sarah McArthur, Marcos Perez, Cindy Hensen, Terry Edwards, Jenna Buffalo, Mariette Fourmeaux, Alexis Dixon, Larry Kesslin, and John Lee.

I was also encouraged—and sometimes surprised—by the consistently positive reactions to the idea of being love-centered in business that I received from colleagues, friends, and even strangers. And to all those whose stories are shared in this book (some with name changes to respect their privacy), a heartfelt thank you.

From a business perspective, I drew deeply on my almost three decades of experience as head of ResearchWorks, a research-based strategy firm. The lessons I learned about what happens when companies, employees, and customers sincerely understand one other, care, and meaningfully connect—and what happens when they don't—were particularly illuminating. Thank you to all my clients and colleagues for these opportunities, as well as to my many employees and collaborators. I also want to express gratitude to the numerous teachers and students I learned from over the years, especially at UCSD, SDSU, and Stanford University.

My writing was greatly informed by both ancient and modern-day thinkers, authors, poets, business leaders, managers, consultants, researchers, and practitioners whose work illuminates the evolving higher level of consciousness that enables a more loving, authentic, inclusive, and collaborative way of being, doing, and having, in business and life.

Contemporary business thinkers who strongly influenced and inspired my work over the years include the late Peter Drucker, Phil Kotler, Brené Brown, Marshall Goldsmith, Ken Blanchard, Jim Collins, Malcolm Gladwell, Steve Farber, Alan Weiss, Denise Lee Yohn, Don Norman, and Chip Conley, to name but a few. I learned a great deal from their work and many other excellent business books, both classic and contemporary, and from numerous *Harvard Business Review* articles and other online resources.

Of special note is *Reinventing Organizations*, by Frederic Laloux. In my view, his work is helping to usher in a new level of spiritual awareness in relation to organizational management. It catapulted my thinking to a higher level and reinforced my belief that I was on the right track. Similarly, the work on Conscious Capitalism and the book *Firms of Endearment* by Raj Sisodia and his colleagues were very uplifting and influential. The latter in particular provided much of the empirical support for demonstrating that the business as love paradigm is highly profitable. I believe the fundamentals of *The Amare Wave* are well aligned with the ideas and findings of these great thinkers. I hope what I wrote will serve the RO and Conscious Capitalism communities well.

Many wonderful spiritually minded books guided my thinking as well. I will draw attention to only a few here for their unique impact. Two ancient sacred books of the East had an especially invigorating influence on me. One was the two-thousand-year-old Hindu scripture, the *Bhagavad Gita*. The other was the even older Chinese text, the *Tao Te Ching*. The timeless wisdom in these spiritual classics, and the incredible interpretations that enabled me to begin to understand them, I found to be nothing short of extraordinary. Relatedly, I also want to call out with gratitude Stephen Cope's book, *The Great Work of Your Life*, which brings to life central principles of the *Bhagavad Gita* as a means of helping people find their dharma, their true purpose in life. I also drew on the wisdom of the Sufi poets Rumi and Hafiz, Rabbi Hillel, Buddha, Gandhi, HH the Dalai Lama, Thich Nhat Hanh, and other revered figures, past and present.

I drew deeply on my own personal spiritual journey of many years. In this regard I want to bring in the energy of all the yogis and yoginis I have been privileged to know, with a special thank you to Saul David Raye; Kenlyn Kolleen, Chiara Stella, and Ryan Stanley of Soul of Yoga; singer/songwriter and voice teacher Katie Wise; and dear friends Ken (Kenesha) and Lidija Diller. I also benefited from healer Donna Keefe and colleagues; Rabbi David Wolpe; Michael Franti; Wayne Dyer, and other teachers and friends on the spiritual path.

One powerful spiritual force that consistently uplifted me throughout the ordeals of writing was Kirtan music. I am indescribably grateful for the high-vibration gift of Kirtan, all the artists who devote themselves to this inspired music, and the beautiful festivals that make it available. This music, along with daily meditating, beach walks, and other activities that helped me stay in alignment, enabled the best part of writing—what I call Guidance. When I could tune into it, ideas and words came through me. I learned to trust and even yearn for that direct inspiration.

Lastly, I am honored to thank Stacey Aaronson, editor and writer extraordinaire. She is the partner I didn't know I needed, because I naively thought writing a book like this was not a big deal. Stacey made the book what it is. Without her generous heart, insightful thinking, and eye for detail, it would be, well, nothing like it is!

In closing, to all my many, many collaborators—whether you knew you were one or not—thank you, thank you, thank you.

INDEX

warlike
  actions/behaviors, 35, 44, 51, 59, 96,
    103, 104, 109, 148, 201
  and Darwinian notions of survival,
    44
  and evil, 59
  approach, 43, 125, 319
  in business, 3, 4, 7, 14, 20, 36, 45,
    51, 59, 90, 233
  language, 63, 65, 146, 201, 244,
    273–75
  mentality/thinking, 36, 41, 55, 59,
    100, 103, 201, 231
  moving away from, 131, 273
  terms, 148
way-shower, 5
Wells Fargo, 57, 58
Whole Foods, 24
wholehearted/wholeheartedness, 73,
    275, 276
Wilde, Oscar, 126
Williamson, Marianne, 145
win-win, 18, 74, 178, 179, 181, 193,
    209, 304, 309
Winfrey, Oprah, 208
Wizard of Oz, The, 50
Wolf of Wall Street, The, 104
Wolfe, David, 27
Wooden, John, 212

Y Combinator, 80
yang
  energy, 35, 43
  epoch, 42, 43, 47
  phase, 34, 35, 43
yin
  energy, 35
  epoch, 42, 43
  phase, 33
Yoga Girl, 327–28

zero-sum game, 206, 309

You may say I'm a dreamer
But I'm not the only one
I hope some day you'll join us
And the world will be as one.

From "Imagine" by John Lennon

DR. MOSHE ENGELBERG inspires businesses worldwide to be their best by thinking different, acting courageously, and leading with love. His innovative ideas and approaches are deeply rooted in a combination of applied behavioral science and diverse wisdom traditions, tested and refined through almost three decades of consulting with world-class organizations. As founder and head of the business strategy consultancy ResearchWorks, his clients include global health and technology companies, federal and state government agencies, large and small nonprofits, foundations, and startups.

Moshe is a teacher at heart who helps others find the deep knowledge and truth they hold within. His extensive academic credentials include a PhD from Stanford University in Communication, and Masters degrees in both Psychology and Public Health. He has published numerous research papers, and designed and taught many executive education and graduate-level courses. As a speaker, Moshe consistently delights and inspires audiences with his innovative thinking, open heart, dry wit, and practical "how-to" tips and techniques.

The Amare Wave converges lessons Moshe learned through years of consulting with a wide array of businesses, mentoring executives, teaching, and his own spiritual journey. His next book in the Amare Way series, *Riding the Amare Wave: Inspired Stories of Leading with Love*, is in the works.

Moshe lives in San Diego with his wife Dana and their pets, and with grown children nearby. He gets his inspiration from family and friends, ocean kayaking, beach walks, anything nature, yoga, and kirtan music.

STACEY AARONSON has been taking writers by the hand since 2011, developing, editing, designing, and publishing over sixty books of excellence with her author clients. She has been a trusted book production partner for some of the most accomplished entrepreneurs, coaches, educators, and writers of inspirational nonfiction and memoir, and her books have won several notable awards, including the National Indie Excellence Award, the Outdoor Writers of Canada Book Award, Gold and Silver Medal IPPY Awards, multiple Book Excellence Awards, and the coveted IBPA Benjamin Franklin Award: Best New Voice, Nonfiction, both in 2015 and in 2018. In addition, Stacey is a ghostwriter who has written two memoirs—one of which is being made into an independent film—in partnership with the authors, and she has been a top layout artist for She Writes Press since 2013. She is also a frequent participant in online writers summits, and has been a guest on multiple podcasts.

A magna cum laude graduate of Scripps College in Claremont, CA, Stacey is a native Southern Californian who now happily resides on Whidbey Island, WA, where she enjoys reading and working on her own novels, as well as forest walks, seeing deer and other wildlife play in the yard, and sharing her life with her amazing partner, Dana, who makes all her creative endeavors possible.

WORKING WITH MOSHE

Moshe is available for keynote speeches, workshops, leadership coaching, and consulting on how to prosper by being more love-centered in business. He will also participate with any book club reading this book—in person if nearby, or virtually. In addition, Moshe leads a limited number of larger research and strategy projects through his consulting firm ResearchWorks (www.researchworks.com).

You can reach him at:
connect@theamarewave.com